ANTITRUST

ASPEN STUDENT TREATISE SERIES

ANTITRUST

DANIEL A. CRANE

Associate Dean for Faculty and Research
Frederick Paul Furth Sr. Professor of Law
University of Michigan Law School

Wolters Kluwer
Law & Business

ISBN 978-1-4548-3799-2

Library of Congress Cataloging-in-Publication Data

Crane, Daniel A. author.
    Antitrust / Daniel Crane.
        p. cm. — (Aspen treatise series)
    Includes bibliographical references and index.
    ISBN 978-1-4548-3799-2 (alk. paper)
1. Antitrust law—United States. 2. Antitrust law. I. Title.

KF1649.C73 2014

343.7307'21—dc23

2013047883

About Wolters Kluwer Law & Business

Wolters Kluwer Law & Business is a leading global provider of intelligent information and digital solutions for legal and business professionals in key specialty areas, and respected educational resources for professors and law students. Wolters Kluwer Law & Business connects legal and business professionals as well as those in the education market with timely, specialized authoritative content and information-enabled solutions to support success through productivity, accuracy and mobility.

Serving customers worldwide, Wolters Kluwer Law & Business products include those under the Aspen Publishers, CCH, Kluwer Law International, Loislaw, ftwilliam.com and MediRegs family of products.

CCH products have been a trusted resource since 1913, and are highly regarded resources for legal, securities, antitrust and trade regulation, government contracting, banking, pension, payroll, employment and labor, and healthcare reimbursement and compliance professionals.

Aspen Publishers products provide essential information to attorneys, business professionals and law students. Written by preeminent authorities, the product line offers analytical and practical information in a range of specialty practice areas from securities law and intellectual property to mergers and acquisitions and pension/benefits. Aspen's trusted legal education resources provide professors and students with high-quality, up-to-date and effective resources for successful instruction and study in all areas of the law.

Kluwer Law International products provide the global business community with reliable international legal information in English. Legal practitioners, corporate counsel and business executives around the world rely on Kluwer Law journals, looseleafs, books, and electronic products for comprehensive information in many areas of international legal practice.

Loislaw is a comprehensive online legal research product providing legal content to law firm practitioners of various specializations. Loislaw provides attorneys with the ability to quickly and efficiently find the necessary legal information they need, when and where they need it, by facilitating access to primary law as well as state-specific law, records, forms and treatises.

ftwilliam.com offers employee benefits professionals the highest quality plan documents (retirement, welfare and non-qualified) and government forms (5500/PBGC, 1099 and IRS) software at highly competitive prices.

MediRegs products provide integrated health care compliance content and software solutions for professionals in healthcare, higher education and life sciences, including professionals in accounting, law and consulting.

Wolters Kluwer Law & Business, a division of Wolters Kluwer, is headquartered in New York. Wolters Kluwer is a market-leading global information services company focused on professionals.

*For my parents, who continued to support me even when
I turned to antitrust.*

Summary of Contents

Table of Contents

Table of Contents

Introduction

On November 9, 2009, the straw finally broke the camel's back. It was an oral argument in the Supreme Court of the United States in *Bilski v. Doll*,[1] a case about the patentability of business methods. Justice Stephen Breyer, who once taught antitrust law at Harvard, asked whether he could patent "a great, wonderful, really original method to teach antitrust law that kept 80 percent of the students awake." Laughter filled the courtroom. Staying awake during antitrust! Funny stuff indeed.

What have we come to when judges in *patent* cases reach out to antitrust as the example of a really boring subject? It was not always this way. Antitrust used to be a magisterial course about economic rivalry, industrial intrigue, and political ideology that packed law school classrooms. In the three-way presidential election of 1912, between William Howard Taft the conservative, Woodrow Wilson the progressive, and Teddy Roosevelt the Bullmoose (I'm not making this up), antitrust was perhaps the defining issue. Trustbusting captured the imagination of generations of Americans and the brightest and best legal minds. Many towering American intellectuals on both sides of the ideological divide including President and, then, Chief Justice Taft, Louis Brandeis, Thurman Arnold, Derek Bok, Phillip Areeda, Richard Posner, Robert Bork, Frank Easterbrook, and Lady Gaga (see, you're still awake) made their early marks in antitrust.

What happened to reduce antitrust to the punch line in patent cases? The answer, in a word, is *economics*. During the 1970s, a revolutionary approach to law and economic regulation (called the Chicago School) swept from the corridors of academia to the courthouse steps. Within a few short years, it had captured the minds of a majority of justices on the Supreme Court. Over time, it diffused throughout the federal judiciary, the antitrust bar, and the antitrust enforcement agencies. By the 1980s, technical economic jargon — marginal cost, freeriding, price discrimination, double marginalization, the Herfindahl Hirschman index — had become the woof and warp of antitrust analysis. Economists, not lawyers, had become the stars of the antitrust show.

So where did that leave the law student who majored in Illyrian Renaissance Sheepherding Fiction, the one who thinks that economies

1. 129 S. Ct. 2735 (2009).

Introduction

of scale is a weight-loss program? Happily, the answer is not so out of the game as you might fear. Unfamiliarity with economics is no reason to avoid taking antitrust. It is a reason to approach it with a strategic mind-set that I will attempt to describe in our brief pages together.

Here, an autobiographical confession is in order. Every year when I teach the basic antitrust course I get a number of e-mails from nervous students along the following lines: "Professor, I don't know any economics. Will I survive antitrust?" These e-mails always make me think back to my own experience in law school at the University of Chicago. I was in a land-use class, arguing about something (I don't remember what) with the professor, the inestimable Richard Epstein, when all of a sudden Epstein burst out with this thick Brooklyn accent, "Your problem, Mistah Crane, is that you're an amateur economist!"

Epstein was wrong. I wasn't even close enough to economics to be an amateur. Before law school, I had taken just one flimsy microeconomics course in college. I knew none of the jargon that is assumed knowledge in antitrust discourse, couldn't tell the x axis from the y axis on a graph, and was terrified of any sentence containing numbers. By all rights, I should have been a sheep to the slaughter in antitrust.

But I wasn't. What I slowly learned is that, for all its economic jargon, antitrust law is still *law*. Lawyers, judges, and law professors have appropriated economic ideas and economic terminology to conduct the same essential enterprise that they conducted in the days that muckraking journalists exposed John D. Rockefeller and the Standard Oil trust, Louis Brandeis railed against the "Curse of Bigness," and Teddy Roosevelt sweated out an antitrust immunity deal with J.P. Morgan to avoid the collapse of the banking and steel industries. As important as economics is to the antitrust enterprise, the backbone of antitrust *law* remains the familiar fabric of law—the push and pull between rules and standards, burdens of proof in the face of uncertainty, profound uneasiness over the boundaries of judicial competence, and deep ideological "priors" over power, freedom, coercion, exceptionalism, and fairness.

This is a book by an amateur economist for amateur economists. To paraphrase FDR, all we have to economize is economics itself. This is not to say that you can succeed in a modern antitrust course without opening your mind to economic reasoning and loosening your tongue to economic jargon. Rather, it is to say that if you are willing to dive into economics, you will find plenty of lawyer work awaiting your skills.

Let me conclude with a few words on this book's pedagogical orientation. There are many ways to study antitrust law, and different casebooks and professors approach the matter differently. Some approach antitrust from a historical perspective, while others dispense with history and teach just modern antitrust doctrine and its economic content. Though I love the

xvi

history and believe that it should be studied in antitrust courses,[2] this book will not dwell too much on history, except insofar as necessary to understand current debates or doctrines. The purpose of this book is to introduce the essentials of modern antitrust law and the economic concepts and lingo that surround it, to put students with no economic background on a level playing field with the econ majors, and to provide a roadmap for every student to navigate the shoals of antitrust problems with confidence.

Organizationally, this book has five parts. Part I introduces foundational concepts. Part II covers agreements in restraint of trade, essentially Section 1 of the Sherman Act. Part III covers exclusionary and exploitative practices, much of which is covered by Section 2 of the Sherman Act. Part IV covers mergers and Part V procedural or quasi-procedural questions like antitrust injury, standing, and jurisdiction and also the two general antitrust immunities — the *Noerr-Pennington* and *Parker* doctrines. Bolded terms are referenced and defined in the glossary.

Oh, about Justice Breyer's little antitrust joke, I'm sure that he was pulling "an Iceland" on us. According to fable, temperate and fertile Iceland was given its dreary name in order to discourage invaders. As soon as you take antitrust and learn the secret handshake, you also will have an interest in discouraging too many others from joining the club. Remember, oligopolists abhor entry! For those in the know, antitrust remains a gem of a course and a gem of an area in which to pursue a career. Just don't spread the word too far — the barbarians may be listening.

2. If you want history, please read my books *Antitrust Stories* (Foundation Press, 2007, with Eleanor Fox) and *The Making of Competition Policy: Legal and Economic Sources* (Oxford University Press, 2012, with Herbert Hovenkamp).

ANTITRUST

PART I
ANTITRUST FUNDAMENTALS

Chapter 1

Foundational Economic Assumptions

Let's face it. *Antitrust* is a horrible word — so negative, so poorly descriptive of the actual field, so antiquated. In most other countries that have an analogue to the United States' Sherman Act, antitrust law is called competition law, a more positive and evocative way of describing the field. (By the way, please, please, *please* don't make the mistake of hyphenating *antitrust* — i.e., *anti-trust* — on your exam or in a brief. This is a clear marker to your professor or the judge that you're an outsider to the field, that you haven't learned the secret handshake. No one in the know has hyphenated *antitrust* for 50 years.)

Put simply, antitrust is the body of rules about how individuals and companies (we'll call them "firms" since that sounds econ-y; the Europeans call them "undertakings") are allowed to compete in order to make money. A basic assumption of the U.S. economic system is that competition is beneficial and that firms should behave "competitively," meaning that they should neither coddle up to competitors nor try to push them out of the market, but rather steer to some middle ground called "competition on the merits." In this introductory chapter, we examine the economic foundations of this assumption

1. Markets, Competition, and Marginal Costs

Imagine an armchair economist — let's just make up a random name and call him "Adam Smith" — surveying the world at the end of the eighteenth century. He's trying to figure out what makes the economic order move. Smith is a realist: he recognizes that goods and services don't appear spontaneously out of nowhere, that people don't go to work for the fun of it or to fulfill a divine calling. Smith jots down a note: "It is not from the benevolence of the butcher, the brewer, or the baker that we expect our dinner, but from their regard to their own interest."[1] People are rational, self-interested actors who produce things in order to make money.

But how will they know what to produce and how to price it? An invisible hand — today we'll just call it "the market" — will guide them. All that sounds very mystical! How does the baker actually know how many loaves he should bake each morning and what price to set? The answer is that he learns by trial and error. If he prices a loaf of bread at even one cent more than his competitor's price, all of his customers will abandon our poor baker and go elsewhere. Since such an error could cost him his living, our baker learns pretty quickly. The mover of the invisible hand is *competition*.

But what determines the competitive price? The answer turns out to be cost — but cost of a particular kind. Suppose that it costs the baker $1 dollar in flour, oil, salt, and heating to bake a loaf of bread. It also takes an hour of his time, during which he could have earned $1 in wages by working for someone else. We can now refer to $2 as the *marginal cost* of producing a loaf of bread. *Marginal* refers to the cost of producing the next loaf. Notice that we are not including in the marginal cost the price that the baker paid for his oven or his bakeshop. Those costs are *fixed*, meaning that they remain the same regardless of how many loaves the baker produces.

According to classic economic theory, competition drives prices down toward marginal costs — in our example, the cost of the baker's raw materials and the opportunity cost of his time. Each baker would, of course, prefer to sell his bread for more than $2. But if one baker set her price at $2.20, another would think, "Well, it costs me only $2 to make another loaf of bread, and I would therefore be better off with any price above $2 for a loaf. So if my competitor is selling for $2.20, I'll sell for $2.19." And then the first competitor thinks, "Gee, I wanted $2.20, but I'll lose all sales if that's my price. I'm better off with any price above $2 than with nothing, so I'll go to $2.18." And this chivying down of the price continues until the market price reaches the marginal cost. The price can't go any lower than the marginal cost, because then no baker would be willing to stay in the business.

---

[1] Adam Smith, *An Inquiry into the Nature and Causes of the Wealth of Nations* 19 (C.J. Bullock ed., P.F. Collier & Son 1909) (1776).

1. Markets, Competition, and Marginal Costs

We have just articulated the foundational and supremely important economic assumption that competition drives prices down to marginal costs. Let's pause for a second and consider three implications of that postulate. First, what if our baker can't get his raw materials for $1 like everyone else? In that case, he can't afford to price bread at $2. In modern parlance, we would say that our baker is less efficient than the market leaders, and hence he should pursue a different calling. Throughout the pages to come, we will see repeated examples of courts showing contempt for less efficient competitors.

Second, if firms priced at marginal cost, wouldn't that mean that they would never earn profits? Yes, but *in competitive markets there are no profits*. When I say things like this in class, a few students invariably pick up their books and head for the door. What do you mean that firms in competitive markets earn no money? Why would anyone ever go into a business expecting always to break even? The answer requires an exposition on the meaning of the word *profit* to economists. Recall that we allowed the baker to include $1 for the value of his time in the computation of marginal cost. We could do the same thing with equipment — say, a mixing machine — that the baker could rent out to someone else for other purposes. If he could get $1 an hour in rental fees for the mixing machine, then he would be forgoing $1 by using the machine to make his bread. Or suppose that the $1 he invested in the raw materials could have earned him five cents of interest if deposited at a bank. You might say that the baker is forgoing "profits" from wages, equipment, or financial investment that he could be earning elsewhere, so when we include those items in the marginal cost and make the market price equal to the marginal cost, we actually see the baker earning a "profit."

To economists, however, those "profits" are simply the opportunity costs of not deploying the baker's labor and capital elsewhere. They are thus "costs," not profits. In this parlance, a "profit" or "rent" is earned only when the seller is able to price an item or service above its cost, including its opportunity costs. To put it another way, recovering the opportunity cost of your investment in a particular industry — an ordinary rate of return on capital — is not equivalent to earning *economic profits*, whatever else your grandmother may believe.

Third, some bright minds may have noticed that our neat little story about the market price equaling the marginal cost means that the baker never covers the cost of his fixed investment in the oven and bakeshop. Why would anyone ever go into the baking business if she knew that she would never recover the basic capital expenditures needed to enter the business?

This turns out to be a bedeviling issue in economic theory with all sorts of complicated answers that, by extension, complicate antitrust law as well. As we shall see, various activities that antitrust law polices, such as price-fixing agreements, price discrimination, and certain monopolization strategies, could be explained as devices to allow the sellers to recover their fixed costs. Keep your eye on this ball!

2.   Market Power, Efficiency, Deadweight Losses, and Wealth Transfers

What happens if the invisible hand goes to sleep? Now our butcher, brewer, and baker are no longer constrained by competition and can charge a price above the competitive level — above the marginal cost of production. In a nutshell, that's what we mean by market power. *Market power* is the power to price without regard to the response of one's competitors or to exclude competitors from the market.

For now, let's not worry about how market power arises; let's simply observe its effects. Suppose that under competitive conditions, a loaf of bread is priced at $2, but then something happens to inhibit competition and the price goes up to $3. Is that bad? Your grandmother (or even you) might say, "Of course that's bad. We don't want prices to go up!" But why not? From the baker's perspective, getting an extra $1 on bread is a good thing. Maybe the baker is poor and deserving and the buyers of bread are all rich and greedy.

To get at the answer, let's observe two things that occur when bread prices go up. First, one group of consumers continue to buy bread as before and pay an extra dollar a loaf. Second, another group of consumers stop buying bread because they find the new price excessive. This second group of consumers now buy something else instead — maybe rice cakes or oatmeal.

Economists describe the economic effect represented by the first group — those who keep buying at a higher price — as a *wealth transfer*. Compared against a baseline of perfect competition, $1 of wealth per loaf is being transferred from consumers to producers.

Is that a bad thing? Cold-hearted economists will tell you that it's not, or at least we don't know. According to economic theory, wealth transfers are neutral from an efficiency perspective because they simply shift money from one person's pocket to another's, and there's no telling whose pocket the money belongs in.

2. Market Power, Efficiency, Deadweight Losses, and Wealth Transfers

We just introduced another term — *efficiency* — that turns out to be critical to antitrust analysis. Efficiency has all sorts of meanings to economists, but antitrust law tends to focus on two particular kinds. *Productive efficiency* refers to the state in which costs of production and/or distribution are minimized. In our bread hypothetical, we are given no facts suggesting that productive efficiency is affected one way or the other by the price increase. *Allocative efficiency* refers to the state in which scarce social resources are put to their most valued uses. Concerns over allocative efficiency often dominate antitrust analysis.

Wealth transfers do not necessarily have any effect on allocative efficiency. In our bread hypothetical, the same transaction in bread continues to occur, so the scarce social resources (the raw materials and labor that went into making the bread) are still put to their most valued uses. The fact that producers are skimming money off of consumers is efficiency neutral, since it is impossible to tell whether that has a positive or negative effect on overall social welfare.

Let's now return to the other class of consumers — those who stopped buying bread when the price went to $3. Their loss is what economists call a *deadweight loss*. Allocations of scarce social resources that would have occurred in a competitive market did not occur. Instead, social resources were devoted to rice cakes and oatmeal, allocations considered second best to bread.

In order to protect the innocent, I have foresworn the use of graphs for this book, but will make one exception. The graph that appears on the next page, which appears in virtually every antitrust case book and treatise, demonstrates the harms caused when prices rise above a competitive level. The graph consists of a demand curve with price on the *y*-axis and quantity demanded on the *x*-axis. The curve (a hypothetical convention) slopes downward from left to right, denoting the fact that as the price of something goes up, people buy less of it.[2] Point C on the demand curve represents the intersection of supply and demand at a competitive price. For the reasons explained above, the competitive price is assumed to equal the sellers' marginal cost. When a firm obtains monopoly power it raises its price to the point on the curve denoted M, the monopoly price. The area between C and M is divided into a square or rectangle representing wealth transfers ("WT") and a triangle representing deadweight losses ("DWL").

---

[2]The Illyrian Renaissance Sheepherding Fiction majors among us may point out that the line in the graph can't be a "curve" because it's quite straight. Sorry, a "curve" to economists is just the line that connects the dots on a graph, whatever its shape.

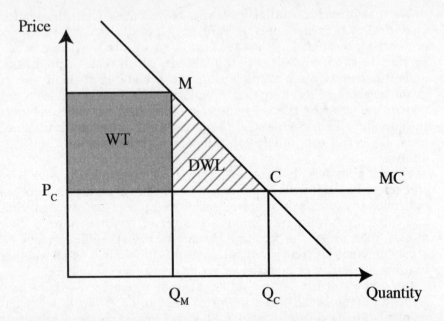

This graph captures the essence of the antitrust project, at least from the perspective of most modern economists. Antitrust law is designed to avoid the deadweight losses and the resulting losses of allocative efficiency that occur when firms with market power raise price above the competitive level. Again, these deadweight losses are thought inefficient because they disrupt the optimal allocation of scarce resources and require consumers to shift to second-best solutions. Wealth transfers do not entail allocative efficiency losses and hence are not considered as lying at the heart of the antitrust project.

3. Consumer Welfare and Other Objectives of Antitrust Policy

As you can imagine, this economist's conception is not free from controversy. Many antitrust scholars would argue that antitrust policy should be designed to protect consumers from exploitive high prices, even those high prices that result in only wealth transfers and not deadweight losses. Historical scholars have argued that in framing the Sherman Act, Congress intended primarily to protect consumers against wealth transfers.[3]

Things often get very confusing when we start talking about what the objectives of antitrust policy should be. On the one hand, there is widespread agreement — in the United States, at least — that antitrust law should exist primarily if not exclusively to advance *consumer welfare*. Indeed, the Supreme Court has described the antitrust laws as a "consumer welfare prescription."[4] One the other hand, different scholars and judges use the term *consumer welfare* to refer to different things. For example, the *Chicago School* of antitrust analysis — associated with scholars such as Richard Posner, Robert Bork, and Frank Easterbrook — tended to argue that antitrust law should seek to advance consumer welfare and nothing else. Bork, however, explicitly excluded wealth transfers from his definition of consumer welfare, instead equating consumer welfare with allocative efficiency and the avoidance of deadweight losses. Some commentators find it a curious practice to define consumer welfare to exclude wealth transfers from consumers to producers. Courts often use the term "consumer welfare" loosely without specifying in which sense they mean to use that term.

Although consumer welfare is an ambiguous term, whether it includes wealth transfers is often inconsequential. This is because the kinds of conduct that cause wealth transfers also cause deadweight losses; hence, antitrust policy makers don't have to stop and worry about the meaning of consumer welfare. (Price discrimination is a thorny exception, but more on that later.) More often than not, the debate is on whether antitrust should be limited to advancing consumer welfare or should include other policy objectives, such as promoting economic rivalry for its own sake, deconcentrating economic power for social and political reasons, protecting smaller business people from overly aggressive rivals, or promoting a level playing field so that people can chose what business or vocation to pursue. These other objectives are often said to be "noneconomic," although they obviously concern economic activity and regulation. It might be better to say that they are objectives that do not directly refer to allocative efficiency.

You may have noticed that the discussion so far has been about the benefits of competition in driving prices toward marginal costs. But surely consumers care not only about price, but also about quality. There is both an easy answer and a hard one. The easy answer is

---

[3] *See* Robert H. Lande, *Wealth Transfers as the Original and Primary Concern of Antitrust: The Efficiency Interpretation Challenged*, 50 Hastings L.J. 871 (1999).

[4] *Reiter v. Sonotone Corp.*, 442 U.S. 330 (1979).

that price and quality are economically interchangeable. If the bakers keep the price of a loaf of bread at $2 but cut out the salt, thus diminishing the quality, that is economically similar to holding the price of bread constant but increasing the price. In theory, the competitive market should determine not only the price but the quality of bread, and losses of market competitiveness can show up as price increases, quality decreases, or both.

The harder answer is that antitrust policy has an uncertain and at times problematic relationship with one particular form of quality—innovation. Some commentators believe that modern antitrust policy is excessively focused on short-run price effects to the neglect of the long-run interest in innovation. Figuring out which policies favor and which ones retard innovation is no easy task and is largely beyond the scope of this book.

4.   Competitive Markets, Monopoly Power, and Forms of Anticompetitive Conduct

Let us return now to Adam Smith's description of the ideal competitive market guided by the invisible hand. Of course, there is virtually no such market in existence anywhere. As Smith himself recognized, every market suffers from imperfections that cause deviations from the ideal of perfect competition. Perfect competition is therefore an idealized baseline, not a fully attainable goal.

All sorts of factors can cause a market to deviate from perfect competition. For expositional ease, let's break them down into two groupings. First, there are *structural* conditions in markets that frustrate the perfect operation of the invisible hand. Think back to our bread example. The bread market may often come close to the competitive ideal because of three important facts about bread: one loaf of bread is pretty much like another, information about bread is pretty simple to obtain, and it's not difficult to set up a bakeshop. But once we change any of these three conditions, it's not hard to see how some degree of market power can arise.

When commercial goods that compete with each other are pretty much the same, we say that they are *fungible, homogeneous,* or *undifferentiated.* Think of commodity futures traded on the Chicago Mercantile Exchange. One bushel of wheat may be pretty much identical to another bushel of wheat. On the other hand, many commercial goods that compete with each other differ in important respects. They are said to be *non-fungible, heterogeneous,* or *differentiated.* Think of Coke and Pepsi. The Coca-Cola and PepsiCo companies spend a huge amount of money on advertising trying to convince consumers that their products are different. Although Coke and Pepsi are obviously competitive products, Coca-Cola and PepsiCo each have some degree of market power by virtue of brand differentiation.[5]

Information costs or *information asymmetries* are another important source of market power. Suppose that you are in a bazaar haggling over a Persian rug. You, the buyer, have a general sense of the market price for the rug you want, and you might get it a little cheaper next door. But you're tired of haggling at different shops and are willing to pay a couple of dollars more than you might have to just to be done with it. Knowing this, the seller may not offer you his *reservation price* — his true bottom line (which presumably equals marginal cost). Such information costs are pervasive in most markets, although they vary in degree.

In our baker story, it would be futile for a baker to raise her price above the competitive level, since that would simply invite more competition. If you were a blacksmith making only a competitive rate of return on capital and you observed that the bakers were all making a handsome economic profit, you might decide to change professions. The lure of monopoly profits, economists say, attracts new entry. But what if entry isn't so easy? Suppose, for example, that being in the baking business is heavily regulated and the Department of Bakeries issues only one new permit a year. Such a *barrier to entry* can facilitate pricing above a competitive level.

Structural conditions such as these are pervasive in real markets and mean that many sellers — perhaps most or all sellers — have some degree of market power. Market power is a matter of degree. Antitrust law can't be concerned with every instance of market power — for example, the power inherent in having a distinctive brand or in information being a little bit imperfect. As we go through various antitrust concepts, we will hear courts trying to signal this fact by bringing up concepts such as "an appreciable degree of market power." We will also hear courts talking about *monopoly power*. There is nothing magical separating market power and monopoly power. Monopoly power is just a very strong form of market power. Exactly where the dividing line falls is unclear — which is why

[5]Economists have different models to explain how firms compete in different kinds of markets. *Cournot competition* occurs when firms sell a homogeneous product and compete by deciding on how much output they will produce. *Betrand competition* occurs when firms sell differentiated goods and compete on price. An economist's choice of a Cournot or Betrand model may influence the assessment of a market's competitiveness — for example, whether the loss or addition of a firm will affect prices or output levels.

11

Chapter 1. Foundational Economic Assumptions

antitrust lawyers can afford to charge lots of money for their services and drive BMWs.

The structural conditions are not anything that antitrust policy can change. They are relevant to discussions about whether firms have market power, but they are pervasive facts. Antitrust policy cannot directly change structure, but it can attempt to prevent *anticompetitive conduct* that enables firms to exercise market power. Broadly speaking, there are three types of anticompetitive conduct.

Collusion refers to an agreement by competitors to diminish the competition among themselves. The simplest form of collusion is a price-fixing agreement, whereby competitors agree on the price they will charge for their goods or services instead of letting the market mechanism determine the price. For example, the lysine cartel depicted in the Matt Damon movie *The Informant!* involved a multi-year conspiracy by Archer Daniels Midland, two Japanese companies, and two Korean companies to set prices on the animal feed additive lysine. Three ADM executives landed in the federal penitentiary.

Exclusion lies at the opposite end of the spectrum from collusion. Instead of cooperating too much, one or more firms engage in anticompetitive acts to drive rivals out of the market. The classic example of exclusion is blowing up a competitor's factory, but we will encounter many other varieties (if you want a quick mental picture, think of the Justice Department's lawsuit against Microsoft). Although exclusion is conceptually the opposite of collusion, its economic effect is largely the same: the thwarting of the invisible hand and the power to charge a price above a competitive level.

Merger refers to the permanent combination of two firms into one, for example AT&T's failed attempt to acquire T-Mobile which the Justice Department blocked. You might think of this as a strong form of collusion since it involves agreement, but there are important legal and economic differences between mergers and collusive agreements. Indeed, after a merger, the two merging firms are deemed a single economic entity for antitrust purposes and are therefore legally incapable of colluding with one another.[6]

We have now introduced the basic economics on which modern antitrust policy is grounded. To recap, antitrust law is designed to prevent certain behaviors that thwart the competitive functioning of the market and hence damage consumer welfare through price increases and/or quality reductions. It now remains to fill out "the details."

[6] *Copperweld Corp. v. Independence Tube Corp.*, 467 U.S. 752 (1984).

Chapter *2*

Triage of Antitrust Problems

Antitrust can be a difficult subject to master. Antitrust novices often find it hard even to frame the questions presented by a fact pattern. Much of the challenge lies in the proper "triage" of the relevant issues. Similar to the way an emergency room intake nurse must decide whether patients should be sent to the outpatient wing or into the operating room, the initial challenge in antitrust cases is to make a few broad-brush categorization decisions about the kinds of analysis that will be required.

This chapter introduces some key branches in the decision tree that will help you to navigate the tangle of legal and economic theory to come. Obviously, you will not be prepared for the triage of antitrust problems until you know more about the substance of antitrust law. But starting with the right framing questions will help you to avoid many of the confusions that entrap the casual student of antitrust.

1. Statutes and Common Law

If you open up the United States Code to Title 15 and begin browsing through the text, you will find scores of pages of statutory text forming a succession of statutes beginning with the 1890 Sherman Act. If you study the annotations, you will encounter the names of a variety of statutes: the Clayton Act, the Federal Trade Commission (FTC) Act, the Robinson-Patman Act, the Celler-Kefauver Act, and the Hart-Scott-Rodino Act, among others.

If you spent, say, five or six hours with the statutory texts, you might think you knew something about antitrust law. Actually, you would know almost nothing, or at least almost nothing that would help you to analyze an antitrust case. This is because antitrust law is mostly a common law overlay on a very broad and open-ended statutory text. In other words, most federal antitrust law is a creation of the courts, particularly the U.S. Supreme Court. Antitrust law is not true common law in the sense that it's a wholesale creation of the courts, but its texture is much more like that of torts or contracts than of truly statutory subjects like taxation, bankruptcy, and environmental law. Until you master the cases and the economic theories they embody, you won't know antitrust law.

Although the statutory texts consume many pages in the United States Code, the meat of the statutes appears in three terse paragraphs: Sections 1 and 2 of the Sherman Act and Section 7 of the Clayton Act. Here they are:

> **Section 1:** Every contract, combination in the form of trust or otherwise, or conspiracy, in restraint of trade or commerce among the several States, or with foreign nations, is declared to be illegal.
>
> **Section 2:** Every person who shall monopolize, or attempt to monopolize, or combine or conspire with any other person or persons, to monopolize any part of the trade or commerce among the several States, or with foreign nations, shall be deemed guilty of a felony. . . .
>
> **Section 7:** No person engaged in commerce or in any activity affecting commerce shall acquire, directly or indirectly, the whole or any part of the stock or other share capital and no person subject to the jurisdiction of the Federal Trade Commission shall acquire the whole or any part of the assets of another person engaged also in commerce or in any activity affecting commerce, where in any line of commerce or in any activity affecting commerce in any section of the country, the effect of such acquisition may be substantially to lessen competition, or to tend to create a monopoly.

Roughly speaking, Section 1 prohibits agreements in restraint of trade, Section 2 prohibits monopolizing behavior by even a single entity, and Section 7 prohibits anticompetitive mergers and asset acquisitions. The statutory texts do contain a few important juridical ingredients. For example, it is clear from the text that there is no Section 1 liability without some sort of agreement (precisely what kind will consume much of our attention in Chapter 5). Section 2 speaks of liability for both attempted monopolization and actual monopolization, which gives rise to some important distinctions about degrees of market power. But despite a few examples where the text matters, most antitrust law proceeds within the broad frame of the statutory category without making much reference to the statutory text.

What about the remaining scores of pages of antitrust statutes? For present purposes, we will largely dismiss them. Where the other statutory provisions are substantive, as in the case of Sections 2 and 3 of the Clayton Act, they have been interpreted to be largely coextensive with Sections 1 and 2 of the Sherman Act. For example, Section 2 of the Clayton Act (as amended by the Robinson-Patman Act) makes price discrimination illegal, but the Supreme Court has held that primary line price discrimination entails nothing different from monopolization through predatory pricing under Section 2 of the Sherman Act.[1] Section 3 of the Clayton Act prohibits certain tying and exclusive dealing arrangements but has been interpreted as being largely coextensive with the common law tests for tying and exclusive dealing developed under Sections 1 and 2 of the Sherman Act. Section 5 of the FTC Act gives the FTC broad powers to prohibit "unfair methods of competition," but the FTC generally confines itself to bringing cases governed by theories developed under Sections 1 and 2 of the Sherman Act.

The upshot is that, unless otherwise instructed, you should not worry too much about the statutory texts and should focus instead on the evolving common law of antitrust, as created by the courts. Most of the time, it will be enough to know whether the relevant case is being decided under Section 1, Section 2, or Section 7. Often, the relevant liability theory will span multiple statutory sections, and the key will be to learn the relevant principles governing the commercial practice at issue (e.g., tying, exclusive dealing, or price fixing) without worrying about what statutory sections it invokes. When it is important to focus on a statutory quirk, we will be sure to draw your attention to it.

2. Rules and Standards

Every year in my student evaluations, one or two students include a comment to the following effect: "I wish he had taught us more of the black letter law." This is the marker of a student who has not "gotten it." There is relatively little black letter law in antitrust law. (Some would say that there is relatively little *law* in antitrust law.) Most of the time, the liability determinants are multifactored and open-ended. A particular offense may have "elements" in a tort law sense, but simply reciting elements will not get you very far. The real work happens in the nuanced outworking of a legal theory, usually heavily seeded with economic theory.

---

[1] *Brooke Group, Ltd. v. Brown & Williamson Tobacco Corp.*, 509 U.S. 209, 222 (1993). The relationship between the Robinson-Patman Act and Sherman Act is discussed in Chapters 8 and 9.

You may have encountered the distinction drawn in legal theory between "rules" and "standards." A rule is a liability determinant that usually focuses on a single dispositive factor. The 55 mph speed limit is an example of a rule. A standard is a liability determinant that focuses on a number of often cumulative factors or an open-ended value judgment to be applied circumstantially. "Drive reasonably under all circumstances" is an example of a standard.

Antitrust is governed much more by standards than by rules. As you will discover in subsequent chapters, there are categories of business behavior that courts call "per se" illegal. The best and clearest example is price fixing, an agreement by competitors to set the price of their products according to an agreed-upon schedule. The "per se" rule seems very rule-like since it is a flat legal prohibition concerning a particular behavior. As we shall see, however, even the per se rule can seem rather standard-like in application. Most other categories of antitrust violation are governed by very general principles.

Practically speaking, this means that you need to be prepared to work nimbly with applied policy tools in relatively unconfined spaces. Once you have identified the relevant analytical category (e.g., the question is whether the joint venture bylaws violated the rule of reason), most of the value you add to the problem will come from asking economic questions: What is the relevant market? Do the defendants have market power? Are there efficiency justifications for the rejection of the competitor's application to join the joint venture?

When we say that these value additions involve "economic questions," we need to recognize that they are economic in a stylized legal way. Case law limits the kinds of economic arguments that parties can raise and may channel economic discussions into fairly formalistic categories. Economists sometimes react with puzzlement at the "economic" assumptions that lawyers and judges make. Still, our job in this book is to help the student learn the economic vocabulary employed by judges and lawyers in litigating and deciding antitrust cases.

3. Precedent and History

Inconveniently, antitrust law did not spring full blown from the head of Congress in 1890. Indeed, antitrust law has been a story of dramatic ideological swings from one epoch to another. It developed rather slowly with an essentially pro-trust bias over its first decade; took off in a new, interventionist direction during the Progressive Era; came largely to a halt during World War I; was radically reformulated three times within the space of a single administration during the

New Deal; took off like a rocket during the postwar boom; was brought rudely down to earth by the Chicago School in the 1970s; and may be in the midst of a post-Chicago revival in the twenty-first century.

That's all fascinating to historians, but what's a law student to do with this information? Many of the older precedents are from eras that do not reflect modern antitrust thinking. When a case has been explicitly overruled, as is true of many of the Supreme Court's vertical restraints precedents, the answer is easy: just disregard the old precedent and follow the new one. But the Supreme Court has not been terribly active in antitrust in recent years and many of the older precedents are still on the books. For example, the Supreme Court has not decided a merger case on the substantive merits since the mid-1970s, yet economic and legal policy about merger law has changed dramatically in the last three decades. (As we shall see in Chapter 11, modern merger law is dominated by the Department of Justice and the FTC's merger guidelines, not by case law.)

The upshot is that some of antitrust law consists of old cases still on the books with questionable predictive power about what the courts would do today. Most antitrust casebooks introduce recent lower court opinions in such circumstances. Still, it is important to keep an eye on the older precedents, since even lower courts that want to distance themselves from those cases' central ideas continue to cite the old cases to create the appearance of adhering to precedent.

It is also important to understand the importance of certain cases as "anti-precedents." As you know from other courses, lawyers and judges often use a particular form of argument: "The argument the dissent makes here is the same kind of argument the Court accepted in *Dred Scott*" or "This is just *Plessy v. Ferguson* repackaged." Antitrust law does not have many cases with the visceral repelling power of *Dred Scott* or *Plessy*, but there are a number of cases that are important for their demonstration of error — or, at least, error in the eyes of contemporary judges or your professor. One case — *du Pont*, or "the *Cellophane* case" — is even known primarily for its "fallacy." So even though, as a general matter, you should emphasize doctrines and precedents thought to be "good law" today, older and overruled cases still play a significant role in illuminating the contours of antitrust law.

4. Vertical and Horizontal Relationships

Much of the trick to learning antitrust law is mastering the economic jargon. (The glossary at the end of this book is there to assist in this endeavor.) One key distinction that will emerge in a variety of contexts is that between *vertical* and *horizontal* relationships.

Two firms are horizontally related if they operate at the same level of production or distribution. That is to say, firms are horizontally related if they are competitors. Coke and Pepsi, Nike and Adidas, and Intel and AMD are horizontally related. Thus, an agreement between Coke and Pepsi would be considered a horizontal agreement.

Two firms are vertically related if they have a business relationship other than a horizontal one. In other words, a relationship is vertical if it concerns firms that operate at different levels of production or distribution. Examples of vertical relationships are supplier-manufacturer, manufacturer-distributor, distributor-retailer, and retailer-customer relationships. Intel is vertically related to Dell since it supplies microprocessors for Dell computers. Dell is vertically related to me, since I bought a laptop from Dell.

Although both vertical and horizontal agreements and relationships can raise antitrust concerns, as we shall see, antitrust law tends to be more lenient toward vertical relationships than toward horizontal relationships. For example, horizontal price fixing is treated more severely than vertical price fixing and horizontal mergers are treated more stringently than vertical mergers. Some in the antitrust community wonder whether antitrust law should scrutinize purely vertical relationships and agreements at all.

As a triage strategy, it is important to keep track of whether vertical or horizontal issues are under consideration at any particular moment. As we shall see, the horizontal and vertical categories interact with our three basic types of relevant conduct: collusion, exclusion, and merger. If a manufacturer blows up its competitor's factory, that's a horizontal exclusion strategy. If it bribes its competitor not to make a new product, that's a horizontal collusion strategy. If a retailer induces its customers not to buy from a rival retailer, that's a vertical exclusion strategy, although the effects may be felt horizontally (i.e., through the diminished sales opportunities of the rival retailer).

Determining whether a particular relationship is horizontal or vertical can be tricky, particularly in the "New Economy" in which industries evolve very quickly. In 2000, Microsoft and Google weren't competitors — their relationship was purely vertical. Microsoft made operating systems and software; Google made search engines. In 2014, there are no two more aggressively competitive rivals than Microsoft and Google. Both companies have evolved into (and often created) market segments that make them competitors and, some would say, mortal enemies.

We shall return to the vertical and horizontal categories frequently throughout this book and expound on their significance. For now, just remain keyed in to the basic distinction and be prepared for further elaboration.

Chapter 3

Market Definition and Market Power

Antitrust law is primarily or exclusively concerned with problems of market power. As we saw in Chapter 1, market power is the power to price without regard to rivals' competitive response, to exclude competitors from the market. Later chapters will be concerned with conduct that enables firms to acquire or maintain market power, whether individually or collectively. This chapter is concerned with two more foundational concepts: (1) what is a market and (2) how do we recognize power in a market? Those concepts—relevant market definition and indicia of market power—cut across most of the questions that will preoccupy us in the rest of this book.

1. Defining Relevant Markets

Traditionally, the first step in analyzing the majority of antitrust problems is to define a relevant market. In later chapters we will discuss more specifically the contexts in which relevant market definition is or isn't required. As a working premise, let's assume that a plaintiff must define and prove a relevant market in all rule-of-reason cases under Section 1 of the Sherman Act, all Section 2 monopolization cases, and all merger cases under Section 7 of the Clayton Act, and that the only time a plaintiff does not have to prove a relevant market is with respect to conduct that is per se illegal under Section 1. While this statement is a little overbroad and does not quite cover all of the possibilities, market definition is undoubtedly a foundational step in most antitrust cases.

Defining relevant markets may be the most difficult task in antitrust analysis. It may also be an ill-conceived task. Prominent antitrust academics have called for the abolition of relevant market as a legal analytical tool,[1] and, as we shall see, the 2010 Horizontal Merger Guidelines sharply downgrade it (more on this in Chapter 11). Still, market definition remains a deeply embedded concept in antitrust jurisprudence and shows no signs of evaporating soon.

The Supreme Court has told us that the purpose of defining relevant markets is to determine the "area of effective competition" in which market power may exist.[2] You might rephrase this to say that market definition is about determining who the defendant's competitors are. If market power is the power to raise prices or reduce output without regard to the competitive response, we have to be able to identify the competitors capable of responding to the defendant's price increases or output reductions in order to decide whether the defendant has market power.

Although the "area of competition" language suggests that market definition is a function of geographic space, there are always two distinct components to relevant market definition: product and geography. If Acme Corp is the only company that sells widgets in Topeka, one might casually say that Acme has a monopoly over widget sales in Topeka. But it might be that Acme—although facing no widget manufacturer rival in Topeka—has absolutely no market power. For example, it may be that there are a hundred companies selling fidgets or gidgets in Topeka, and customers think of fidgets and gidgets as completely interchangeable with widgets. Or it may be the case that there are plenty of competitive widget sellers in Kansas City, and customers in Topeka are indifferent about whether they purchase widgets in Kansas City or Topeka. In the former case, we would say that widgets is too narrow a product market definition and in the latter we would say that Topeka is too narrow a geographic market definition.

The relevant case law does not suggest a systematic, step-by-step approach to defining relevant markets. Broad principles—many of them flawed and contradictory—can be derived from three major Supreme Court decisions.

1.1. The *Cellophane* Fallacy

In *United States v. du Pont*[3]—known simply as "the *Cellophane* case"—the Supreme Court had to decide whether du Pont had unlawfully monopolized the cellophane market. That, in turn, required determining whether cellophane even was a relevant market or whether the

---

[1] Louis Kaplow, *Why (Ever) Define Markets?*, 124 Harv. L. Rev. 437 (2010).
[2] *Brown Shoe v. United States*, 370 U.S. 294, 324 (1962).
[3] *United States v. E.I. du Pont de Nemours & Co.*, 351 U.S. 377 (1956).

market should be considered wider, including other flexible packaging materials like Pliofilm, glassine, foil, polyethylene, waxed paper, and Saran Wrap. If the relevant market was just cellophane, du Pont, with 75 percent of all domestic cellophane sales, would probably have been considered a monopolist. But if the relevant market included all flexible packaging materials, then du Pont had less than 20 percent of the market and certainly would not be considered a monopolist.

The Supreme Court began by explaining that, in order to be condemned for having "monopolized," du Pont would need to be shown to possess monopoly power. It then defined monopoly power (as we did in the last chapter) as the power "to control prices or exclude competition." Could du Pont control cellophane prices or exclude competitors from selling cellophane?

The answer, the Court explained, turned in large part on how consumers perceived the reasonable substitutability of various products. If purchasers of flexible packaging materials viewed cellophane and, say, Saran Wrap as reasonably substitutable, then du Pont wouldn't have monopoly power even if it controlled a large percentage of cellophane sales. If du Pont tried to increase the price of cellophane above marginal cost, buyers would just substitute away to Saran Wrap. So long as consumers perceive Saran Wrap and cellophane as being reasonably substitutable, those two products should be considered as being parts of the same relevant market for antitrust purposes.

But how do we know whether consumers view Saran Wrap and cellophane as reasonably substitutable? Here, the *du Pont* Court resorted to some fancy economic jargon. Two products are reasonably interchangeable from a consumer perspective if there is a high degree of *cross-elasticity of demand* between the two products. There's a lot packed into this, so let's break it down.

First, let's look at simple *demand elasticity*. Demand elasticity refers to the relationship between a change in price and a change in the quantity demanded. Say the price of sugar goes up by 20 percent and that as a result, the amount of sugar that people are willing to buy falls by 10 percent. In that case, economists would say that the elasticity of demand for sugar is 0.5. If the price goes up 10 percent and the quantity demanded falls by 20 percent, demand elasticity would be 2.

Conventionally, if demand elasticity is above 1, economists say that demand is *elastic*. This means that price changes result in comparatively large decreases in the amount desired. Conversely, if demand elasticity is below 1, economists say that demand is *inelastic*. Here price changes result in comparatively small decreases in demand. Demand elasticity is an important concept in antitrust policy, and we will encounter it frequently.

Now back to *cross*-elasticity. Cross-elasticity refers to the relationship between a change in the price of one product and the amount of demand for another. Suppose that people eat chocolate sauce only on vanilla ice cream and eat vanilla ice cream only if they have chocolate sauce. Suppose that the price of chocolate sauce goes up by 30 percent. What will happen to the demand for vanilla ice cream? If our information is correct, demand for vanilla ice cream must go down. People consider vanilla ice cream and chocolate sauce to be *complements* that they consume in relatively fixed proportions. If the price of one of the complements goes up, the demand for the other complement must go down, since the price of the overall "ice cream and chocolate sauce" consumption experience has gone up. Thus, where complements are involved, there is *negative* cross-elasticity of demand between the products.

But now think about raspberry ice cream and strawberry ice cream. Sure, there are people who really must have one or the other, but lots of berry ice cream aficionados would be happy with either flavor. Suppose the economic data showed that a 10 percent price increase in raspberry ice cream (due to a drought in raspberry fields in the Pacific Northwest) resulted in a 10 percent increase in the demand for strawberry ice cream. In that case, we would observe a *positive* cross-elasticity of demand between raspberry and strawberry ice cream.

Back to the *Cellophane* case. According to the Supreme Court, the best way to determine whether consumers consider two products reasonably substitutable is to ascertain whether there is a positive cross-elasticity of demand between them. If so, then consumers are telling us through their purchasing behavior that the two goods are substitutes. If the two goods are substitutes, then they belong in the same relevant market, because they compete with one another.

So far so good. But now we come to a cruel difficulty of application. In *du Pont*, the Supreme Court looked at the record and found evidence of positive cross-elasticity of demand between cellophane and other flexible packaging materials. Based on historic pricing data, it found that any increase in the price of cellophane would make people start buying Saran Wrap and other packaging materials instead. Based on this finding, the Court found that cellophane and other flexible packaging materials were in the same relevant market, that du Pont (with its less than 20 percent of market share) did not have monopoly power in that market, and therefore du Pont could not be guilty of monopolizing that relevant market. Judgment for du Pont.

Wrong, wrong, wrong. The virtually universal consensus today is that the Court committed a fundamental theoretical error. Note well: The consensus is not that du Pont was actually a monopolist because cellophane was its own relevant product market. Rather, the consensus is that the Court's approach did not exclude the possibility that cellophane should have been declared its own relevant market and, therefore, that du Pont was a monopolist.

Why? Well, suppose the following occurred. Thirty years ago there were hundreds of competing cellophane producers. The market price of cellophane was $1 a roll. No one thought that other flexible packaging materials were a good substitute for cellophane. But then du Pont began to do naughty things. Systematically, it bought out its competitors, drove them out through predatory pricing, murdered their executives, and blew up their factories. As of 25 years ago, du Pont was the last cellophane producer left.

Obviously, du Pont's profit-maximizing strategy once its cellophane competitors were eliminated would be to raise its price. But how high? Well, to the point that any further price increase would be unprofitable. Du Pont doesn't know the answer initially. So it raises the price from $1 to $2. A few people stop buying, but most people grudgingly continue to buy cellophane. Why? They consider other flexible packaging materials not to be reasonable substitutes.

But at what price? As Judge Learned Hand explained in *United States v. Alcoa*, "substitutes are available for almost all commodities, and to raise the price enough is to evoke them."[4] In other words, one should not ask the substitutability question generically (i.e., are orange juice and lemonade good substitutes?) but with an identified price point for each item compared (i.e., would consumers consider orange juice and lemonade substitutes if their price was the same, if orange juice was $1 and lemonade $2, and so on?).

Back to our hypothetical. Buoyed by its success at $2, du Pont raises the price to $3. Now it sees a sudden and precipitous drop in demand for cellophane. Customers say, "At *that* price, I'll take Saran Wrap instead." Chastened, du Pont drops its price to $2.50. At that price, most people still buy cellophane. In economic parlance, du Pont has discovered its *profit-maximizing monopoly price* — the point where any further price increase would be unprofitable because customers would substitute other products.

The price stays at roughly $2.50 until the date of the monopolization lawsuit. Discovery occurs. All the evidence shows that for the past 20 years, any time du Pont raised its price above $2.50, customers started buying other products. In other words, the evidence shows positive cross-elasticity of demand between cellophane and other flexible wrapping materials. Employing the *du Pont* rule, a court would have to conclude that du Pont was not a monopolist.

What? *Not* a monopolist after the company carried out dastardly deeds to drive out all of its competitors and then raised the price 150 percent?

---

[4]*United States v. Aluminum Co. of America*, 148 F.2d 416, 426 (1945).

This is the infamous *Cellophane* fallacy: examining cross-elasticity of demand at current prices may result in false negatives (i.e., exonerate monopolizers) because the defendant may already be charging the profit-maximizing monopoly price such that any further price increase would invoke a shift of demand to substitutes. The fact that cellophane and other flexible packaging materials displayed cross-elasticity of demand at then-current prices may reflect nothing more than the fact that du Pont was a smart monopolist — that it had fully exercised its monopoly power by raising the price to the profit-maximizing level at which point any further price increase would be unprofitable because customers would begin to substitute other flexible packaging materials.

The *Cellophane* fallacy is a good reason to be wary about using cross-elasticity of demand to determine reasonable interchangeability in monopolization cases. Still, *du Pont* remains one of the leading Supreme Court decisions on market definition, cited hundreds of times, so we must pay it close attention in antitrust cases. Further, and alas, the alternative methods for defining relevant markets are fraught with peril also.

1.2. *Grinnell* and Unique Customer Preferences

In *United States v. Grinnell Corp.*,[5] the Supreme Court had to answer the same question it answered in the *Cellophane* case: was the defendant a monopolist? As in *du Pont*, this required defining the relevant market. Despite paying lip service to its earlier decision in *du Pont*, the Court conducted a very different analysis in *Grinnell*.

Grinnell and its affiliated companies provided accredited central service station functions such as fire and burglary protection. These services involved the installation of a hazard-detecting device at the customer's place of business with a direct link to a central service station that could notify the police or fire department in case of an alarm. The key issue was whether *accredited* central service station activities were in a product market distinct from other forms of fire and burglary protection, including unaccredited services and other, self-help forms of protection (installing alarms, buying a German Shepherd, etc.).

The evidence showed that at least some customers valued accreditation highly because it resulted in a reduction in their property insurance premiums. The Court conceded that some customers didn't care about the insurance premium reduction and would gladly

[5] 384 U.S. 563 (1966).

substitute a cheaper, unaccredited service. But to the Court, this was not a sufficient reason to find that the relevant market included unaccredited services: "Though some customers may be willing to accept higher insurance rates in favor of cheaper forms of protection, others will not be willing or able to risk serious interruption to their businesses, even though covered by insurance, and will thus be unwilling to consider anything but central station protection." Hence, accredited central station services would serve as the relevant product market.

In contrast to the *du Pont* approach, which examines reasonable interchangeability by focusing on the relationship between changes in prices and changes in demand for possibly substitutable products, the *Grinnell* approach examines reasonable interchangeability by focusing on the peculiar preferences of various individuals who purchase the defendant's products. The Court essentially looked for direct evidence that subpopulations of customers did not consider the two products to be reasonably interchangeable for their purposes. Finding that a subpopulation of buyers did not consider accredited and unaccredited services reasonably interchangeable, it found accredited services to be a separate relevant market.

We noneconomists might be drawn to the *Grinnell* approach since it seems to avoid the *Cellophane* fallacy and rely on direct evidence of the kind lawyers are accustomed to working with. It also seems more intuitive and accommodating of human nature than the aloof cross-elasticity test. Alas, it also presents some potential pitfalls.

Most fundamentally, just because *some* customers don't view product A as a reasonable substitute for product B does not mean that product B and product A aren't competitive products. Recall that our basic goal with market definition is to determine which products constrain the makers of other products from raising their prices. In many cases, sellers can't take into account the idiosyncratic preferences of a few customers when setting their prices. The fact that Aunt Gertrude will never buy life insurance from Met Life because she once had a bad date with a Met Life salesman who had false teeth and a toupee doesn't mean that Met Life is immune from competition with other life insurance companies. Sellers have to think about the big picture: would a price increase be profitable, or would enough customers switch to another product to make it unprofitable?

Suppose, for example, that Grinnell has 1,000 customers. Fifty of them happen to purchase expensive property insurance and really value the insurance discount they receive by being accredited service station customers. But the other 950 customers are indifferent to the insurance premium discount. Further assume that Grinnell doesn't know which customers are the 50 and which are the 950. In that case, it will almost certainly price its services to be competitive with unaccredited services. The mere fact that some customers have idio-syncratic preferences wouldn't govern its decision.

So one might reasonably take the view that the *Grinnell* approach — looking at the unique demand preferences of some subset of customers — isn't good enough. Without knowing how large the sub-population with the unique demand preferences is and what effect, if any, that subpopulation would have on the seller's overall pricing decision, we can't intelligibly define markets.

Some readers are probably itching to respond that it doesn't matter how large the subpopulation is; whatever their number, they are entitled to protection from monopoly, too. Sure, but buyers with idi-osyncratic preferences usually *are* protected from monopoly by the non-idiosyncratic preferences of all the other buyers. Even though Aunt Gertrude would never dream of buying a Met Life policy, when she buys her Aetna policy she finds (or would find, if she studied eco-nomics) that the price is lower than it would be if Met Life didn't exist. This is because Aetna sets its rates by thinking about how most cus-tomers — not just Aunt Gertrude — view reasonable substitutability.

Unless, that is, Aetna, or Grinnell, practices *price discrimination*. Fasten your seatbelts. We're in for another wild ride.

Up until now, we've been assuming that the seller doesn't know which of its customers have idiosyncratic preferences. But suppose that Grinnell does know which of its customers especially value its services because they're accredited. Now Grinnell may be able to charge them a higher price than it charges other customers. That is all that economists mean by price discrimination — charging a higher price based on a greater willingness to pay. In that case, Grinnell would effectively have monopoly power over some customers in the market even though it technically doesn't have monopoly power over customers.

Before you get all excited and announce that the *Grinnell* Court was on to something after all, observe that it is not enough for Grinnell to be able to identify which of its customers have unique demand prefer-ences. It also has to be able to charge them a higher price and make it stick.

This is not always as easy as it sounds. Suppose that a brick man-ufacturer with a patent on purple bricks (no, you can't really patent purple bricks) figures out that 10 percent of its customers really value the purple ones because these customers build in a town that requires purple brick facades on all government buildings. The rest of the cus-tomers plan to mortar over the bricks and don't care what color they are. The brick company now tries to charge a higher price for its bricks to the 10 percent than it charges to the 90 percent. But then some enterprising souls in the 90 percent figure out the game and start resel-ling their bricks to the 10 percent at a lower price than the discriminatory price charged by the company. This is an example of *arbitrage* — buying in one market and reselling in another. Arbitrage tends to erode price discrimination and make it unprofitable. The purple-preferring buyers soon figure out that there's no reason to buy directly from the manufacturer.

So, in order to conclude that the seller can exploit a unique subpopulation through price discrimination, you must establish that at least two conditions are present: (1) the seller must be able to separate the sheep from the goats, that is, to identify the customers with the idiosyncratic preferences; and (2) arbitrage must not undermine the price discrimination. The *Grinnell* Court did not discuss these factors, and the case would have been far more satisfying if it had. We don't know whether Grinnell was able to identify the customers who valued its services distinctly because of their accreditation.

On the other hand, it's a pretty good guess that if price discrimination occurred, arbitrage would not have undermined it in the fire and burglary protection market. As a rule of thumb, arbitrage is possible with goods (since they can be resold to others) but not with services (which cannot be resold to others). Thus, if we want *Grinnell* to make economic sense, we could conjecture that it is a case in which the seller was able to engage in price discrimination without fear of arbitrage. But that would be putting many words into the Court's mouth.

Let's shift gears for a minute and examine another issue in *Grinnell*. So far we've talked mostly about defining relevant product markets. But, as we noted at the outset, a relevant market always has two dimensions: product and geography. Saying that accredited services was the relevant product market would not allow a determination of whether Grinnell had monopoly power unless we knew the geographic area in which to examine the question.

In *Grinnell*, the Court concluded that the relevant market was national. The Court conceded that individual stations generally served only customers within a 25-mile radius. It nonetheless noted that Grinnell engaged in national planning; that the challenged agreements were national; and that price, rate, and term schedules were national. Thus, the Court found that a national market "reflected the reality" of how Grinnell did business.

In dissent, Justice Fortas aptly charged the majority with concocting a "strange red-haired, bearded, one-eyed man-with-a-limp [relevant market] classification." Though politically incorrect, he had a point. In *du Pont* and the product market portions of *Grinnell*, the Court instructed the legal community to define relevant markets by examining how *customers* viewed the question of what products are reasonably interchangeable. In most geographic market definition cases, we do the same thing. We ask whether customers would view sellers in geographic location A as reasonable substitutes for sellers in geographic location B. Obviously, people who buy fire protection services in Seattle do not view service stations in Key West as reasonable substitutes. But in the second half of *Grinnell*, the majority suddenly shifted its focus from the demand side to the supply side and identified a national market because of the way the seller, rather than the buyer, perceived the market.

Despite Justice Fortas's well-aimed objection, courts routinely consider both demand-side and supply-side factors in defining relevant markets.[6] The highly influential Areeda-Hovenkamp treatise puts it this way: "Two products, A and B, are in the same relevant market if substitutability at the competitive price is very high as measured from either the demand side or the supply side. To have separate markets, one must find that a significant price increase beyond the competitive level in the A price would neither induce customers of A to buy B instead, nor induce B producers to make A."[7] In defining relevant markets, it is permissible to consider how sellers might reposition their products in response to a price increase.

So where do we end up on *Grinnell*? As with *du Pont*, we're given new tools to work with, but no systematic or consistent method of defining markets.

1.3.   *Brown Shoe* and Submarkets

The third major Supreme Court case on relevant market definition, *Brown Shoe*,[8] was decided before *Grinnell* but falls third on the list because it is most useful as a refinement of some of the themes raised in *Grinnell*. *Brown Shoe* (i.e., the first *Brown Shoe* case; there was a later *Brown Shoe* decision in a case brought by the FTC) involved a challenge by the Justice Department to a merger between the Kinney and Brown Shoe companies, which were both involved in shoe manufacturing and retailing. The market definition issue was whether the market should be considered as broad as all shoes; divided into three parts—men's, women's, and children's shoes; or further segmented into smaller components (e.g., sports shoes for active boys, expensive shoes for older women).

---

[6] For a more recent case exploring the use of supply-side factors in market definition, *see In re Live Concert Antitrust Litig.*, 247 F.R.D. 98 (C.D. Cal. 2007).

[7] 2B Phillip E. Areeda, Herbert Hovenkamp & John L. Solow, Antitrust Law: An Analysis of Antitrust Principles and Their Application ¶ 561 at 360 (3d ed. 2007).

[8] *Brown Shoe v. United States*, 370 U.S. 294, 324 (1962).

The Court settled on an intermediate classification. It acknowledged that there might be a broad "all shoes" market at some level. But it also noted that shoes were conventionally divided into men's, women's, and children's lines. Assuming that some evidence of supply and demand interchangeability showed up in both the broad and narrower markets, how should a court decide which one should count as the relevant market? The answer, said the Court, was that there could be both a broad general market and narrower "submarkets": "[W]ithin this broad market [all shoes], well-defined submarkets may exist which, in themselves, constitute product markets for antitrust purposes. . . . The boundaries of such a submarket may be determined by examining such practical indicia as industry or public recognition of the submarket as a separate economic entity, the product's peculiar characteristics and uses, unique production facilities, distinct customers, distinct prices, sensitivity to price changes, and specialized vendors."

Brown Shoe thus gives rise to the possibility of defining broader and narrower markets simultaneously (and not merely as alternatives). Although *Brown Shoe* gave us relatively few tools to figure this out, more recent cases have suggested the following approach. Submarkets should be employed when the seller could engage in discriminatory pricing within a broader market. Thus, even though most purchasers of product A might consider product B a perfectly good substitute, if the seller could identify sellers who have idiosyncratic preferences for product A and charge them a higher price, then it is proper to define a relevant submarket around the purchasers with idiosyncratic preferences for product A.

As you may see, the process of defining submarkets invokes some of the themes we discussed with respect to *Grinnell*. Particularly, (1) can the seller identify the buyers with idiosyncratic demand preferences, and (2) can it charge them a higher price, or will arbitrage undermine the price discriminatory scheme?

Example: Acme Corp makes synthetic down sleeping bags. Most campers happily substitute between synthetic and natural down when choosing sleeping bags. However, high-elevation campers insist on synthetic down since it's much lighter to carry and stays warmer at extreme temperatures. Acme proposes to merge with Beta Corp, which also makes synthetic down sleeping bags. Acme's market share of all sleeping bags is 10 percent, but its share of synthetic down sleeping bags is 40 percent. Beta's share of all sleeping bags is 5 percent, and its share of synthetic down sleeping bags is 20 percent. The evidence shows that Acme and Beta compete on price with regard to natural down sleeping bags, and that a general price increase in synthetic down sleeping bags would not be profitable because of competition from natural down. It also shows that they have ways of identifying high-altitude campers. For example, market research suggests that

29

most high-altitude campers frequent specialty outdoor gear stores. Thus, postmerger, it is possible that Acme-Beta will attempt to selectively raise its prices to specialty outdoor gear retailers in the hopes of capturing some monopoly profits from the unwillingness of high-altitude campers to buy natural down sleeping bags.

What's the correct market definition? It seems clear that there is a relevant market for all sleeping bags. But there is arguably also a submarket for synthetic down sleeping bags sold to high-altitude campers. If there is such a submarket, the merger may be in trouble because the Acme-Beta share in that market would be 60 percent (more on this in Chapter 11). The one thing we don't know is whether arbitrage might undercut price discrimination in this market. Sleeping bags are goods, so arbitrage is presumptively possible. If Acme-Beta raised prices just to outdoor gear stores, other retailers, such as Walmart and Target, might decide to make some money by reselling sleeping bags at wholesale to the specialty stores. Do Acme and Beta have plausible strategies to counteract this sort of arbitrage? For example, can they impose contractual restrictions prohibiting their big-box purchasers to resell at wholesale? These are the sorts of questions that one should ask to determine whether high-elevation campers are vulnerable to price increases postmerger and hence deserve to be considered a relevant submarket.

1.4.   Putting It All Together: A Market Definition Toolkit

The case law on market definition is a mess. It fails to leave us with a consistent, systematic approach to defining relevant markets. At best, the courts give us a potpourri of questions to ask. In *Brown Shoe*, the Court suggested that judges should proceed "by examining such practical indicia as industry or public recognition of the submarket as a separate economic entity, the product's peculiar characteristics and uses, unique production facilities, distinct customers, distinct prices, sensitivity to price changes and specialized vendors." Great. What if price sensitivity points one way and the product's "peculiar characteristics and uses" point the other?

Given the prevailing case law, one must approach market definition issues inductively rather than deductively. Instead of starting with a theory and finding facts to fit it, one needs to examine the facts and then work back to a theory that fits them. One needs to approach market definition with a toolkit consisting of various adaptive concepts and vocabularies and then deploy them as the facts seem to suggest. Whether or not this is intellectually satisfying, it is the role of the lawyer working through a market definition issue.

What's in the toolkit? First, it is never wrong at the beginning of a market definition exercise to articulate a broad statement of purpose. Say that the essential function of market definition is to determine (1) the group of products or services and (2) the geographic locations that provide those products or services that customers perceive as reasonably substitutable.

Next, if the facts contain evidence of cross-elasticity of demand — data on shifts in the demand for one product when the price of another changed — explore the possibility of using the *Cellophane* approach. Here the game is usually to determine whether using the cross-elasticity approach would entail the *Cellophane* fallacy. Note well that not all uses of cross-elasticity of demand entail the *Cellophane* fallacy. In particular, watch out for three scenarios in which using cross-elasticity does *not* implicate the fallacy:

(1) The price of the defendant's product went up, but demand for other products did not increase. Here the data show us that the defendant's products and other products are *not* competitive. Whether the defendant has already monopolistically charged the profit-maximizing price is irrelevant, since the data show us that the other products aren't yet substitutes.

(2) The cross-elasticity data are from a period *before* the defendant is alleged to have obtained monopoly power. For example, suppose the plaintiff claims that the defendant blew up all of its competitors' widget factories in 2012 and thus obtained a monopoly over widget production. Suppose there are price elasticity data from 2011 showing that the widget manufacturers all raised their prices by 10 percent and that demand for gidgets increased by 15 percent. There are no *Cellophane* fallacy implications in saying that gidgets belong in the same relevant market as widgets.

(3) A merger is unconsummated. This is just an extension of the last point, but it's worth underlining. Given the Hart-Scott-Rodino premerger notification requirement (see Chapter 10), most merger decisions are made before the merger is finalized. Since the potentially anticompetitive event has not yet occurred, the well cannot yet have been poisoned. Using cross-elasticity data therefore does not entail the *Cellophane* fallacy.

Next in the toolkit is the *Grinnell* approach. Look for direct evidence that some customers do or don't think about products as substitutes. Market research studies, statements by buyers, technological constraints, and practical evidence of the uses and limitations of products may be useful. When defining geographic markets, be attentive to transportation costs, which often give sellers at a particular location advantages over their rivals. Evidence that sellers or buyers conventionally understand the market in a certain way (think of the conventional "men's, women's, and children's" breakdown in *Brown Shoe*) may be relevant.

When you work with this sort of direct evidence, consider whether it is pointing in the direction of a general market definition or a submarket definition. If you observe that some buyers don't seem to consider fidgets a substitute for widgets while others do, first ask whether the buyers who don't view fidgets as a substitute are such a large or important group of customers that the seller would be inclined to raise its price across the board, even if that meant losing some sales to people willing to substitute to fidgets. In that case, the "idiosyncratic" preferences of the fidget haters aren't so idiosyncratic—they're market-determining.

On the other hand, if it seems unlikely that the seller would set a general market price based on the fidget haters' preferences, you need to entertain the possibility that fidget haters are a submarket. Remember your two questions: (1) can the seller identify the fidget haters in order to charge them a higher price, and (2) will arbitrage undermine the effort at price discrimination? If the fidget haters can be identified and charged a higher price, and arbitrage is unlikely to undermine the price discrimination scheme, you have a relevant submarket.

Although throughout these exercises you will usually be focusing on demand-side considerations, don't ignore supply-side factors. Evidence that machines could be quickly retooled to make a different competitive product, that sellers plan and organize a market nationally, or that new technologies are on the horizon may all be pertinent to defining relevant markets, even though these factors do not involve viewing the market through the lens of customer preferences.[9]

Finally, look for ways that your "facts on the ground" may reinforce a particular market definition under different theories. You may score a home run if you can show that fallacy-free cross-elasticity data tell the same story as direct evidence of consumer preferences and uses, and that supply-side considerations bolster the story. When stories seem to point in different directions, ask which story is more helpful in answering the question with which you began: Which products are reasonable substitutes and hence practically constrain the pricing power of other suppliers?

---

[9]When we examine market definition under the merger guidelines in Chapter 11, we will see that these sorts of supply considerations are separate from market definition and considered as evidence on the question of market power. However, in other antitrust cases, they may come under market definition — as *Grinnell* suggests.

2. Market Power

Once you have a properly defined product and geographic market, the next step in many antitrust cases is to determine whether the defendant or defendants have market power in that market. Market power questions are less conceptually tricky than market definition questions, although there are pitfalls here as well. Most mistakes occur because of imprecision about why you are asking the market power question. We'll look at specific uses of market power questions in later chapters. For now, observe that market power questions generally arise in three circumstances:

1. Actual monopolization cases, where the question is whether the defendant is a monopolist. As we previously observed, monopoly power is just a strong version of market power.
2. Attempted monopolization cases, where the question is whether the defendant — although not yet a monopolist — was dangerously close to becoming a monopolist. Many of the factors relating to market power are useful in determining whether the defendant was close to becoming a monopolist.
3. Rule-of-reason and merger cases, where the defendant need not have monopoly power to violate the relevant statutes, but where lesser amounts of market power are still relevant to determining liability.

In all three kinds of cases, we look for the same categories of information. The differences are largely ones of degree: how much power is necessary for finding liability of the variety at issue.

2.1. Market Share

The most important determinant of market power is the defendant's share of the market. The relevant share may be that of an individual company, or it may be that of a group of companies or individuals if the group's actions are under investigation. For example, in joint ventures or association cases, it is usually the cumulative market share of the joint venturers or association members that is relevant, since it is generally the joint actions of the venturers or the bylaws or rules of the association that are attacked as anticompetitive. In those cases, the question is whether the collective share of the group points toward group market power.

Sometimes the facts simply reveal market shares and the only question is in interpreting their significance. In other cases there may be a struggle over what the relevant market shares are. Usually, this occurs because of differences between units sold and revenues. A Mercedes-Benz dealer may sell 10 percent of all cars sold in a particular region but have 20 percent of all revenues from automobile sales; this is obviously because a Mercedes is more expensive than most other cars. Assuming that automobile sales in this particular region is the appropriate relevant market, which figure — 10 or 20 — is the right market share number to assign?

There is no general answer to this question in the case law. As we shall see in Chapter 11, the Horizontal Merger Guidelines suggest that revenues are generally appropriate for calculating market shares, but sometimes other factors like units sold or produced or productive capacity may be more appropriate.

Once we know the relevant market shares, we must interpret their significance. As a rule of thumb, a market share above 70 percent is required for a finding of monopoly power. In *Alcoa* Judge Hand stated that a share above 90% would constitute a monopoly but that "it is doubtful whether sixty or sixty-four persent would be enough; and certainly, thirty-three percent is not. Although Judge Hand basically pulled these numbers from thin air, the *Alcoa* pronouncement has stuck.

In attempted monopolization cases, there is no hard and fast rule on how large a share of the market the defendant must have had to be guilty of the offense. Often in attempt cases, it is the trend in the share — that is, was defendant's share increasing or decreasing — that is most probative. We will return to attempted monopolization particulars in Chapter 7.

What market share is required for a defendant to have market power in a rule-of-reason case under Section 1 of the Sherman Act? Again, there is no hard and fast rule. A survey of the cases suggests that a 30 to 40 percent share is roughly the threshold for market power, although courts sometimes find market power when the defendant has a lesser share and other factors strongly point toward the existence of market power.

2.2.   Entry Barriers

The second most important factor in market power analysis is the presence or absence of entry barriers. Suppose that the defendant has a 50 percent market share, and hence presumably some degree of market power. Hypothesis 1: If the defendant raised its price 10 percent, six new suppliers would come into the market, attracted to the lure of the defendant's extraordinary profits like bugs to a light. Hypothesis 2: If the defendant raised its price 10 percent, no one would enter, because entry into this market is difficult. Which hypothesis we believe is true colors our view of the significance of the defendant's large market share as demonstrating market power.

Alas, a juridically unresolved definitional question intervenes. What exactly is an entry barrier? Is it just anything that makes entry difficult or expensive? If that's the case, then many markets are subject to entry barriers. However, a much narrower definition of entry barriers has support in influential quarters. One of the key tenets of the Chicago School is that only expenses incurred by new entrants but not by incumbents should be considered entry barriers.

For example, suppose that it costs a billion dollars to design a new sonar system for submarines. There are currently two sonar system suppliers. They had to incur the cost of a billion dollars necessary to enter the market and have to reincur that expense whenever they create a new generation of sonar. To the Chicago School and its adherents, the fact that it's very expensive to get into the sonar business is not an entry barrier, since anyone in the market has to incur that expense.

Under the Chicago School definition, what are examples of entry barriers? Well, the most likely culprit is governmental regulation favoring incumbents — say, a land use restriction with a grandfather clause for existing businesses. Other examples might include access to scarce resources that the incumbents have already tied up and various other first-mover advantages. Strong buyer brand preferences arising through happenstance rather than investment in brand promotion are another example.

The Chicago School view is not written in stone. Many judges are probably willing to find entry barriers based on considerable expenses or difficulties to enter a market, whether or not the incumbents share in those difficulties or expenses. Just be prepared to flag this definitional issue, where appropriate, in discussing market power issues.

Entry barriers in high-technology markets are a popular focus of discussion in recent years and deserve some introductory mention. In particular, the modern antitrust student should pay close attention to the theory of *network effects*, which receive quite a bit of attention in high-tech cases like *Microsoft* (more on this in Chapter 7). A network effect occurs when one party's use of a particular technology or infrastructure makes another party's use more valuable. The classic example is the telephone. When Alexander Graham Bell called his assistant Thomas Watson on March 10, 1876, the telephone was basically a toy. But when a second line was connected, the value of Bell's telephone grew, because there were more people to call. Each new connection added to the value of the system — not just to the newly connected user, but to everyone else with a telephone.

Network effects can act as entry barriers, because they tend to standardize technology along the parameters set by the first firm to enter the market. Subsequent entrants might have a better technology, but find it difficult to peel away customers from the incumbent since the incumbent's network has so many customers and hence so much value to the user. In the *Microsoft* case, the D.C. Circuit found that operating system users and programmers writing applications for operating systems were both attached to Microsoft's Windows operating system because of strong network effects.[10] The more users that an operating system had, the more willing programmers were to write programs for that operating system. The more programs written for an operating system, the greater the number of those willing to use it. This "chicken and egg" problem allegedly made it difficult for rival operating systems to displace Microsoft.

2.3. Other Factors

Beyond market share and entry barriers, courts and antitrust agencies often turn to a smattering of other buyers in determining a defendant's market power. Short of an exhaustive recitation, here are some of the other factors to consider.

- **Powerful or sophisticated buyers.** Where buyers are relatively few in number, economically powerful, or highly sophisticated, the defendant may find it difficult to raise its price even though it faces little or weak competition.
- **Changing technology.** The defendant may have been dominant for the past 50 years, but new technologies are emerging that threaten to displace its market position. Conversely, a defendant may have a relatively small market share today, but may be sitting on a technology that is likely to become dominant shortly. In that case, a court might conclude that the defendant has market power despite its relatively small present market share.
- **Changing consumer demand.** Changes in customer demand for products can make historical market share numbers seem less significant than predictions about how the players in the market will be repositioned in the future.
- **Diminishing reserves or future capacity constraints.** In *United States v. General Dynamics*,[11] a large coal producer bought a rival coal producer in a transaction that, superficially, appeared to result in significant market concentration.

[10]*U.S. v. Microsoft Corp.*, 253 F.3d 34 (2001).
[11]415 U.S. 486 (1974).

36

Nonetheless, the Supreme Court allowed the acquisition on the ground that the acquired firm had virtually no coal reserves that it hadn't already committed to customers under long-term contracts. Thus, the acquired firm's current share of the market had very little power in predicting the firm's market power in the future. More generally, evidence that a large producer today faces future capacity constraints may be relevant to determining its true market position.

- **Demand elasticity.** We have already seen that demand elasticity is an important criterion for defining relevant markets. It may also be an important factor for determining whether the defendant has market power in the relevant market. Where demand is relatively elastic—that is, where relatively small increases lead to fairly large drops in the quantity demanded—sellers have relatively little power to impose monopolistic price increases. Conversely, where demand is highly inelastic, sellers may have considerable power, since they can increase prices considerably without inducing customers to substitute to other products.

2.4. Profits: The Non-Factor

The alert reader may have noticed that the foregoing discussion contained no discussion of profit margins as evidence of monopoly power. This may strike some as odd. If the monopolist's goal is to earn supracompetitive profits, shouldn't evidence of monopoly profits be the best indication of economic power? The answer is no. Focusing on monopoly profits would produce both false positives and false negatives: it would find monopoly power that isn't present, and it would fail to locate monopoly power that is present.

First, just because a firm earns a large rate of return on capital invested doesn't mean that the firm has a monopoly of the kind that should be of interest to the antitrust lawyers. The problem with focusing on profits actually earned is that it fails to take into account the ex ante risk that the profits would never materialize. Suppose, for example, that an inventor invests in a highly speculative research and development project that has only a 1-in-5 chance of panning out. For every $1 she invests, she has to expect that the invention will yield $5 in profits just to make her investment break even on an expected value basis. If her investment does break even, she will earn five times her investment and hence look like a monopolist using a profitability test. But now suppose that the investor is a big pharmaceutical company that makes many such investments, most of which fail but a few of which turn into blockbuster drugs. Across the board, the company may earn no more than an "ordinary" rate of return on capital, even though it has some hugely successful drugs in its portfolio. So looking at profitability can lead us to believe falsely that a firm is a monopolist when all that is showing up is the successful outcome of a risky investment.

Now consider the flip side: the firm that does not earn an abnormal profit. Does that mean that the firm lacks the power to price above a competitive level or exclude competitors? Before answering, consider two well-known antitrust aphorisms. Nobel Laureate John Hicks once wrote that "the best of all monopoly profits is quiet life."[12] In *Alcoa* Judge Learned Hand stated that "[m]any people believe that possession of unchallenged economic power deadens initiative, discourages thrift and depresses energy; that immunity from competition is a narcotic, and rivalry is a stimulant, to industrial progress; that the spur of constant stress is necessary to counteract an inevitable disposition to let well enough alone."[13] What Hicks and Hand are saying is that monopolists often get lazy and extravagant and internally consume their monopoly profits. Instead of giving back monopoly profits to shareholders, the firms' managers decorate their corporate offices, pay for fancy country club memberships, and lease corporate jets. On the balance sheets, it looks like the company is earning a normal profit, even though it is a monopolist in the economic sense.

There you have it. Market power will be an important threshold question in most antitrust cases, and it is tough sloughing. Consider yourself fortunate if called upon to analyze a fact pattern subject to the rule of *per se* illegality, where market definition and market power are not relevant.

[12]John R. Hicks, Annual Survey of Economic Theory: *The Theory of Monopoly*, 3 Econometrica 1, 8 (1935).

[13]*United States v. Aluminum Co. of America*, 148 F.2d 416, 427 (2d Cir. 1945).

PART II

AGREEMENTS IN RESTRAINT OF TRADE

Chapter 4

Juridical Categories

In this chapter and Chapters 5 and 6 we examine the set of issues that arise under Section 1 of the Sherman Act. As we saw in Chapter 2, Section 1 of the Sherman Act prohibits "contracts, combinations . . . and conspiracies in restraint of trade" — agreements that restrict competition. Unfortunately, the statute tells us very little about how to identify or judge such agreements. That has been the subject of over a century of case law development that we will attempt to unpack in this and the following two chapters.

For organizational purposes, we will begin in this chapter by surveying the issue of juridical categories or analytical modes — the broad patterns that courts use to assess Section 1 claims. In Chapter 5 we will drill down to more specific case law treatment of particular categories of *horizontal* agreements, such as cartel or "naked" price-fixing agreements, group boycotts, information exchange agreements and other facilitating practices, and joint venture agreements. We will also consider the question of when there is an agreement for purposes of Section 1. Finally, in Chapter 6 we will look at Section 1 treatment of vertical contractual restrictions — a subject that has become less important because of case law developments in recent years.

1. Historical Development

Most students of U.S. antitrust law are introduced to Section 1 of the Sherman Act by looking at the Supreme Court's early efforts to pour content into the statute and the gradual systematization of the doctrine over the course of the twentieth century. We can't afford the luxury of a detailed historical exposition here, but let's take a quick peek at the history from 30,000 feet in order to set the stage.

After the passage of the Sherman Act in 1890, the initial problem facing the Supreme Court was a textual one. Section 1 prohibits all agreements that "restrain trade," without exception. But all kinds of ordinary agreements restrain trade. Imagine a partnership agreement

41

between two doctors who agree to pool their business assets, patient lists, and time and to work as a team rather than as competitors. The doctors fix a common fee for their services and make all business decisions jointly. The doctors have literally agreed to restrain competition; indeed, they have agreed to stop competing against each other completely. But no one believes that all such agreements should be illegal. To interpret Section 1 of the Sherman Act as barring every agreement that restrains trade in any way would be to forbid a myriad of arrangements clearly necessary to economic prosperity and stability.

In its first major Section 1 opinion, *Trans-Missouri Freight Association*,[1] the Supreme Court suggested that it would take an absolutist position and prohibit literally every agreement restraining trade. But the Court quickly retreated from that position and recognized that certain "restraints of trade" were reasonable and should be upheld. With its landmark *Standard Oil* decision in 1911,[2] the Court finally put to rest its absolutist suggestion from *Trans-Missouri* and held that only unreasonable restraints of trade are illegal under Section 1. Thus was born the *rule of reason*.

Although recognizing that only unreasonable restraints of trade should be declared unlawful, the courts did not want to have to deal with the slippery concept of reasonableness in every Section 1 case. So, over time the courts began to recognize certain categories of agreement that were so likely to be anticompetitive and so unlikely to have any redeeming virtues that they should be declared conclusively illegal. In the leading case, *Socony-Vacuum*,[3] the Supreme Court described the essential character of these nakedly anticompetitive agreements as follows: "Any combination which tampers with price structures is engaged in unlawful activity. . . . Under the Sherman Act a combination formed for the purpose and with the effect of raising, depressing, fixing, pegging, or stabilizing the price of a commodity in interstate or foreign commerce is illegal per se." Thus was born the rule of per se illegality.

In *Socony*, the Court explained that when a restraint of trade is deemed illegal per se, there essentially are no justifications that can be offered for it. It doesn't matter that the defendants might have had good reasons (such as reacting to depressed economic conditions and stabilizing production) for the restraint. The fact that defendants lacked economic power, that prices weren't on average higher, or that the plaintiff failed to identify a relevant market or adverse economic effects also is unavailing as a defense. Further, it is not necessary to

[1] *United States v. Trans-Missouri Freight Ass'n*, 166 U.S. 290 (1897).
[2] *Standard Oil Co. of New Jersey v. United States*, 221 U.S. 1 (1911).
[3] *United States v. Socony-Vacuum Oil Co.*, 310 U.S. 150, 221 (1940).

per se illegality that the defendants literally agree on a price. As noted, any arrangement that tampers with market-determined pricing structures is "price fixing" and per se illegal.

For a long time—roughly between 1940 and the mid-1970s—law school students learned that Section 1 cases fall into two categories—per se cases and rule-of-reason cases. But there's a problem with the dichotomous approach to Section 1 adjudication—the problem of all rule-based systems. In order to know which rule to apply, the system has to create categorization rules. And it's often very hard to frame and apply those categorization rules without doing the work that the analytical categories (rule of reason and per se) are supposed to be doing. Thus, much of the time spent figuring out whether a restraint of trade should be assigned to the per se or rule-of-reason category requires asking some of the factual questions that the per se rule was intended to preclude.

Consider the leading "characterization" case, *BMI*.[4] ASCAP and BMI are the two leading "performance rights" organizations in the United States. They essentially act as clearinghouses for the transmission of copyright permissions from music copyright owners to users like television and radio stations (and, today, often Internet media companies) that want to publicly perform the copyrighted music. ASCAP and BMI typically issue "blanket licenses" for entire musical repertoires at fees established by them (not the copyright holders). In the 1970s CBS became unhappy with the fees that ASCAP and BMI were charging and the form of their licensing agreement, and the broadcaster brought an antitrust suit challenging the blanket licensing structure as a per se illegal price-fixing agreement among the copyright holders.

Was it? Literally, there was "price fixing." Justice White conceded as much in his opinion for the Supreme Court: "[T]he blanket license involves 'price fixing' in the literal sense: the composers and publishing houses have joined together into an organization that sets its price for the blanket license it sells." But, said Justice White, "[l]iteralness is overly simplistic and often overbroad." Whether a restraint of trade involves price fixing "is not a question simply of determining whether two or more potential competitors have literally 'fixed' a 'price.' As generally used in the antitrust field, 'price fixing' is a shorthand way of describing certain categories of business behavior to which the *per se* rule has been held applicable."

The Court then went on to explain that ASCAP and BMI's blanket licensing system was not "price fixing" in the antitrust sense and hence merited rule-of-reason rather than per se treatment. The key fact in this "characterization" decision was that blanket licensing is

---

[4]*Broadcast Music, Inc. v. CBS*, 441 U.S. 1 (1979).

characterized by tremendous efficiencies. The transaction costs of individual licensing negotiations between copyright holders and users meant that there would be far less licensing, and hence far fewer lawful public performances of copyrighted music, if blanket licensing were prohibited. Hence, the Court concluded that ASCAP and BMI were not truly coordinating price fixing among their copyright owner clients, but were creating a "different product" — the blanket license — and then deciding its price.

Here's the paradox: Per se analysis prohibits consideration of the efficiencies of a restraint of trade and requires no showing that it raises prices or leads to diminished output. But to determine whether something is "price fixing" and hence condemned as "per se illegal," courts sometimes have to determine whether the restraint in practice is justified by any efficiencies and whether it has positive or negative effects on price or output. Thus, in at least some cases, the *characterization* stage of analysis will allow the defendants to make arguments about the efficiencies and procompetitive effects of the restraint, arguments that would be inadmissible once a practice is deemed "price fixing" and hence per se illegal.

One consequence of this broad characterization stage is that the label *per se illegal* often becomes more of a conclusion than a real analytical category. Courts say "this is per se illegal" after asking precisely the kinds of questions — about competitive effects, justifications — that they aren't supposed to be asking about per se illegal restraints.

Closely related to the development of a characterization stage of analysis, reflected in *BMI*, was the development of an intermediate category of Section 1 analysis, residing somewhere between open-ended rule-of-reason analysis and inflexible per se analysis. In *NCAA*[5] the Supreme Court struck down a restriction by the NCAA on the television broadcasting of intercollegiate football games. The district court and court of appeals had found that the restriction amounted to a per se illegal price-fixing and output restriction agreement. The Supreme Court, however, held that some restraints were essential in intercollegiate athletics and hence declined to apply the per se rule. Under conventional analysis, this should have led to full rule-of-reason analysis, including a requirement that the plaintiff prove that the defendant has market power and that anticompetitive effects result from the restraint. But the Supreme Court stopped short of requiring full rule-of-reason analysis. Citing the prominent antitrust scholar Philip Areeda, it noted that "the rule of reason can sometimes be applied in the twinkling of an eye" and without "elaborate industry analysis."

---

[5]*National Collegiate Athletic Association v. Board of Regents*, 468 U.S. 85 (1984).

NCAA and several other decisions gave rise to a "quick look" Section 1 analysis, which we shall discuss in greater detail below. For purposes of this overview, the essential point is that many commentators, and some judges, think that the broadening of the characterization stage and the introduction of the "quick look" approach has undone the dichotomous approach — or, rather, revealed that the dichotomy never applied. In other words, they contend that these Section 1 modes of analysis aren't really discrete categories into which cases are dropped, and that all Section 1 analysis is really on a continuum from presumptively unlawful agreements to presumptively lawful ones.

Consider the D.C. Circuit's decision in *Polygram*.[6] The "Three Tenors," José Carreras, Placido Domingo, and Luciano Pavarotti, put on concerts coinciding with the World Cup soccer finals in 1990, 1994, and 1998. Polygram distributed recordings of the 1990 concert, Warner of the 1994 concert. The two labels cooperated to promote the 1998 recording. As part of their cooperation, they agreed not to market or discount the 1990 and 1994 recordings during the early period of their joint promotion of the 1998 recording.

The FTC brought suit, viewing the agreement as "inherently suspect" and ultimately finding it unlawful. The D.C. Circuit affirmed, offering a sweeping perspective on the development of Section 1 "categories" over the last few decades. The court explained that "the Supreme Court has steadily moved away from the dichotomous approach — under which every restraint of trade is either unlawful *per se*, and hence not susceptible to a procompetitive justification, or subject to full-blown rule-of-reason analysis — toward one in which the extent of the inquiry is tailored to the suspect conduct in each particular case." Although some commentators and courts had viewed the quick look as creating an intermediate category of analysis, the D.C. Circuit saw "quick look" developments as revealing the decline of "categories" altogether in favor of a more continuous approach: "It would be somewhat misleading, however, to say the 'quick look' is just a new category of analysis intermediate in complexity between '*per se*' condemnation and full-blown 'rule of reason' treatment, for that would suggest the Court has moved from a dichotomy to a trichotomy, when in fact it has backed away from any reliance upon fixed categories and toward a continuum."

To be certain, the Supreme Court and the lower courts continue to employ the categories. There are still cases that turn on whether a particular restraint is per se illegal or subject to rule-of-reason analysis. But it is also undoubtedly true that case law developments have

---

[6]*Polygram Holding, Inc. v. FTC*, 416 F.3d 29 (D.C. Cir. 2005).

revealed that the categories are not hermetically sealed—that lots of substantive antitrust analysis, including analysis about the costs and efficiencies of certain practices, is performed at the triage stage, when courts are deciding how to classify the practice. In that sense, legal analysis of all restraints of trade falls along a continuum, even though the categories of analysis are recognized.

2.   Triage of the Categories

Suppose that you are called upon to analyze the legality of a restraint of trade under the antitrust laws. Given the tension between the categorical and continuous styles of analysis described in the previous section, how do you start?

The first step is to identify the restraint at issue. Exactly what is the agreement being challenged? At this stage, it's very important to give as precise and technical a definition as possible to the restraint at issue. In good lawyerly fashion, this involves stripping the parties and facts of some of their identities and particular characteristics and assigning them generic antitrust labels. For example, take the facts of *Polygram*. A journalistic account of the agreement might read something like this: "Warner and Polygram, two major record labels, agreed to jointly market *Three Tenors 3*. They also agreed that, while they were jointly marketing *Three Tenors 3*, they wouldn't lower their prices on *Three Tenors 1* (owned by Polygram) or *Three Tenors 2* (owned by Warner)." Let's rewrite in antitrust legalese: "Horizontal competitors in a joint venture agree to suspend price discounting outside the joint venture for a limited time while jointly promoting the joint venture."

What we've done is to reduce the agreement to its legally important form, stripping out facts and characteristics that might be eventually important (e.g., competition in music is different from competition in corn) but might also distract us from the initial categorization exercise. What's important in the facts is that we have horizontal competitors who are in a probably lawful joint venture and are agreeing to suspend price competition outside the joint venture. Let's look at each of those elements in turn.

First, the fact that we have horizontal competitors is crucially important to the characterization. As already noted, antitrust law tends to treat restrictions among horizontal competitors with considerably greater suspicion than it does restrictions among vertically related firms. With the exception of some "tying" cases we'll discuss in Chapter 8 as exclusionary practices, the per se categories are usually reserved for agreements among horizontal competitors.

Second, the fact that the parties are in a lawful joint venture is important. Any restrictions between parties within the scope of a bona fide joint venture are analyzed under the rule of reason.[7] That is because the restrictions are "ancillary" (a term of art) to an otherwise lawful agreement. The opposite of *ancillary* is *naked*, and generally only "naked" restraints are per se illegal.

Third, the restriction is on price discounting and promotion. That's important because an agreement between competitors not to compete on price generally meets the definition of "price fixing" under *Socony* and is therefore per se illegal.

So everything comes down to the last observation, that the "price fixing" is occurring with respect to products that are not part of the joint venture. The question now is whether to classify the restraint as price fixing on the ground that it falls outside the scope of the space otherwise protected by the joint venture (JV).

This would be a good moment to think about the *BMI* and *NCAA* type of cases. Because of the presence of the JV, there's some doubt as to the classification of the restraint. The defendants will likely be permitted to make an argument that the restriction is necessary to advancing the socially desirable aspects of the JV. For example, they might argue that since the parties are jointly promoting a very closely related product, they should be allowed some leeway on restraints of trade outside the scope of the JV. Otherwise, each member of the JV might be tempted to free-ride on the other member's promotional activities, which would undermine the joint promotion agreement.

One could view that kind of argument as a "characterization" argument: the defendants are saying, "This isn't price fixing, because it's actually output expanding." Or it could be an opportunity for a quick look at the justification, where the defendants bear an initial burden of proving that a restraint that is prima facie suspect is actually justified by some special circumstance. In any event, following the identification of precisely what the restraint is, the moment arises for arguments about how it should be classified for purposes of Section 1 analysis.

The result of this analysis is still likely to be a decision to put the restraint into one of two buckets: (1) per se illegal, in which case the defendants simply lose; or (2) rule of reason, in which case many more facts need to be discussed. At the end of this initial stage of analysis it may seem that the per se and rule-of-reason categories are very important. But seeing everything that goes into making the initial determination makes it clear that the categories are not self-defining and that, even in cases that end up as per se illegal, there's lots of initial room to talk about efficiencies and justifications.

---

[7] *Texaco, Inc. v. Dagher*, 547 U.S. 1 (2006).

We now turn to some more specific remarks on each of the three "categories."

3. The Per Se Rule

Despite all of this talk about the difficulties of assigning restraints of trade to "categories," there are still some core cases where, if the restraint is proven, there will be little question that it is per se illegal. (In those cases, the big money is often on whether or not there was an agreement—a subject discussed in the next chapter.) Generally, the per se rule will be applied to the following categories of horizontal agreement.

3.1. Naked Price-Fixing Agreements

Naked here means that the price fixing is the whole point of the agreement; it's not ancillary to some other agreement, like a joint venture, the sale of a business, or the settlement of a dispute. Recall that under *Socony*, price fixing is a broad concept, including any scheme designed to tamper with the market mechanism for setting prices.

3.2. Bid Rigging, Market Manipulation, Output Reduction, and Related Market Distortion Schemes

Under *Socony*'s broad definition, schemes that fall short of agreement directly on prices but specify mechanisms to subvert market pricing—such as by colluding on bids, shutting down factories, disseminating false information, or "cornering" a market—can be instances of per se illegal price fixing.

3.3. Naked Market Division Agreements

If two competitors agree that A will do business in Georgia and B will do business outside of Georgia, and they won't enter each other's market, that is naked market division and is per se illegal.[8] The same applies to an agreement that A will sell product X and B will

[8]*Palmer v. BRG of Georgia*, 498 U.S. 46 (1990).

sell product Z, and they each won't sell the other's product. Or that *A* will sell to customers 1 to 3 and *B* will sell to customers 4 to 6, and they won't "poach" each other's customers. It's illegal per se to divide up geographic or product markets or customers and agree not to compete in each other's "territory."

3.4. Buyer Price Fixing or Market Division

Most antitrust cases focus on seller-side schemes, but it is also per se illegal for buyers to collude to drive down the prices of their purchases. For example, if two buyers at an auction agree to refrain from competing with each other in the bidding so that they can acquire the goods at a lower than competitive price, that is per se illegal (although note that if the parties are submitting a joint bid to have an opportunity to participate in an auction they otherwise could not afford, that may look procompetitive rather than anticompetitive).

3.5. Horizontal Group Boycotts

The final per se category is tricky, and we will discuss it in greater detail in the next chapter. For now, simply observe that there is such a thing as per se illegal horizontal agreements to boycott competitors.

4. The Quick Look

Suppose that you are analyzing an agreement in restraint of trade that does not seem to fit squarely into one of the traditional per se categories but seems pretty close — perhaps like the *Polygram* agreement. The agreement is horizontal, it has a fairly immediate and obvious effect in increasing prices or reducing output, and it's not integral to a joint venture or other lawful business relationship. You have a candidate for application of the *quick look* approach.

The quick look is a confusing area of doctrine because the Supreme Court has not clearly identified its parameters. But let's do our best to give the doctrine some content. In the most important "quick look" case to date, — *California Dental*,[9] the Supreme Court held that the quick look approach applies to restraints of the type not previously held to be per se illegal but that "an observer with even a rudimentary

---

[9]*California Dental Association v.* FTC, 526 U.S. 756 (1999).

understanding of economics could conclude ... would have an anti-competitive effect on customers and markets." If a court determines that the restraint falls within the quick look category, then the defendant is called upon immediately to proffer a procompetitive justification for the restraint. If she succeeds in offering such a justification, then full rule of reason should apply to the restraint. If she fails, then the restraint is condemned as per se illegal.

Let's walk through these steps. Suppose you observe a restraint and initially want to know whether it's within the traditional per se categories. Since we've already seen in *Socony* and *BMI* that whether a restraint is "price fixing" is not about literal application of the label, this won't always be obvious. But here are some markers for kinds of restraints that, while similar to the traditional per se illegal ones, would likely be subject to quick look review.

4.1.   Ethical Rules or Professional Codes of "Learned Professions"

Many professional groups, such as doctors, lawyers, engineers, and architects, adopt ethical rules or professional codes that restrict competition among their members. In *California Dental*, for example, the dental association prohibited its members from engaging in certain kinds of advertising on price or quality. Restrictions not to compete on price or quality advertising sound a lot like price fixing, within *Socony*'s capacious definition. But the Supreme Court has typically been reluctant to apply the per se rule to efforts at professional self-policing, so in many "professions" cases the quick look will apply.

4.2.   Cases Where Some Restraints on Competition Are Inherent

In *NCAA* the Supreme Court declined to apply the per se rule because operating intercollegiate sports leagues inherently involves agreeing on some restrictions on competition. Following this reasoning, one might apply the quick look to cases of fairly obvious restrictions on price or output occurring in the context of necessary restrictions on competition.

4.3.   Agreements with Noncommercial Motivations

Nonprofit status—for example, of hospitals, universities, or religious organizations—does not confer immunity from the reach of the Sherman Act. Nor, as a general matter, does a noncommercial objective justify restricting competition. However, courts may be less inclined to apply the per se rule when the actors are noncommercial or are pursuing noneconomic objectives. For example, in *United States v. Brown*,[10] the Third Circuit applied the quick look to an agreement between MIT and eight Ivy League schools to determine collectively the amount of financial assistance designated for admitted students. As in most other quick look cases, one could easily characterize this as a form of price fixing, but the court wanted to hear MIT's explanation in search of some plausible and socially desirable objective—such as increasing the diversity of the student body—behind the agreement in question.

4.4. Complex Agreements About New Circumstances or Technologies

The Supreme Court has repeatedly stated that the per se rule is reserved for kinds of restraints with which it has long experience.[11] This does not mean that price fixing of computer tablets would be acceptable, because the Court doesn't have experience with tablets. It's experience with the practice, not the industry or technology, that is important. But it's often the case that new technologies or changed economic or social circumstances bring slight variations to old themes before the courts. For example, an agreement between Internet search companies with respect to the confidentiality of user data in sales to marketing companies might entail concerns related to price fixing, but the overall set of circumstances might be sufficiently different from established and known patterns that a court would apply the quick look rather than the per se rule.

Suppose your analysis has revealed that the restraint in question is far enough from the traditional per se categories that it doesn't require the defendant to go straight to jail, but is suspicious enough to a person "with a rudimentary understanding of economics"—imagine a judge with foggy memories of his introduction to microeconomics in college 27 years ago—that it's slotted for quick look review. What next? The defendant gets one chance to avoid application of the per se rule by offering a procompetitive justification for the restraint. Observe, critically, that the justification coming out of the defendant's mouth cannot be any of the usual defenses in a rule-of-reason case, such as "But I don't have market power," or "But you haven't proven a relevant

---

[10] *United States v. Brown*, 5 F.3d 658 (1993).
[11] *See, e.g.*, *BMI*, 441 U.S. at 9.

market," or "But where's the evidence of anticompetitive effects?" No, the only thing that the defendant is allowed to say is "Your Honor, before you throw my restraint into the per se prison, hear my justification for the restraint. It's good because. . . ."

If the court accepts that the justification is procompetitive and plausible, then the case proceeds to the full rule of reason, discussed next. If the court rejects the justification as not really a procompetitive one (see further below) or one without any support, then the court may find the restraint per se illegal—meaning that no further analysis of the market or competitive effects is required.

5.   The Rule of Reason

The *rule of reason* is the residual category of analysis for contracts in restraint of trade that are not tossed into the per se category or that from triage are sent through the quick look and found to have a plausible procompetitive justification. At its core, the rule of reason asks whether, on balance, the restraint is good or bad for competition. At its worst, the rule of reason feels like a completely amorphous and unstructured inquiry into all the motivations behind the restraint and its alternative and economic effects. However, rule-of-reason cases often turn on much narrower considerations.

The classic articulation of the rule of reason appears in Justice Brandeis's 1918 opinion in *Chicago Board of Trade.*[12] The Chicago Board of Trade (CBOT) had adopted a "call rule" prohibiting members of the exchange from purchasing "to arrive" wheat, corn, oats, or rye at any price other than the closing price of that commodity on the previous day. This was literally a form of price fixing, since it involved competitors agreeing on a common pricing formula, but Justice Brandeis was quick to find that the agreement was justified by its creation of a level playing field and open market for the purchase and sale of agricultural commodities. For Justice Brandeis and the Court, "[t]he true test of legality is whether the restraint imposed is such as merely regulates and perhaps thereby promotes competition or whether it is such as may suppress or even destroy competition."[13] And to answer that question, said Justice Brandeis, "the court must ordinarily consider the facts peculiar to the business to which the restraint is applied; its condition before and after the restraint was imposed; the nature of the restraint and its effect, actual or probable. The history of the

[12]*Board of Trade of City of Chicago v. United States*, 246 U.S. 231 (1918).
[13]*Id.* at 238.

restraint, the evil believed to exist, the reason for adopting the particular remedy, the purpose or end sought to be attained, are all relevant facts."[14]

This classic rule-of-reason articulation reads like a kitchen sink test. Over time, however, the rule of reason has become somewhat more structured. Unfortunately, there is no canonical Supreme Court or lower court decision articulating the analytical framework with precision. Many courts refer to a three-step test, others to a four-, five-, or even six-step test. The precise number of steps is relatively unimportant, since "steps" are often divisible into substeps or assume that other steps have already been taken. For purposes of analytical convenience, we may describe modern rule-of-reason analysis as follows.

Initially, the plaintiff must prove the existence of an agreement in restraint of trade. In many cases, the existence of the agreement is plain and uncontested. For example, the CBOT's call rule was an officially promulgated and written rule, and proving its existence was simple. As we shall see in the next chapter, however, in some cases proving the existence of a horizontal agreement is everything.

Next, the plaintiff must ordinarily define a relevant product and geographic market and prove that the defendant(s) had some degree of power in that market. Here caution is warranted. In *Indiana Federation of Dentists*,[15] the Supreme Court held that the plaintiff in a rule-of-reason case need not define and prove the existence of a relevant market if it can offer direct proof that the agreement in restraint of trade had anticompetitive effects. The Court reasoned that the relevant market definition and market power analysis are merely tools to proving anticompetitive effects, so if there's direct evidence of anticompetitive effects, why bother with the intermediate steps?

This statement may be more confusing than helpful. Many commentators understand *Indiana Federation of Dentists* as a covert quick look case in which the defendants failed to offer an adequate procompetitive justification, and hence proof of relevant market and market power wasn't essential. In any event, it is rare to find a true rule-of-reason case in which a court lets the plaintiff get away without defining and proving a relevant market and showing that the defendant had power in that market. As the First Circuit has stated, "It is not easy to think of a rule of reason analysis that does not depend on showing adverse effects on competition in a properly defined relevant market."[16] It is

---

[14]*Id.*

[15]*FTC v. Indiana Federation of Dentists*, 476 U.S. 447 (1986).

[16]*Stop & Shop Market Co. v. Blue Cross & Blue Shield of Rhode Island*, 373 F.3d 57, 69 (1st Cir. 2004).

quite common to see rule-of-reason cases dismissed for failure to prove the presence of a relevant market or market power in the relevant market (as was true in the remand from the *Leegin* resale price maintenance case, to be discussed in Chapter 6).[17]

The next step is for the plaintiff to prove the existence of anticompetitive effects in the relevant market. Typically, this requires the plaintiff to show that the restraint of trade has resulted in higher prices, reduced output, or diminished quality.

Once the plaintiff has proven the restraint, shown market power in a relevant market, and demonstrated anticompetitive effects, the burden shifts to the defendant to rebut the showing of anticompetitive effects by showing redeeming procompetitive effects. Of course, the defendant is also entitled to dispute the plaintiff's showing on any of the prior steps, but the procompetitive showing is the first instance where the defendant bears the burden of proof and has to make its own affirmative case as opposed to merely poking holes in the plaintiff's theory. For example, if the plaintiff has argued that the restraint resulted in a price increase, the defendant might show that the price increase was more than justified because the restraint resulted in the goods becoming a technically superior and more durable product.

If the defendant rebuts the plaintiff's showing by offering a procompetitive justification, the burden then shifts back to the plaintiff to show one of two things: (1) that the anticompetitive effects "outweigh" the procompetitive virtues or (2) that the procompetitive effects could have been achieved in a manner less restrictive of competition.

Although the first option, the balancing of virtues and vices, makes sense in theory, it is seldom actually done in antitrust cases. In order to balance procompetitive and anticompetitive effects, the fact finder has to assign them weights. This turns out to be a serious challenge. Suppose that a joint venture between pharmaceutical companies results in a new drug that is 30 percent more effective for 10 percent of the relevant patient population, but also increases the pharma companies' market power so they are able to raise their prices to everyone by 7 percent. How does one assign weights to these effects in order to assess their relative magnitudes? The upshot is that although rule-of-reason analysis nominally includes this kind of balancing, it is not a major factor in rule-of-reason cases.

Option 2 of the plaintiff's rebuttal case is significantly more important. In this step, the plaintiff seeks to show that the efficiencies created by the restraint of trade could have been achieved in a manner less restrictive of the competitive process. To return to the previous example, suppose that the pharma companies argue that the new

---

[17]*PSKS, Inc. v. Leegin Creative Leather Prods., Inc.*, 615 F.3d 412 (5th Cir. 2010).

drug resulted from the challenged joint venture agreement, but the plaintiff is able to show that the joint venturers could have pooled their research and development efforts without any agreement on marketing, and hence without increasing their market power. In that case, the joint venture agreement might be illegal on least-restrictive-alternative grounds.

This kind of "means-ends fits" reasoning is pervasive in law. In such analysis, the question is always how tight the fit between means and ends must be. In constitutional law, the courts generally require that governmental restrictions on "suspect" groups such as racial or ethnic groups be justified as strictly necessary to achieve a compelling governmental interest. In contrast to that "strict scrutiny" approach, courts apply "rational basis" review to governmental socioeconomic classifications or regulations: the regulation need only be a rational means of achieving a legitimate objective. Between these poles lie a variety of possible intermediate tests.

It is not well settled in antitrust law whether the "means-ends" stage of rule-of-reason analysis falls closer to the strict scrutiny or rational basis side of the ledger. Although courts often describe this stage as a least-restrictive-alternative test, it is rarely applied as such in practice. As one court has explained, "In a rule of reason case, the test is not whether the defendant deployed the least restrictive alternative. Rather the issue is whether the restriction actually implemented is 'fairly necessary' in the circumstances of the particular, case or whether the restriction 'exceed(s) the outer limits of restraint reasonably necessary to protect the defendant.'"[18] Perhaps the clearest exposition of the consensus standard is contained in the Justice Department and Federal Trade Commission's 2005 Guidelines on Collaborations Among Competitors:

> The Agencies consider only those efficiencies for which the relevant agreement is reasonably necessary. An agreement may be "reasonably necessary" without being essential. However, if the participants could have achieved or could achieve similar efficiencies by practical, significantly less restrictive means, then the Agencies conclude that the relevant agreement is not reasonably necessary to their achievement. In making this assessment, the Agencies consider only alternatives that are practical in the business situation faced by the participants; the Agencies do not search for a theoretically less restrictive alternative that is not realistic given business realities.[19]

---

[18] *Fleer Corp. v. Topps Chewing Gum, Inc.*, 658 F.2d 139, 151 n.18 (3d Cir. 1981) (citation omitted).

[19] *See http://www.ftc.gov/os/2000/04/ftcdojguidelines.pdf*, §3.36(b).

If the plaintiff meets her prima facie burden of proving anti-competitve effects in a properly defined relevant market and is successful in rebutting the defendant's efficiencies defense, then she wins. Such cases are rare. According to one study, defendants win over 99 percent of all rule-of-reason cases.[20] Still, in recent years plaintiffs have won some important rule-of-reason cases, such as the Justice Department's challenge to Visa's and MasterCard's exclusivity rules[21] and the FTC's challenge to realtor groups' restrictive Web site policies.[22] Perhaps as we see the continuing decay of the categorical approach to Section 1 analysis and transition toward the continuum approach previously described, the number of plaintiff victories on the rule-of-reason end of the continuum will increase.

6. The Meaning of *Procompetitive*

As we have seen, the idea of a procompetitive justification for a restraint of trade is central to much Section 1 analysis. It allows the defendant to escape per se condemnation in a quick look case and to rebut a showing of anticompetitive effects in a rule-of-reason case. So let's make sure that we understand what we mean by a "procompetitive" effect.

Recall that in *Chicago Board of Trade*, Justice Brandeis distinguished between restraints that "regulate[] and perhaps thereby promote[] competition" and those that "destroy" it. If you were a literalist, you might believe that *procompetitive* means "makes the market more competitive" or "makes it possible for more firms to compete in the market or for firms to do so more vigorously." To be sure, that kind of evidence is consistent with a restraint's being "procompetitive." In antitrust usage, however, *procompetitive* has come to mean something more than just making the market more competitive. It means, in the broadest sense, "good for consumers."

For example, in *BMI* the justification for the blanket licensing that induced the Court not to condemn the practice as illegal per se was that blanket licensing radically lowered the costs of negotiating for performance rights licensing and hence led to the broader and cheaper dissemination of performance rights. Nothing in this analysis turned on

---

[20] Michael A. Carrier, *The Rule of Reason: An Empirical Update for the 21st Century*, 16 Geo. Mason L. Rev. 827, 829 (2009) (examining all 222 rule-of-reason cases that reached final judgment in the previous decade and finding that the defendant won 221, or 99.6 percent).

[21] *United States v. Visa U.S.A., Inc.*, 344 F.3d 229 (2d Cir. 2003).

[22] *Realcomp II, Ltd. v. FTC*, 635 F.3d 815 (6th Cir. 2011).

the market for dissemination of music copyrights becoming more "competitive" in a literal sense. ASCAP and BMI were the only games in town, and, pursuant to a consent decree, they were (and still are) closely monitored by the federal courts to ensure that their licensing terms were reasonable and nondiscriminatory. If their licensing arrangements were "procompetitive," it was because they reduced transactions costs and hence increased output, not because they literally increased competition. Thus, in making "procompetitive" arguments in a quick look case or anywhere else, one is not limited to proving that the restraint made it possible for there to be more competitors or more competition.

On the other hand, there is a particular kind of argument that is never allowed as a "procompetitive" justification. Indeed, whenever this argument is made, courts tend to view it as an admission that the restraint in question is anticompetitive. The argument is labeled *ruinous competition*, and here's how it goes.

Going back to the very earliest Sherman Act cases, defendants often tried to argue that a restraint on competition was unreasonable because competition was itself unreasonable. Around 1900, this argument had strong support in the economics profession. Economists believed that competition forced prices down toward marginal costs, which was unsustainable in a world of industrialization and mass production with very high fixed costs. Hence, competition led to boom and bust cycles. The only antidote—the only means of making production stable and sustainable—was for the competitors to fix prices or otherwise combine to avoid "ruinous competition." So long as prices were "reasonable," the lawyers advocating this position argued, the restraint should be lawful under the Sherman Act.

In a landmark lower court opinion, Judge William Howard Taft (later President and Chief Justice of the Supreme Court) rejected this theory. He explained that allowing "ruinous competition" claims to justify naked restraints on competition would require courts to decide the reasonableness of prices, which was far beyond the ability of judges. Such a move, said Judge Taft, would cause judges "to set sail on a sea of doubt."[23]

Ever since the earliest cases, "ruinous competition" has been an epithet that judges apply to proffered justifications by defendants that assume that overcoming competition through a restraint of trade is a permissible choice. Consider the Supreme Court's decision in *Professional Engineers*.[24] The Society of Professional Engineers adopted a canon of ethics prohibiting its members from engaging in

[23]*United States v. Addyston Pipe & Steel Co.*, 85 F. 271 (6th Cir. 1898).
[24]*National Soc. of Professional Engineers v. United States*, 435 U.S. 679 (1978).

competitive bidding—that is, offering a price for engineering work before the engineer has been selected by the client. The anticompetitive effects of such a restriction are obvious, but the Court declined to apply the per se rule because this was a professional society's efforts at self-regulation. However, when the Court asked the engineers to justify their rule, the proffered justification served to condemn, rather than sustain, the restraint. The engineers argued that they were trying to prevent price competition from eroding the quality of work done by engineers, which ultimately could endanger public safety. The Supreme Court would have none of it. As the Court saw it, the engineers were attacking the Sherman Act's "legislative judgment" that competition is good: "The assumption that competition is the best method of allocating resources in a free market recognizes that all elements of a bargain—quality, service, safety, and durability—and not just the immediate cost, are favorably affected by the free opportunity to select among alternative offers. Even assuming occasional exceptions to the presumed consequences of competition, the statutory policy precludes inquiry into the question whether competition is good or bad."

The lesson of *Professional Engineers* and similar cases is that the "procompetitive" category is broad, but it is not all-encompassing. Challenging the assumption that competition is a good thing— arguing that competition is in some way "ruinous"—is a sure way to lose a Section 1 case. Thus, in advancing a "procompetitive" argument, a party does not need to show that the market becomes literally more competitive, but she dare not suggest that the market's becoming less competitive is a good thing.

Chapter 5

Horizontal Restraints

Chapter 4 laid the groundwork for Section 1 analysis by describing the generic patterns of analysis. In this chapter we look more closely at Section 1 analysis of certain categories of horizontal agreement, specifically cartel agreements, other "price-fixing" agreements, market division, group boycotts, information exchanges and other facilitating practices, joint ventures, and other ancillary restraints.

1. Cartels

A *cartel* agreement is a "naked" price-fixing agreement that is usually conducted in secret. Once the existence of a cartel agreement is proven, its legal treatment is simple: it's per se illegal under *Socony* and its progeny. Individuals and corporations involved in cartels are criminally prosecuted; fines and private damages suits often run into the hundreds of millions or billions, and executives actually serve hard prison time.

The catch in most cartel cases is not proving the illegality of the agreement but proving the agreement itself. Because most cartel agreements (OPEC excepted, but that's another story) are secret and the members of the cartel have strong incentives to keep it secret, direct evidence of the price-fixing agreement — the proverbial smoking gun — is often lacking. This raises complex questions of proof and of the meaning of the agreement ("contract, combination, . . . or conspiracy") requirement for purposes of Section 1.

Proving the existence of a cartel from purely circumstantial evidence is tricky because of the following theoretical paradox. Suppose that you look at a market where there are four competing sellers who all charge the same price for widgets. Suppose further that on a certain date, all four sellers raise their price by an identical 10 percent. What conclusion can you draw from this fact?

I know what you're thinking. This is an antitrust course, so the answer must be collusion! Why would all four companies raise their prices in unison unless they had secretly agreed on a coordinated price increase? Their behavior is inherently suspicious.

Maybe, but isn't the opposite conclusion equally plausible? Suppose that the market is characterized by truly perfect competition. Each firm is pricing exactly at marginal cost and must be exactly as efficient as every other firm in the market in order to stay in business. Now, say some exogenous shock hits the suppliers. Maybe the price of one of their inputs doubles. If the firms simply react like theoretically rational "price takers" — firms that have no control over price but simply charge established market prices — each will automatically incorporate the same input price increase into the price of widgets. Without any collusion at all, the 10 percent simultaneous price increase could occur.

So here's the paradox: externally observed parallel behavior by firms in a market is, without additional information, equally consistent with two opposite hypotheses — collusion and a perfectly competitive market. The job of antitrust law is to figure out which one of those two hypotheses is more likely to be true in a particular case. In a long line of cases, courts have wrestled with two related and often indistinguishable questions: (1) As a matter of substantive antitrust law, when have two or more parties "agreed" within the meaning of Section 1? (2) What kind of circumstantial evidence is sufficient to support a finding of agreement?

The Supreme Court answered the first question in *Interstate Circuit*.[1] The question was whether a group of movie studios had agreed among themselves to fix the price of "first run" and "subsequent run" movies shown in theaters in certain regions of Texas. The evidence showed that Interstate, a powerful Texas movie theater chain, had sent each of the studios a letter, copied to the other studios, demanding that they impose certain pricing restrictions on movie theaters in the relevant region. Representatives of the studios attended meetings in which Interstate repeated these demands. There was no direct evidence that the studios agreed among themselves, but they all acquiesced to Interstate's demand.

The Supreme Court found that the evidence sufficed to find that the studios had conspired horizontally. It found that the facts that the studios were solicited jointly by Interstate, that they engaged in substantially identical pricing conduct, that it was a substantial change from prior practice, and that they offered no counter-explanation for their new pricing requirements were sufficient to sustain the verdict. These facts supported an inference of agreement within the meaning of Section 1.

---

[1] *Interstate Circuit v. United States*, 306 U.S. 208 (1939).

Toward the conclusion of its opinion, the Court made a further observation that seemed to expand the scope of Section 1 considerably: "While the District Court's finding of an agreement of the distributors [studios] among themselves is supported by the evidence, we think that in the circumstances of this case such agreement for the imposition of the restrictions upon subsequent-run exhibitors was not a prerequisite to an unlawful conspiracy. It was enough that, knowing that concerted action was contemplated and invited, the distributors gave their adherence to the scheme and participated in it." This language could easily be read to mean that actual agreement is not required under Section 1 — that it's enough if competitors decide to engage in parallel conduct knowing or expecting that the other firms in the industry will follow suit.

The problem with this broad interpretation of Section 1 is that it would criminalize lots of pricing decisions made unilaterally and perhaps unavoidably by firms in concentrated markets. Imagine the conundrum facing the gasoline retailer whose competitors have all raised their prices ten cents. If she goes along, she may be guilty of price fixing. If she doesn't, her shareholders will call her an idiot and fire her.

The Supreme Court backed away from this broad reading of *Interstate Circuit* in another movie theater case (antitrust lawyers love the movies, except dumb ones about antitrust like the 2001 "thriller" *Antitrust* starring Ryan Phillippe), *Theater Enterprises*.[2] The Court explained that mere parallel behavior — even if consciously undertaken with the assumption that competitors would follow — was not enough to constitute agreement under Section 1: "Circumstantial evidence of consciously parallel behavior may have made heavy inroads into the traditional judicial attitude toward conspiracy; but 'conscious parallelism' has not yet read conspiracy out of the Sherman Act entirely."

Following *Theater Enterprises*, the following doctrine has emerged. Consistent with *Interstate Circuit*, explicit agreement is not required; tacit agreement may suffice. However, mere *conscious parallelism* — a common reaction of "firms in a concentrated market [that] recogniz[e] their shared economic interests and their interdependence with respect to price and output decisions"[3] — is not sufficient.

Where direct evidence is lacking, how does a plaintiff meet its burden of proving that parallel conduct was the product of at least a tacit agreement and not mere conscious parallelism? The answer is

[2]*Theater Enterprises, Inc. v. Paramount Film Distributing Corp.*, 346 U.S. 537 (1954).
[3]*Brooke Group, Ltd. v. Brown & Williamson Tobacco Corp.*, 550 U.S. 209, 227 (1993).

plus factors, evidence "tending to exclude the possibility of independent action."[4] Although there is little authoritative Supreme Court precedent on this point, lower courts have held that "plus factor" evidence typically falls into two categories: (1) evidence that the alleged conspirators were "motivated" to enter into a conspiracy and (2) evidence that the alleged conspirators acted contrary to their economic interests.[5] A word is in order on each prong, since they're quite confusing as typically worded.

First, it's obviously true that all firms are "motivated" to get rich. If this were an Agatha Christie novel, a body murdered by an anonymous price-fixing conspiracy had been discovered[6] and the question was "Who had a motive to do this?" the answer would be "anyone who wants to make more money." However, motivation in the plus factors context has a narrower meaning. Motivation is found when the idea of collusion has been suggested to, or clearly considered by, the alleged conspirators. For example, the studios in *Interstate Circuit* were "motivated" since they all got the same letter, all sat in the same room hearing Interstate's pitch, and all clearly had the possibility of undertaking concerted action on their minds. The motivation prong is often satisfied by evidence that the alleged conspirators had conversations about possible collaborative pricing, that an executive stood up in a trade convention when competitors were present and suggested that everyone raise prices, that the competitors exchanged sensitive pricing information (more on information exchange below), or something similar.

The second prong — action against economic self-interest — is also quite misleading as stated. When firms enter a cartel, they are not acting against their economic self-interest unless one assumes that the illegality of the behavior and the concomitant sanctions if the cartel is discovered make the conduct irrational. What this prong of the test refers to is the possibility that the pricing decision adopted by each of the allegedly conspiring firms *would be* irrational but for an understanding that all other firms were committed to following suit.

---

[4] *Bell Atlantic Corp. v. Twombly*, 550 U.S. 544, 554 (2007).

[5] *In re Baby Food Antitrust Litig*, 166 F.3d 112, 122 (3d Cir. 1999).

[6] This example may be a *wee bit* hyperbolic, but attempted murder to enforce a price-fixing cartel is not unknown to the law, particularly in the unpleasant trash collection business. *See Sanitation and Recycling Indus., Inc. v. City of New York*, 107 F.3d 985, 990 (2d Cir. 1997) ("According to the indictment, this cartel; restrains competition by acts of violence including attempted murder, assault and arson; allocates customers to particular carters and directs substantial compensation in instances when one carter loses a customer to another; and treats carters operating outside the existing trade associations as outlaws, subjecting them to violence and threats if they compete for an established customer of a trade association member.").

Suppose, for example, that a gasoline retailer suddenly raises his price ten cents even though nothing has happened to the gasoline supply, costs, or demand. It may very well be that this behavior makes no sense unless the retailer has good reasons to believe that his competitors will also raise their prices ten cents. In that case, "action against economic self-interest" would be found. Conversely, if the behavior would likely be profitable even if other firms didn't follow suit, then the conduct is not "against economic self-interest."

In addition to these two plus factors, the structure of the relevant market is very important in determining the credibility of a claim that a cartel has formed. Economists generally assume that cartels can form only when certain market attributes are present:

- *A concentrated market.* The fewer the firms in the market, the easier it is to form, coordinate, and enforce a price-fixing conspiracy.
- *Fungible or homogeneous goods.* It's very hard for firms to fix prices unless their goods are very similar. If goods are heterogeneous or differentiated, firms will have to negotiate intensively over which prices apply to which products, and cheating on the agreement will be easier.
- *Policing and punishment mechanisms.* Firms in a cartel face tremendous incentives to cheat. This is because an agreement to increase price generally has to include an agreement to decrease output (if demand is at all elastic). Each firm is making more money by selling fewer products at the elevated price, but each firm faces a temptation to expand output slightly and make more sales at the seductively higher price. If this sort of cheating breaks out, cartels fall apart quickly. Hence, in order for a cartel to be stable, the members must impose mechanisms to detect and punish members who cheat.
- *Pricing transparency.* Even though we usually think about transparency as a good thing, this is not the case when it comes to cartels. In a "transparent" market, where buyers and sellers have easy access to information about other buyers' and sellers' prices, it's easier for the members of the cartel to detect cheating and hence stabilize the cartel. Conversely, where the market is characterized by pricing opacity, cheating is harder to detect, so it is less plausible that firms would try to fix prices in the first place.
- *Demand elasticity.* Where demand is elastic within the market, the firms in the market have relatively little power to impose price increases through collusion. Buyers will simply substitute other products. Conversely, where demand is relatively inelastic, collusion is very profitable and the temptation may be strong.

How, then, do you analyze a fact pattern involving circumstantial evidence suggestive of collusion? Start by stating that a court may find collusion with direct evidence if the circumstantial evidence tends to exclude the possibility of independent action. Explain that the plus factors generally used to show this fall into two categories — motivation and action against economic self-interest — and then explore the applicability of these to the facts. Finally, discuss whether the structure of the market is economically conducive to cartelization. Then hope your argument made some sense.

2. Other Naked Restraints

The classic form of per se illegal price fixing is an agreement by sellers on the price they will charge to their customers. However, the Supreme Court has interpreted *Socony*'s capacious price-fixing principle as reaching a variety of restraints on trade besides the classic seller's cartel. Without attempting to develop an exhaustive catalog, let us briefly consider three varieties of per se illegal agreements that might not seem like price fixing at first blush.

2.1. Buyer Cartels

Buyer cartels, like seller cartels, are per se illegal under Section 1 of the Sherman Act.[7] This might not be immediately obvious. If one assumes that the purpose of the antitrust laws is to promote consumer welfare, then how does an agreement by buyers to *lower* the price of goods sold fit within the objectives of the antitrust laws? This question is not limited to the Section 1 context. We later raise similar questions about monopsonization as an offense under Section 2 (see Chapter 8) and mergers that create overly dominant buyers (see Chapter 11). For present purposes, we make two observations, one legal and one economic.

The legal observation is that despite all the language celebrating the antitrust laws as a "consumer welfare prescription," the Supreme Court has generally assumed that the antitrust laws apply equally to buyers and sellers, without articulating how increases in buyer power fit within the overall normative scope of the antitrust laws.[8]

---

[7] *Mandeville Island Farms, Inc. v. Am. Crystal Sugar Co.*, 334 U.S. 219 (1948).
[8] *See, e.g., United States v. Griffith*, 334 U.S. 100 (1948).

The economic observation is that even if one is concerned solely about consumer welfare, anticompetitive acts by buyers can sometimes harm consumer welfare. Assume, for example, that two firms compete in the sale of widgets. An essential component of a widget is a gidget. The two firms buy gidgets in competition with one another. The firms then secretly agree to depress the price of gidgets by bidding less aggressively against each other. Suppose that the price of gidgets goes down 10 percent as a result. Isn't this great for consumers, since the firms will lower their costs and pass on their savings to widget purchasers? Probably not. Assume, as in most markets, that the supply of gidgets is somewhat elastic — meaning that as the price of gidgets goes down, gidget sellers produce and sell fewer of them. As a result of their colluding on input prices, the widget makers will have to decrease the amount of gidgets they purchase. And since gidgets are an essential component of widgets, this means they will have to decrease the number of widgets they sell. Thus, the effect of the buyer collusion will be to reduce output and, in all likelihood, raise prices of widgets, to the detriment of consumers.

2.2. Maximum Price Setting

Just as one might be tempted to overlook collusion among buyers, one might be tempted to forgive agreements by sellers to cap the prices they charge to buyers. For example, suppose that a doctors' association in a particular region sets a maximum fee the doctors can charge insurance companies for providing certain medical services. Since the doctors are able to charge a price below the cap, shouldn't antitrust law smile on this maximum price setting?

Whether or not it should, it doesn't. In *Maricopa*[9] the Supreme Court considered precisely the doctors' agreement mentioned above and declared it per se illegal. And for good reason. While maximum price setting by competitors may seem beneficial or innocuous, it can have exactly the same anticompetitive effects as ordinary price fixing. The maximum prices may become the doctors' pricing benchmark and hence the de facto prices in the market. For example, suppose that the market price for a procedure had previously been $9 and the doctors collectively agree that henceforth, they may charge no more than $10 for it. There is an implicit yet powerful suggestion in this that everyone raise their price to $10, which is often what happens in these situations. Hence, price fixing is price fixing, whether it is of the maximum or minimum variety.

[9]*Arizona v. Maricopa County Medical Association*, 457 U.S. 332 (1982).

2.3. Agreement on Pricing Components

Sometimes competitors agree to standardize pricing components without agreeing to set an overall price. For example, in *Catalano*[10] a group of beer wholesalers agreed not to extend short-term credit to retailers, essentially requiring them to pay in cash on delivery or in advance. The retailers complained that this was per se illegal price fixing — and won. True, the wholesalers hadn't fixed the prices of beer, but they had eliminated competition over one pricing component — credit — and thus had fixed prices within the meaning of the per se rule. (Whether antitrust law should be used to increase the output of *beer* is another question!)

In this vein, recall that in *Socony* itself the major oil companies had not directly fixed *any* pricing component, but had simply divided up independent refiners to serve as their "dancing partners" and buy up excess or "hot" oil so it would not depress market prices. The Supreme Court found this sufficient to be price fixing. In analyzing potential price-fixing cases involving naked agreements by competitors, do not limit the reach of the per se rule to literal fixing of the full price charged to customers.

2.4. Market Division

Market division, like price fixing, is per se illegal. Like price fixing, market division can take a number of forms. Probably the three most common forms are dividing geographic territories, dividing customers, and dividing products. For example, in the most recent Supreme Court decision on market division, *Palmer*,[11] the Supreme Court held per se illegal an agreement between BarBri and another bar review service that allocated Georgia to the other service and the rest of the country to BarBri. In other cases, the parties might agree that one of them will sell exclusively to corporate buyers while the other sells to governmental agencies (customer market division), or that one of them will sell only five-inch ball bearings while the other sells only seven-inch ball bearings (product market division). If horizontal and naked, any of these agreements is per se illegal.

The trick in many of these cases is determining when the market division is really horizontal and when it is vertical, and also when it is naked and when it is ancillary to some other, lawful agreement. Consider two somewhat dated Supreme Court opinions in this regard.

---

[10]*Catalano, Inc. v. Target Sales, Inc.*, 446 U.S. 643 (1980).
[11]*Palmer v. BRG of Georgia, Inc.*, 498 U.S. 46 (1990).

In *United States v. Sealy*,[12] a group of 30 competitive mattress producers got together to form the Sealy Corporation, which owned the Sealy mattress trademark. Sealy then "licensed" each of its participant companies the right to use the Sealy brand in an exclusive territory. The upshot was that the mattress companies didn't compete with each other — at least as to Sealy brand mattresses — outside their assigned territories. The government challenged the arrangement as per se illegal market division. Sealy responded in essentially two ways.

First, it argued that the market division was not horizontal but vertical, since the exclusive territory contracts were all between Sealy and individual licensees, not among the licensees. The Supreme Court rejected this argument, finding that the economic substance of the transaction was that Sealy was the "instrumentality" of the competitor mattress companies who were, in essence, using the Sealy Corporation as a shell for horizontal market division.

Second, Sealy argued that the agreement, even if horizontal, wasn't really naked, since the exclusive territories were necessary to the companies' joint advertising efforts. The Supreme Court rejected this argument summarily, but it would play a much greater role in later cases and case criticism. In short, the Court held that the Sealy arrangement was a naked, horizontal market division agreement and therefore per se illegal.

A much more controversial market division case arrived at the Supreme Court five years later. In *Topco*[13] the Supreme Court confronted an arrangement by a group of medium-size regional grocery chains to form a joint buying and branding association. Topco's essential function was to serve as a purchasing agent for about 1,000 food and nonfood items for its members and then make them available to participating chains to be sold as Topco-branded items. Topco then granted each participating chain an exclusive territory in which to sell Topco-branded items. As in *Sealy*, the government challenged this arrangement as market division.

This time, the argument for legality was much stronger than in *Sealy*. The district court made a set of dream findings for Topco: Topco's members had no market power; they competed against larger and more powerful national supermarket chains that had their own private labels; the territorial exclusivity did not harm competition; and enjoining the territorial exclusivity would weaken the ability of the regional chains to compete against the big national chains and hence weaken competition in the grocery market.

---

[12] *United States v. Sealy*, 388 U.S. 350 (1967).
[13] *United States v. Topco Associates, Inc.*, 405 U.S. 596 (1972).

The last finding deserves some explanation, since it wasn't well articulated in the majority opinion and is only hinted at in Justice Burger's dissenting opinion. The issue is *free riding*, which is a critically important theme in the vertical cases we will study in Chapter 6. The question is why would Topco's members need contractual protection from other Topco members selling in their territory? ? Here goes the argument: If Topco's members want to become more competitive with the national chains, they will have to invest in advertising the Topco brand. Topco itself could do that advertising on a national basis, but it might be better for the individual Topco members to advertise the Topco brand on a local market basis, since they know their customers and local market conditions best. However, each Topco member may be concerned that if it invests in advertising the Topco brand, other Topco sellers may enter its market and take advantage of its advertising. To avoid this sort of free riding, and hence to make possible local advertising, Topco has to grant each member an exclusive territory.

Unfortunately for Topco, the Supreme Court was in no mood to entertain economic theory. In a striking footnote celebrating the value of per se rules, Justice Marshall dissed a rule-of-reason approach as "leav[ing] courts free to ramble through the wilds of economic theory in order to maintain a flexible approach." Lions and tigers and bears, oh my! Economic theory is a jungle. The Court struck down the Topco exclusive territory system as per se illegal market division.

Topco has been much criticized over the years for failing to pay attention to the free-riding possibility, and it is doubtful whether the Supreme Court would rule the same way today. Judge Richard Posner has described *Sealy* and *Topco* as "dead as dodos."[14] Still, if one wants to jettison *Topco*, one needs a doctrinal explanation. The simplest end-run would be to describe *Topco* as involving horizontal agreement, yes, but not a naked restraint on trade. Since the Topco buying cooperative was akin to a joint venture to create a new brand, and (perhaps unlike the case in *Sealy*) meaningful economic integration was achieved through the joint venture, the exclusive territories should be understood as ancillary to the lawful purposes of the joint venture, and judged under the rule of reason. In light of later "characterization" cases like *BMI*, that avenue certainly would be open today.

One final note is applicable to not only market division but all horizontal restraints. Complex commercial agreements often involve a combination of vertical and horizontal elements. As we saw in Chapter 2, and will see again in Chapter 6, horizontal agreements are generally judged more stringently than vertical agreements. Where both vertical and horizontal elements are present, the agreement is judged

---

[14]Richard A. Posner, *Antitrust Law* 189 n.62 (2d ed. 2001).

by the more stringent standards applicable to horizontal agreements. Thus, for example, in *General Motors*[15] three associations of Chevrolet dealers in the Los Angeles area pressured General Motors to prevent its dealers from reselling to unfranchised "discounters," who were supposedly undermining the prices of Chevrolets. Nominally, the prevention took the form of General Motors enforcing "location clauses" in its vertical contracts with dealers. However, because a horizontal agreement between GM and the associations was also present, the Court treated the overall scheme as a horizontal agreement and declared it per se illegal. So don't be distracted by the vertical aspect of an agreement if a horizontal element is also present; the stricter rules governing horizontal agreements will control.

2.5. Group Boycotts

Yet another category of agreement in restraint of trade treated as per se illegal is the horizontal group boycott. This category of horizontal restraint is the trickiest of all to identify because it involves a number of identification elements quite different from the other per se offenses. Further, although this per se category persists in Section 1 doctrine, its domain has shrunk considerably over time.

Unlike price fixing, which is relatively easy to identify in theory, the idea of a "boycott" is theoretically indefinite. Or, at least, the idea is susceptible to a broad range of interpretations. For example, suppose that two companies agree not to allow a third company to join their joint venture. In a colloquial sense, one might say that the joint venturers have "boycotted" the third party. But it obviously wouldn't do to make it per se illegal for two joint venturers to refuse membership to a third party. There are all sorts of legitimate reasons not to allow a third party to join. Even if we think it might sometimes be anticompetitive to deny competitors access to a joint venture's facilities (a matter considered further under "Joint Ventures" below), if a court is going to consider the legitimacy of the reasons for the denial of access, it will have to proceed under the rule of reason and not the per se rule, since the per se rule prohibits inquiry into the justifications for the restraint. So, to make a per se prohibition on group boycotts operational, we're going to have to give the rule a fairly restrictive scope.

Before trying to define the scope of the rule in general terms, let's consider three fact patterns in which the Supreme Court found a per se illegal horizontal group boycott.

---

[15] *United States v. General Motors Corp.*, 384 U.S. 127 (1966).

- **Suppliers agree to boycott retailer's rival.** In *Klor's*[16] a department store chain in San Francisco went to its major appliance suppliers—General Electric, RCA, Admiral, Zenith, and Emerson—and got them to agree not to supply a small appliance store (Klor's) situated next to a Broadway-Hale store on Mission Street. The Supreme Court held the agreement per se illegal as a group boycott.
- **Trade association members agree to boycott retailers cooperating with "pirates."** In *Fashion Originators Guild of America (FOGA)*[17] a trade association of designers, manufacturers, distributers, and retailers of women's garments developed an elaborate system for identifying "style pirates" and prohibiting their members from doing business with such pirates. Any retailers who sold "pirated" garments would be blacklisted by FOGA, and FOGA's members agreed not to supply fashions to the blacklisted retailers. The Supreme Court held this system per se illegal.
- **Trade association members agree not to do business with nonmembers.** In *Montague*[18] an association of San Francisco tile dealers adopted a bylaw prohibiting members of the association from selling tiles to nonmember dealers, except on onerous terms. The Supreme Court invalidated the restraint.

These are just a selection of the "boycott" patterns that the Supreme Court held illegal over the course of the first 70 or 80 years of the Sherman Act's existence. Over time, the Court began to worry about the need to construct a general set of principles governing the group boycott categories. The occasion for announcing those principles arrived in *Northwest Wholesale.*[19] A retail office supply store sued a nonprofit buying cooperative, claiming that it had been expelled from membership for anticompetitive reasons and without being accorded due process. The Ninth Circuit took the group boycott principle to its logical conclusion and held that expulsion by competitors from a membership organization without "procedural safeguards" was a per se illegal group boycott. Concerned about the possibility of transforming the Sherman Act into a code of procedures for cooperative organizations, the Supreme Court rejected this approach. More generally, it offered some observations meant to cabin the reach of the group boycott per se principle:

[16] *Klor's, Inc. v. Broadway-Hale Stores, Inc.*, 359 U.S. 207 (1959).
[17] *Fashion Originators Guild of America v. FTC*, 312 U.S. 457 (1941).
[18] *W.W. Montague & Co. v. Lowry*, 193 U.S. 38 (1904).
[19] *Northwest Wholesale Stationers, Inc. v. Pacific Stationery and Printing Co.*, 472 U.S. 284 (1985).

Cases to which this Court has applied the per se approach have generally involved joint efforts by a firm or firms to disadvantage competitors by "either directly denying or persuading or coercing suppliers or customers to deny relationships the competitors need in the competitive struggle." . . . In these cases, the boycott often cut off access to a supply, facility, or market necessary to enable the boycotted firm to compete, . . . and frequently the boycotting firms possessed a dominant position in the relevant market . . . . In addition, the practices were generally not justified by plausible arguments that they were intended to enhance overall efficiency and make markets more competitive.

Packed into this paragraph are several apparent criteria for the application of the per se rule: (1) a competitive relationship, meaning that at least one of the parties involved in the boycotting scheme must be a competitor of the boycotted party; (2) denial of some facility necessary for competition; (3) market power by the boycotting firms; and (4) the absence of a plausible efficiency justification. Clearly, this is not the ordinary per se rule, where there is no need to show market power or to discuss the efficiency of the restraint.

Later cases further cabined the reach of the group boycott per se rule.[20] In *Sharp*[21] an electronic calculator retailer in Houston complained to the manufacturer, Sharp, that another retailer was pricing below Sharp's suggested resale price. The retailer demanded that Sharp cut off the "cheating" retailer, and Sharp agreed. The terminated retailer then sued Sharp, charging that it had been the victim of a per se illegal boycott akin to the one in *Klor's*. The Supreme Court rejected this argument, explaining that *Klor's* had involved a horizontal element not present on the facts of *Sharp*. Critically, in *Klor's* the major appliance suppliers had agreed not only with Broadway-Hale but among themselves not to do business with Klor's. Hence, there was a horizontal group boycott in *Klor's*.

---

[20] A note of caution: In *FTC v. Indiana Federation of Dentists*, 476 U.S. 447 (1986), the Supreme Court tried to summarize *Northwest Wholesale* by stating that "the per se approach has generally been limited to cases in which firms with market power boycott suppliers or customers in order to discourage them from doing business with a competitor." This confuses *Northwest Wholesale* and the Court's other group boycott cases in one important respect: In most cases, the "boycott" is directed not against the "customers or suppliers" but directly against the competitor. For example, in *Klor's* Broadway-Hale did not threaten to "boycott" its manufacturer suppliers. It got them to boycott Klor's. While the application of coercive pressure on customers or suppliers to get them to boycott a competitor may be an ingredient of some cases, as for example in *FOGA*, that is not an essential component of the group boycott rule. The Supreme Court's misstatement in *Indiana Federation of Dentists* was probably inadvertent.

[21] *Business Electronics Corp. v. Sharp Electronics Corp.*, 485 U.S. 717 (1988).

Putting *Sharp* and *Northwest Wholesale* together, to be a candidate for the per se rule, the alleged boycott must involve some agreement between competitors, that is, a horizontal agreement. Importantly, the horizontal agreement need not be at the level of the boycotted firm; it can be at the level of the firm's suppliers or customers. *Klor's* involved a horizontal agreement among Klor's suppliers procured by a competitor, and hence met both *Sharp*'s insistence that there be a horizontal agreement and *Northwest Wholesale*'s that at least one of the conspirators have a competitive relationship with the boycotted firm. A boycott can also take the form of a firm's getting its customers to agree not to do business with the firm's rivals. In *FOGA*, for example, the retailers who were the customers of the alleged pirates agreed with other style designers not to do business with the pirates. The important point is that both a horizontal agreement and competitive relationship need to be present.

The group boycott per se rule survives, but it's not your grandma's per se rule. If called upon to analyze a potential boycott pattern, walk through the *Northwest Wholesale* factors, as informed by *Sharp*. If you conclude that the restraint meets those criteria, feel free to call it "per se illegal," recognizing that the actual test feels much more like a highly structured rule-of-reason analysis.

3.   Information Exchanges and Other Facilitating Practices

We transition now to horizontal restraints that are judged under the rule of reason rather than the per se rule. The first major category — facilitating practices — can be tricky because facilitating practices can show up in either per se or rule-of-reason cases.

A *facilitating practice* is a practice that facilitates conscious parallel or collusive pricing or other interdependent competitive decisions by competitors. Note one very important thing about this definition. A facilitating practice need not facilitate conduct that is illegal. If it merely facilitates conscious parallelism, as you already know from the discussion above with respect to cartels, the conscious parallelism is not even considered an agreement for purposes of Section 1 and hence is not illegal.

Does that mean that facilitating practices are legal so long as they do not facilitate actual horizontal agreement, but only conscious parallelism? No. If two or more competitors agree to the facilitating practice, then we have a horizontal agreement for purposes of Section 1. If the result of the agreement is that the firms are better able to engage in conscious parallelism and hence to raise prices, the agreement to engage in the facilitating practice may be challenged under Section 1, even though the resulting conscious parallelism may not.[22]

There are many possible forms of facilitating practices, including most favored nation clauses, meeting competition clauses, early announcement of pricing changes, and arbitrary pricing terms such as base point pricing. To keep this discussion manageable, we will focus here on only the most commonly challenged facilitating practice: horizontal information exchange.

Competitors exchange information all the time. Adam Smith famously quipped that "[p]eople of the same trade seldom meet together, even for merriment and diversion, but the conversation ends in a conspiracy against the public, or in some contrivance to raise prices."[23] Information exchange can be used to raise prices and harm consumers. Yet it can also be used for legitimate purposes. For example, knowing some of your competitor's production plans may allow you to plan your own production more efficiently. In consequence, the Supreme Court has held that pure information exchange is not per se illegal.[24]

When challenging information exchange as a violation of Section 1, a plaintiff may choose one of two theories.[25] First, she may challenge the agreement to exchange information as itself violating Section 1 of the Sherman Act. Such a claim is judged under the rule of reason. Second, she may allege price fixing and use the information exchange agreement as a plus factor to help prove the existence of the price-fixing agreement.

Which path is easier? Either one, depending on your facts. As we know from Chapter 4, rule-of-reason claims typically involve proving market power in a relevant market and anticompetitive effects, and the defendant may rebut by showing efficiencies. Given these obstacles, why wouldn't plaintiffs always choose to bring per se challenges on a price-fixing theory? The answer is that absent direct evidence of a price-fixing agreement, the plaintiff will have to convince the judge or jury that the evidence of information exchange together with other

---

[22] Conversely, facilitating practices that are unilaterally adopted are generally outside the reach of the antitrust laws. During the 1970s and early 1980s, the FTC brought several challenges to unilaterally adopted facilitating practices, such as base point pricing, and the courts rejected the challenges due to the absence of horizontal agreement. *See, e.g., E.I. du Pont de Nemours & Co. v. FTC*, 729 F.2d 128 (1984); *Boise Cascade Corp. v. FTC*, 637 F.2d 573 (9th Cir. 1980).

[23] 1 Adam Smith, *An Inquiry into the Nature and Causes of the Wealth of Nations* 117 (E.P. Dutton & Co. 1914) (1776)

[24] *United States v. Citizens & Southern National Bank*, 422 U.S. 86, 113 (1975).

[25] Judge Sotomayor's opinion in *Todd v. Exxon Corp.*, 275 F.3d 191 (2d Cir. 2001), helpfully traces the contours of these two different legal theories.

plus factors tends to disprove the possibility of independent action. That can be very difficult also.

Whichever legal theory the plaintiff adopts (and the plaintiff may plead both in the alternative), there are several criteria concerning the information exchange that are often important in assessing its legality. Among these are the following.

- **The timing of the data exchanged.** Information about past prices or production decisions is considered far less problematic than the exchange of information about present or future prices or production decisions.
- **Specificity or disaggregation.** The exchange of aggregated data — such as the average price for a product — is considered less problematic than the exchange of more specific or disaggregated data, such as the price quoted to a particular customer or class of customers.
- **Public dissemination of the information.** If the competitors share the information not only with each other but with the world at large, courts are likely to treat the exchange with greater leniency.
- **Meetings or contacts beyond information exchange.** Suppose two competitors exchange detailed pricing information by fax every Friday at noon, and the telephone logs show that the sales managers of the two companies speak by telephone for a half hour every Friday after the faxes go out. Without knowing what was said in the calls, we can't prove that there was collusion, but these contacts certainly color the information exchange in a more suspicious hue.

In addition to these factors, the criteria usually relevant to determining whether a market is conducive to cartelization (fungibility, concentration, demand elasticity, etc.) or whether a restraint violates the rule of reason (market power, concentration, etc.) continue to apply.

4. Joint Ventures

Competitors often enter into joint ventures for legitimate reasons, such as to obtain economies of scope or of scale from joint production, research and development, or distribution. However, joint ventures can sometimes create market power and hence raise antitrust concerns.

Cases in which a plaintiff (government or private) challenges the fact of a joint venture, as opposed to some bylaw or practice in the venture, are rare. If a challenge to the fact of a joint venture occurs—essentially, an argument that the entire joint venture is illegal—it will typically be analyzed under the horizontal merger principles discussed in Chapters 10 and 11.[26] For present purposes, we will consider several common antitrust questions that arise in joint venture cases where the fact of the joint venture is not being challenged.

One threshold question is whether the challenged agreement should be analyzed under the per se rule or the rule of reason. The Supreme Court has held that any agreement within the scope of a lawful joint venture should be analyzed under the rule of reason and not the per se rule.[27] Hence, when Texaco and Shell formed the Equilon joint venture for purposes of jointly refining and selling gasoline in the western United States, their joint decisions on the pricing of Texaco and Shell brands of gasoline at retail was not "price fixing" in an antitrust sense because it occurred within the scope of the joint venture.[28]

Two further questions arise from this general principle. The first is whether even the rule of reason applies to certain kinds of agreements within the scope of a joint venture, or whether they are simply off limits to antitrust scrutiny. As noted in Chapter 1, when two firms have economically integrated through merger, they become a single entity for purposes of Section 1 analysis. Thus, even though a parent corporation tells its subsidiary how to set its prices, and the parent and subsidiary are hence engaged in "price fixing" in a literal sense, the two companies are not even "agreeing" for purposes of Section 1 analysis.[29] Seizing on this idea, the National Football League (NFL) argued that when the league's 32 teams granted Reebok an exclusive 10-year license to produce NFL-branded headwear, the teams were acting as a single entity and were hence exempt from being charged with creating an anticompetitive agreement. The Supreme Court unanimously disagreed, holding that the intra-venture agreement should be analyzed under the rule of reason.[30] As a result of the NFL case, agreements within the scope of a joint venture are immune from per se challenge, but not from rule-of-reason challenge.

The other question is when are agreements within the scope of a joint venture? This takes us back to the "Three Tenors" case discussed in Chapter 4. Warner and Polygram argued that the agreement to discontinue promotions for *Three Tenors 1* and *Three Tenors 2* was necessary to the joint marketing of *Three Tenors 3*. Recall that the

---

[26] *See FTC & DoJ Antitrust Guidelines for Collaborations Among Competitors* (2000), *http://www.ftc.gov/os/2000/04/ftcdojguidelines.pdf*, §1.3.

[27] *Texaco, Inc. v. Dagher*, 547 U.S. 1 (2006).

[28] *Id.*

[29] *Copperweld Corp. v. Independence Tube Corp.*, 467 U.S. 752 (1984).

[30] *American Needle, Inc. v. National Football League*, 130 S. Ct. 2201 (2010).

FTC and D.C. Circuit largely dodged the question of whether the per se rule or rule of reason applied, finding that this "dichotomous" approach to Section 1 analysis was inconsistent with the modern "continuum" approach. Nonetheless, to the extent that a court still finds it important to decide a case like the "Three Tenors" one by initially allocating the agreement to either the rule of reason or the per se rule, it will be important to discuss whether the horizontal agreement at issue is "within the scope" of the joint venture, that is, relates to the subject matter of the joint venture or falls outside it.

A second major issue in joint venture analysis is whether the restriction at issue is reasonably necessary to the joint venture's lawful objectives. Many of the discussions over "least restrictive alternative" analysis, discussed in Chapter 4, arise in joint venture cases. Thus, for example, the MasterCard and Visa payment card networks long imposed rules prohibiting their member banks from issuing other credit cards, such as American Express, Discover, or Diner's Club. The Justice Department prevailed in a lawsuit alleging that these restrictions violated Section 1 under rule-of-reason analysis.[31] Visa and MasterCard argued that these restrictions were necessary to promote "cohesion" within their networks. The courts disagreed, finding no evidence that allowing member banks to carry other cards would damage network cohesion.

The final major issue is whether joint ventures have special obligations to provide access to rivals on nondiscriminatory terms. In framing this issue, consider two legal doctrines that bookend questions of competitor access to joint venture facilities. First, we have already seen that it is not a per se illegal group boycott for a joint venture to kick out or otherwise deny access to a competitor. Second, as explored in greater detail in Chapter 8, there is no "duty to deal" with competitors under Section 2, except perhaps under very narrow circumstances. The question, then, is whether joint ventures could ever violate Section 1 of the Sherman Act under a rule-of-reason analysis by refusing access to rivals. The answer is yes. Under some circumstances, it is a violation of Section 1 for a joint venture to deny access or discriminate against rivals of one or more of the joint venturers.

Consider two cases in which the Supreme Court found that a joint venture acted unlawfully by excluding or discriminating against competitors. In *Terminal Railway*[32] the railroad entrepreneur Jay Gould had organized an association of 14 competing railroads to create a unified terminal system at the Mississippi River at St. Louis, Missouri. The new terminal system replaced three earlier inefficient terminals.

[31] *United States v. Visa U.S.A., Inc.*, 344 F.3d 229 (2d Cir. 2003).
[32] *United States v. Terminal Railway Ass'n of St. Louis*, 224 U.S. 383 (1912).

When the association began to charge discriminatory rates to nonmembers of the association, the government complained and called for the association to be dissolved. While finding a violation of Section 1 based on "arbitrary" discrimination against competitors, the Supreme Court recognized the superior efficiency of the unified terminal system and refused to order it dissolved. Instead, the Court ordered the terminal to provide access to all comers on reasonable and nondiscriminatory terms.

In *Associated Press (AP)*[33] the Associated Press news collection association adopted a bylaw allowing any member to block its nonmember competitor from membership. As in *Terminal Railway*, the Supreme Court did not doubt that the Associated Press joint venture was lawful. However, it found that the inability of a competitor newspaper to buy news from the country's largest news agency could have "the most serious effects on the publication of competitive newspapers" and enjoined operation of the exclusionary bylaw.

Commentators frequently contend that *Terminal Railway* and *AP* reflect the application of an "essential facilities" doctrine in the joint venture context (although the Supreme Court did not make this explicit in either case). We shall return to the essential facilities doctrine as a Section 2 issue in Chapter 8. For now, observe that the Supreme Court has never explicitly recognized the doctrine, but various lower courts have held that the following criteria apply: "(1) control of the essential facility by a monopolist; (2) a competitor's inability to duplicate the facility; (3) denial of the use of the facility to a competitor; and (4) the feasibility of providing the facility."[34] Where a facility is deemed essential under these criteria, the joint venture may have an obligation to make it available to competitors on reasonable and nondiscriminatory terms.

Joint ventures among competitors face pervasive antitrust scrutiny and require careful monitoring by antitrust lawyers. Sports leagues, professional associations, technology consortiums, and standard-setting bodies are a few examples of joint ventures that come under constant scrutiny. In many cases, there are significant bodies of antitrust law governing particular types of joint venture arrangements—NCAA rules on student athletes, patent pooling in the technology standardization context, fee arrangements among real estate agents, etc.

[33]*Associated Press v. United States*, 326 U.S. 1 (1945).
[34]*Gregory v. Fort Bridger Rendezvous Ass'n*, 448 F.3d 1195, 1204 (10th Cir. 2006) (citation omitted). For a fuller discussion of the essential facilities doctrine, see Robert Pitofsky, Donna Patterson & Jonathan Hooks, *The Essential Facilities Doctrine Under U.S. Antitrust Law*, 70 Antitrust L.J. 443 (2002).

5.   Other Ancillary Restraints

Facilitating practices and joint ventures are the two most important categories of horizontal restraints judged under the rule of reason. However, there are a variety of other, non-hardcore horizontal restraints that antitrust law must sometimes address. Putting together a comprehensive catalog here isn't feasible. Some examples of other horizontal restraints governed by the rule of reason are covenants not to compete accompanying the sale of a business or employment relationship, ethical rules by professional associations, and membership rules in industry groups. Just be aware that if you observe an agreement among competitors that doesn't neatly fit into one of the rule-of-reason categories and, after triage under a categorization or quick look approach, it isn't assigned to the per se category, you will need to apply the rule of reason using the methods discussed in Chapter 4.

Chapter 6

Vertical Restraints

Section 1 law governing vertical restraints used to be as elaborate and important as the law governing horizontal restraints, addressed in Chapter 5. However, following several transformative Supreme Court opinions in the last several decades, particularly the *Leegin* decision in 2007, that is no longer the case. Vertical restraints have shrunk severely in importance as a doctrinal matter, although many interesting theoretical issues remain. It is possible, of course, that U.S. law will once again change and that vertical restraints will return to a prominent place in antitrust policy. In the meantime, we will consider vertical restraints relatively briefly.

1. Types of Vertical Restraints

The vertical restraints nomenclature is inherently confusing, so let's clarify categories at the outset. Most generally, a *vertical restraint* is any competitive restraint that appears in a vertical contract. But there are many different varieties. Consider three examples: (1) A manufacturer and retailer agree that the retailer will be the manufacturer's exclusive franchisee in San Antonio, Texas, meaning that the manufacturer would be in breach of contract if it made any other retailer its franchisee in that city. (2) A manufacturer and retailer agree that the retailer will exclusively carry the manufacturer's shoes, meaning that the retailer would be in breach of contract if it carried a competitor manufacturer's shoes. (3) A manufacturer requires a canning customer to buy its salt from the manufacturer if it wants to lease the manufacturer's patented salt injection machine.

These are all vertical restraints, but the reasons that we might want to prohibit them are quite different. The first is a purely *intrabrand* restraint, meaning that it applies solely to competition within a particular manufacturer's brand. Later we will consider theories of harm from intrabrand vertical restraints, which generally involve concern over collusion between competing manufacturers or retailers.

The second example is an *interbrand* restraint, meaning that it constrains the ability of one of the parties to carry multiple competitive brands. As we shall see in greater detail in Chapter 8, this sort of vertical restraint is of concern primarily because of its potential to exclude competitors from the market. Exclusionary vertical restraints are generally studied in connection with monopolization offenses, and we will do the same in this book.

Finally, the third example — an example of contractual tying — is also considered an interbrand restraint. If we hold this particular tying arrangement unlawful, it could be because we are worried about excluding competitors in the salt market or simply because we believe that such tying arrangements can be used to exploit customers by extracting consumer surplus.[1]

Courts and commentators often confuse the categories and the terminology. In this chapter, we will study just the line of cases and policy questions raised by the first example: intrabrand vertical restraints. Interbrand restraints, raising either exclusion or exploitation concerns, will be addressed in Chapter 8.

2.   A Brief Historical Sketch

We noted in the introduction that antitrust history is largely beyond the scope of this book. Intrabrand vertical restraints, however, present a case where knowing something about the doctrinal development over the last century is important to understanding the framework of contemporary Section 1 doctrine.

The story begins with *Dr. Miles*,[2] a 1911 Supreme Court decision that established the rule of per se illegality for *resale price maintenance*, or RPM. Dr. Miles was a manufacturer of proprietary medicines sold to jobbers or wholesalers, who then resold to retailers, who in turn resold to the consuming public. Dr. Miles not only fixed the price charged to wholesalers, but also specified contractually the resale prices charged by wholesalers to retailers and by retailers to the general public. The Supreme Court invalidated this RPM scheme as a violation of Section 1. Following *Dr. Miles*, RPM was considered per se illegal until *Leegin*[3] in 2007.

Dr. Miles spawned a long line of cases on how to identify RPM and how far the rule of per se illegality extended. Early on, the Supreme

---

[1] There are also theories regarding tying arrangements as collusion devices, but we will not have the chance to consider them in this book.

[2] *Dr. Miles Medical Co. v. John D. Park & Sons Co.*, 220 U.S. 373 (1911).

[3] *Leegin Creative Leather Prods., Inc. v. PSKS, Inc.*, 551 U.S. 877 (2007).

Court carved out a major exception that would have doctrinal, rhetorical, and ideological implications outside of the vertical restraints context. In *Colgate*[4] the Court held that when a manufacturer sets a suggested resale price (MSRP) and then prospectively refuses to do business with any wholesaler or retailer that deviates from that price, the manufacturer is simply exercising its "independent discretion as to parties with whom he will deal." Reflecting the freedom of contract ideology then in vogue, the Court observed that a manufacturer "of course [] may announce in advance the circumstances under which he will refuse to sell. 'The trader or manufacturer, on the other hand, carries on an entirely private business, and can sell to whom he pleases.'"

Colgate created a strange dichotomy in franchising and distribution. If a manufacturer and retailer contractually agreed on the retailer's resale price, that was per se illegal under *Dr. Miles*. However, if the manufacturer merely exercised its "*Colgate* rights" by announcing an MSRP and cutting off any franchise or retailer who deviated — which is often identical in economic substance to RPM — there wasn't even an agreement for purposes of Section 1. Thus, small variations in the form of manufacturer-dealer relationship resulted in drastic swings between per se illegality and per se legality, with no middle ground for consideration of the justifications for and effects of the agreement under the rule of reason. Over the years, a line of cases addressed the question of whether *Dr. Miles* or *Colgate* applied, with the Supreme Court limiting *Colgate* to the narrow circumstance of announcement of an MSRP and prospective refusal to do business with nonconforming downstream firms.[5]

A second line of cases dealt with the question of whether consignment contracts — where the manufacturer nominally retains title to the goods until they are sold at retail and calls the retailer its distribution agent — fell within the *Dr. Miles* per se prohibition. The Supreme Court ruled that ostensible consignment cases that were essentially attempts to avoid *Dr. Miles* treatment through formal gamesmanship were per se illegal,[6] but left open the possibility that true consignment relationships would be judged less harshly.

[4]*United States v. Colgate Co.*, 250 U.S. 300 (1919).
[5]*See United States v. Parke, Davis & Co.*, 362 U.S. 29 (1960) (applying *Dr. Miles* rather than *Colgate* where manufacturer tried to coerce retailers to abide by MSRPs by cutting off wholesalers who dealt with "cheating" retailers); *Albrecht v. Herald Co.*, 390 U.S. 145 (1968) (applying *Dr. Miles* where newspaper publisher cut off distributor who charged price higher than MSRP and offered to deliver paper to affected customers itself).
[6]*Simpson v. Union Oil Co.*, 377 U.S. 13 (1964).

Another question that arose over time was whether it was illegal under *Dr. Miles* for a manufacturer to establish a maximum resale price, leaving the retailer free to charge any price below the ceiling if it so chose. In *Albrecht*[7] the Court held such maximum resale price setting per se illegal under *Dr. Miles*.

The cases discussed thus far have involved vertical restraints on price. In *Schwinn*[8] the Supreme Court extended the per se rule to certain non-price vertical restraints. The restrictions in *Schwinn* prohibited the franchised retailer from selling the manufacturer's goods outside of its assigned territory or to nonfranchised retailers.

Thus, as of the 1960s a broad swath of vertical restrictions on price and non-price decisions by downstream firms (wholesalers and retailers) were per se illegal. During the 1970s the ascendant Chicago School and its adherents on the Supreme Court began to jettison the prohibitions. The watershed case — *Sylvania* — arrived in 1977.[9] Articulating a number of Chicago School themes that we will examine in the next section, the Court jettisoned *Schwinn* and declared that all non-price intrabrand vertical restraints should be judged under the rule of reason rather than the per se rule. As a practical matter, this meant that non-price intrabrand vertical restraints were lawful, since plaintiffs almost never win rule-of-reason cases challenging them.

Although much of the majority's reasoning in *Sylvania* applied logically to *Dr. Miles* as well (as the *Sylvania* dissenters grumpily pointed out), the Supreme Court continued to adhere nominally to the per se prohibition on price-based vertical restraints until 1997, when it decided *Khan*.[10] *Khan* involved a gasoline supplier's maximum resale price constraints on its franchised retailer. In a delicious irony, Judge Richard Posner — perhaps the best-known Chicago School academic and judge — got the case in the Seventh Circuit and was forced by precedent to apply *Albrecht*, which he nonetheless proceeded to deride as ignorant and stupid. The Supreme Court unanimously reversed, thanking Judge Posner for his fidelity to precedent and agreeing that maximum price setting could be beneficial to consumers and should therefore be left to rule-of-reason adjudication.

After *Khan* the handwriting was on the wall for *Dr. Miles*, and the only question was how long it would take the Supreme Court to jettison the last rule of per se illegality for intrabrand vertical restraints. Given the relative infrequency with which the Supreme Court decides antitrust cases, the answer turned out to be a decade. Finally, in 2007, the

---

[7] *Albrecht v. Herald Co.*, 390 U.S. 145 (1968).
[8] *United States v. Arnold, Schwinn & Co.*, 388 U.S. 365 (1967).
[9] *Continental T.V., Inc. v. GTE Sylvania, Inc.*, 433 U.S. 36 (1977).
[10] *State Oil Co. v. Khan*, 522 U.S. 3 (1997).

Supreme Court decided *Leegin*, overruling *Dr. Miles* and sweeping all intrabrand vertical restraints into the rule of reason. The only surprise was that four Justices voted to retain *Dr. Miles* — although that may have had much to do with ideologically charged discussions over the importance of stare decisis and that doctrine's implications for controversial areas of constitutional law.

As of 2007, then, all intrabrand vertical restraints are judged under the rule of reason. There has been precious little case law exploring the new framework since that time, as most plaintiffs' lawyers think that bringing a rule-of-reason challenge to intrabrand vertical restraints is a fool's errand. However, *Leegin* is hardly the end of history. Some states continue to treat RPM as per se illegal under their own antitrust statutes. Further, the economic evidence of the effects of *Leegin* is only starting to trickle in.[11] The pendulum on RPM may swing once again.

3. Economic Considerations

Why would a manufacturer impose a resale price restriction on a downstream firm such as a retailer? Many students instinctively answer, "Well, the manufacturer obviously wants her goods to sell at the highest price possible, so why wouldn't she do everything possible to jack up their price?" But this answer misinterprets the question. Obviously, the manufacturer wants to get the highest possible price for her goods, and she is free to charge the retailer whatever price the market will bear. The price the manufacturer can charge the retailer is a function of the retailer's elasticity of demand, which is itself a function of the elasticity of demand at the retail level. Once the manufacturer has charged the highest price she can to the retailer, she makes no further profits by insisting that the retailer mark up the goods even more when reselling to consumers.

Indeed, it's just the opposite. Once the manufacturer has sold the goods to the retailer and taken whatever profits she can, her incentive is for the retailer to mark up the goods as little as possible. To see why, suppose that the profit-maximizing wholesale price (i.e., the price the manufacturer charges the retailer) is $10. By definition, if the manufacturer tried to charge a higher price to the retailer, her profits would fall

---

[11] One of the first empirical papers on the effects of *Leegin* — from the University of Chicago Department of Economics of all places — find that the use of RPM increases prices and decreases output. Alexander McKay & David Aron Smith, *The Empirical Effects of Minimum Resale Price Maintenance on Prices and Output*, http://home .uchicago.edu/~davidsmith/research/Leegin_and_MRPM.pdf.

since the retailer would want to buy fewer units of the product. Now suppose that the retailer is himself a monopolist and can therefore mark up the goods at retail a fair amount since no retailer competitor will undercut him. Suppose that he marks up the goods from $10 to $15, even though the cost of providing retail distribution is only $2. The manufacturer is worse off with the retailer charging a higher than competitive price at retail. Indeed, the manufacturer would prefer the retail market to be competitive, in which case the retailer would not be able to mark up the price of the goods to more than its cost, would sell the goods for $12, and, given consumer elasticity of demand, would therefore want to buy more of the goods from the manufacturer.

Or think of it this way. Suppose that instead of relying on retailers to distribute its goods, the manufacturer integrated forward into retail distribution and ran its own retail outlets. Would the manufacturer prefer to pay a lot or a little for its retail employees and real estate? Obviously, it would like to pay as a little as possible, since a lower cost structure would maximize its profitability. The retail distribution function — whether performed "in-house" within the manufacturing corporation or outsourced to retailers — is, to the manufacturer, just a cost of getting its goods to customers.

This thought experiment leads to one of the fundamental tenets of the Chicago School on intrabrand restraints, explained as follows in *Leegin:* "[I]n general, the interests of manufacturers and consumers are aligned with respect to retailer profit margins. The difference between the price a manufacturer charges retailers and the price retailers charge consumers represents part of the manufacturer's cost of distribution, which, like any other cost, the manufacturer usually desires to minimize." Given this observation (or belief), the entire tradition of judicial hostility to manufacturer efforts to control retailer prices and practices seems wrongheaded. If the manufacturers have no interest in creating market power at the retail level, and indeed have every interest in preventing it, then why should antitrust policy be concerned with these vertical restraints? Their rationale must be procompetitive and benign rather than anticompetitive.

Having debunked the claim that manufacturers would willingly do something to create retailer market power, the Chicago School offered several procompetitive reasons for vertical restraints. Chicago School academics and judges pointed out that manufacturers might decide to establish RPM or exclusive territories in order to persuade retailers to begin carrying their brands. Or they might do so to encourage new retailers to enter the market.

Most significantly in the Chicago School account, vertical restrictions are often efforts by the manufacturer to incentivize retailers to promote the manufacturer's brand without fear of free riding by other retailers selling the same brand. We encountered this theme with respect to *Topco* in Chapter 5. Suppose Audi wants to incentivize its franchised retailers to invest in promoting the Audi brand. Audi would like its dealers to have fancy showrooms, educated salespeople knowledgeable about Audi's fine fleet of German-engineered cars, and an excellent service department so that customers can buy their cars with confidence. All of this costs money, and dealers will be discouraged from making these investments if a discounting Audi dealer with no showroom, no educated salespeople, and no service department — but with cheaper Audis — sets up across the street. To give assurances that free riding won't happen, Audi then requires its dealers not to sell for less than an established price.

According to the Chicago School perspective, any loss of intrabrand competition that results from vertical restraints is more than offset by gains in interbrand competition. Although Audi dealers may compete a little less against each other after Audi institutes RPM, Audi cars will become better positioned to compete against BMW and Mercedes-Benz. Beginning with *Sylvania*, the Supreme Court has repeatedly stated that the Sherman Act is primarily concerned with competition between different brands, and that a little loss of intrabrand competition in exchange for stimulation of interbrand competition is just fine.

The logical end of the Chicago School perspective is the abolishment of any legal prohibition on intrabrand vertical restraints, even the toothless rule of reason. But the Supreme Court has thus far refused to go that far. Indeed, in *Leegin* the Supreme Court acknowledged three competitive risks that RPM might entail — risks that justified leaving the rule of reason in place as at least a minimal check.

First, RPM might be used as a device to stabilize a cartel among rival manufacturers. As we saw in the previous chapter, a cartel needs a method to detect cheating by its members. Suppose that BMW, Audi, and Mercedes have conspired to fix the prices of their mid-size sedans (quick review — not very likely since luxury automobiles are highly differentiated goods). The prices they initially set are their wholesale prices to dealers. But those prices tend not to be transparent to the outside world, and it will be difficult for the cartelists to verify that the others have stuck to the agreement. So now they agree to fix not only the wholesale price, but also the retail price (which they will have to implement through RPM). Now each company will be able to check very easily whether there is cheating on the cartel agreement: they just have to ask for price quotes from dealers.

Second, RPM might be used to stabilize a cartel among rival retailers. Suppose that three dominant Audi dealers in Denver would like to collude on prices (much easier to do than in the earlier example, since Audi A6's are pretty fungible). Like any cartel, they need an enforcer. So they ask Audi itself to enforce their agreed-upon prices by mandating them through a vertical contract. Audi should be reluctant to do this for the reasons previously discussed, but maybe the three dominant dealers are powerful enough to force Audi's hand. Audi goes along, and becomes the reluctant cartel ringmaster. Between the two collusion stories—retailer or manufacturer—the *Leegin* majority said that it worried more about the retailer story, and hence would find retailer-initiated RPM particularly suspect.

Finally, in *Leegin* the Supreme Court recognized that RPM might have unilateral anticompetitive effects—that is, effects not predicated on horizontal collusion. "A dominant retailer, for example, might request resale price maintenance to forestall innovation in distribution that decreases costs" and hence empowers the retailer's smaller rivals. Or a "manufacturer with market power . . . might use resale price maintenance to give retailers an incentive not to sell the products of smaller rivals or new entrants."[12]

4.   The Current Landscape

To keep things simple, we have focused here on just a top-level exploration of the most important themes in the currently prevailing RPM cases. There are many critiques of the Chicago School reasoning that influenced *Sylvania, Kahn, Leegin*, and related decisions, but they will have to await another day. For now, an apparently tepid rule of reason is all that stands between intrabrand vertical restraints and freedom.

In conclusion, let us make three observations about how vertical intrabrand issues may play out post-*Leegin*.

First, *Leegin* frames the primary concern as the possibility that RPM will be used instrumentally to enable the formation of either a manufacturer or retailer cartel. This suggests that RPM may be most legally relevant under either a facilitating practice analysis or as a plus factor tending to exclude the possibility that the manufacturers or retailers acted independently. RPM may thus continue to have some relevance insofar as it establishes horizontal agreement or facilitates conscious parallelism. As of this writing, the Justice Department's Section 1 case against Apple and several major book publishers over e-book pricing has much of this flavor.

Second, to the extent that RPM cases ever reach the stage of rule-of-reason analysis where the defendant has to prove the procompetitive justification as opposed to simply relying on a theoretical one, it will be interesting to see how well the free-rider arguments in particular stack up against reality. Academic commentators have pointed out that

[12]551 U.S. at 893-94.

many of the goods on which RPM was used required precious little point-of-sale promotion, which calls into question the accuracy of the free-rider justification.

Finally, even though *Leegin*'s repudiation of *Dr. Miles* may have mooted much of the importance of *Colgate*, there is still the doctrinal possibility that a simple pattern of a manufacturer setting an MSRP and cutting off a cheating retailer does not even involve an agreement sufficient for the invocation of Section 1. The stakes on this question are low in practice, since post-*Leegin* all that happens if the manufacturer exceeds its *Colgate* rights is rule-of-reason analysis, which usually means the manufacturer wins. Or at least that's what the cognoscenti are predicting post-*Leegin*.

PART III

EXCLUSIONARY AND EXPLOITATIVE PRACTICES

The General Tests for Monopolization

We now make the transition from Section 1 of the Sherman Act to Section 2, which prohibits monopolizing, conspiring to monopolize, and attempting to monopolize. In this chapter we will consider the general elements and foundational doctrines of Section 2 analysis. In the next chapter we will move category by category through various species of conduct prohibited as monopolistic. As we shall see, many of those species of conduct can also be considered unlawful exclusionary or exploitive acts under Section 1 or other antitrust statutes. In this chapter, however, we will stick to Section 2 fundamentals.

1. Monopolization Fundamentals

Monopolization law is simple! According to the Supreme Court, "The offense of monopoly under §2 of the Sherman Act has two elements: (1) the possession of monopoly power in the relevant market and (2) the willful acquisition or maintenance of that power as distinguished from growth or development as a consequence of a superior product, business acumen, or historic accident."[1] A two-element offense. What could be easier?

Alas, I've once again lied. Monopolization law is far from simple. Its two-element doctrinal specification masks unfathomed miseries of economic exposition. Compared to the Section 1 analysis of the last few chapters, Section 2 analysis tends to feel lawless — as if the judges are making it up on the fly based on free-floating economic theories. Still, there is some doctrine to be observed, some lawyer work to be done, in analyzing Section 2 problems.

[1]*United States v. Grinnell Corp.*, 384 U.S. 563, 570-571 (1966).

Chapter 7. The General Tests for Monopolization

The first order of business is to differentiate clearly between monopolization and attempted monopolization theories. The *Grinnell* test cited above is the test for actual monopolization. The test for attempted monopolization is different, and we shall come to it momentarily. Conspiracy to monopolize turns out to be an unimportant prong of Section 2. The reason is that virtually anything that can be reached under a conspiracy-to-monopolize theory could also be reached under a Section 1 theory—and more easily. As discussed in Chapter 3, monopoly is a higher degree of economic leverage than the market power necessary for rule-of-reason offenses, so a conspiracy to restrain competition that violates the conspiracy-to-monopolize prong of Section 2 will have easily violated the rule of reason. Hence, for present purposes, we will focus solely on actual monopolization and attempted monopolization.

Actual monopolization comes in two shades: acquisition of a monopoly and maintenance of a monopoly. An acquisition theory claims that the wrongdoer did not have monopoly power prior to engaging in the unlawful conduct but obtained the monopoly through anticompetitive means. Thus, John D. Rockefeller supposedly monopolized the oil industry by driving out, or buying up, his principal rivals. A monopoly maintenance theory assumes that the defendant obtained its monopoly lawfully, but then maintained its monopoly power unlawfully. Thus, in suing Microsoft, the government did not claim that Bill Gates became a monopolist in the computer operating systems market through nefarious means. Rather, the charge is that having become a monopolist through a combination of historical accident and ingenuity, Gates and Microsoft allegedly kept competitors from challenging Microsoft's dominance, and hence unlawfully maintained a monopoly.

The distinction between monopoly acquisition and maintenance is simply expositional, a pointer about two different patterns that can amount to monopolization under Section 2. Unlike European law, which recognizes monopoly maintenance but not monopoly acquisition, there are no doctrinal differences between the two theories under U.S. law. What's important for Section 2 analysis is to identify a moment at which the defendant possessed monopoly power and to be able to attribute his possession of that power to an anticompetitive act.

Conveniently, we discussed the meaning of monopoly power in Chapter 2 and hence have already mastered the first element of the *Grinnell* test. For a recap, recall that the accused's market share is the predominant factor in assessing whether the accused has monopoly power, that a share of at least 50 percent (and often more like 60 or 70 percent) is required by most courts, and that other factors—such as entry barriers, technological changes, customer strength, and demand elasticity—also bear on the analysis.

One point of note on the first prong of the *Grinnell* test: In order to prove "the possession of monopoly power in the relevant market," it seems necessary to prove the presence of a relevant market. Hence, most courts routinely assume that failure on the part of a plaintiff to define and establish proof of a relevant product and geographic market is fatal to the claim. However, in a few cases, courts have held that proof of a relevant market may not be necessary if the plaintiff comes up with "direct evidence" of monopoly power.[2] This is not the occasion to explore this exception or rant about the confusion it has caused. For those of you trying to learn antitrust law to pass an exam, consider making subtle inquiries to your professor about whether he or she is aware of these "direct evidence" cases and expects you to discuss them. If your professor is not aware of them, then for the sake of your fellow students and the welfare of mankind, please don't alert him or her to their existence. Assume that market definition will be an integral part of *Grinnell* prong 1 in all monopolization cases and move on.

We should now be as comfortable as we're going to get on the monopoly power prong. Time for prong 2.

2. The Anticompetitive Conduct Element

One of the few joys of being an antitrust lawyer is sneering at the ignorance of journalists on those rare occasions when a big antitrust case manages to displace analysis of Justin Bieber's hairstyle in the newspaper headlines. When the occasional headline about Microsoft, Google, Intel, or Apple comes along, it reads something like "Justice Department accuses Bill Gates of being a monopolist" or "Google denies it's a monopolist." Sure, denying the existence of monopoly power under prong 1 of *Grinnell* can be a successful strategy in many Section 2 cases since it knocks out one of the required elements, but it is not the case that the government can sue someone just for *being* a monopolist. The newspapers often seem to assume that *being* a monopolist is illegal. The core of *Grinnell* prong 2 is that monopolization is not a status offense; it's OK to be dominant.

The hard part is to distinguish between the kinds of actions that result in monopoly lawfully and those that result in monopoly unlawfully — to flesh out the distinction between "the willful acquisition or maintenance of that power" and "growth or development as a consequence of a superior product, business acumen, or historic accident." The classic case on this question is Judge Hand's *Alcoa* decision, which we encountered on the question of monopoly power. Among the

---

[2] *See, e.g., Broadcom Corp. v. Qualcomm, Inc.*, 501 F.3d 297, 307 (3d Cir. 2007).

many legal questions in *Alcoa* was whether Alcoa had monopolized the virgin aluminum ingot market by excluding competitors through anti-competitive means. Alcoa hadn't done anything obviously evil like blowing up a competitor's factory or forcing its customers not to buy from competitors. Mostly, it had built out new factory capacity — what Judge Hand called "doubling and redoubling its capacity before others entered the field." This had the effect of discouraging new entry.

Judge Hand ultimately found that Alcoa's conduct was anticompetitive. Figuring out exactly why is a challenge. What *Alcoa* leaves us with is a set of commonly used, albeit incomplete, expressions for thinking about prong 2 of *Grinnell*.

First, Judge Hand made clear that Section 2 is not a status offense. *Monopolize* is an "active verb," he explained. Firms can become monopolists in several ways that do not violate Section 2. For one, "persons may unwittingly find themselves in possession of a monopoly, automatically so to say: that is, without having intended to put an end to existing competition, or to prevent competition from arising when none had existed; they may become monopolists by force of accident." If you want a mental image here, think of Tom Hanks as Forrest Gump riding out Hurricane Carmen on a shrimping boat with Gary Sinise as crazy Lieutenant Dan, only to find that after the storm theirs is the only boat left afloat.

Historical accident is the easy case to make for nonliability. The harder case is the one where a firm fights hard to get ahead and wins. Judge Hand commonsensically explains that "[t]he successful competitor, having been urged to compete, must not be turned upon when he wins." Hence, the producer who obtains a monopoly by "superior skill, foresight, and industry" is a lawful monopolist. A company that obtains a monopoly by building a better mousetrap shouldn't be condemned.

What words, then, should we use to describe the bad category — unlawful monopolizing conduct? Judge Hand never gives us a convincing set of words. He tells us that "Alcoa's size was 'magnified' to make it a monopoly" and that Alcoa "utilized its size for 'abuse,'" but that doesn't help very much. Why wasn't "doubling and redoubling" capacity just the product of "superior skill, foresight, and industry"?

Alas, the Supreme Court has never given us a definitive answer either, apart from the very general set of words from *Grinnell* that largely tracks the *Alcoa* formulation. However, the Court has dramatically reinforced the dividing line between monopoly and monopolization, particularly in its 2004 *Trinko* decision.[3] We shall revisit *Trinko* in the next chapter as a case about the "duty to deal." One aspect of

---

[3] *Verizon Commc'ns Inc. v. Law Offices of Curtis V. Trinko LLP*, 540 U.S. 398 (2004).

2. The Anticompetitive Conduct Element

Trinko deserves special mention now, however. In the context of discussing why Verizon did not violate Section 2 of the Sherman Act by dragging its feet in fulfilling its statutory obligation to share its telephone network with competitors, Justice Scalia offered the following perspective on monopolization and Section 2:

> The mere possession of monopoly power, and the concomitant charging of monopoly prices, is not only not unlawful; it is an important element of the free-market system. The opportunity to charge monopoly prices — at least for a short period — is what attracts "business acumen" in the first place; it induces risk taking that produces innovation and economic growth. To safeguard the incentive to innovate, the possession of monopoly power will not be found unlawful unless it is accompanied by an element of anticompetitive conduct.[4]

Justice Scalia is far too skilled, careful, and intentional a craftsman of legal prose to have employed the triple negative — "not only not unlawful" — without the most intense of purposes. *Trinko* communicates that monopolists should not be on the defensive, that their achievements are largely to be celebrated, and that monopoly condemned because of *Grinnell* prong 2 will be the rare exception rather than the rule. And that has certainly been the Supreme Court's course in the Chicago School era, as we shall observe in greater detail in the next chapter. Having a monopoly and charging monopoly prices isn't illegal.

Despite *Trinko*'s celebration of monopoly, it did not advance the ball very far in terms of defining the distinction between "superior skill, foresight, and industry" and anticompetitive conduct. In recent years, academic commentators have spilled considerable ink trying to articulate a unifying theory of Section 2's anticompetitive conduct element. Since there is no general consensus in the academic literature or case law on this issue, let us focus briefly on just two of the more commonly proposed tests.

One test that has received a good bit of scholarly support is the *profit sacrifice* or *"no economic sense"* test. Under this test, an act should be deemed exclusionary and illegal if it would have been rational for the accused to undertake only on the assumption that it would produce monopoly profits. The classic example of an anticompetitive act that meets this definition is predatory pricing. A firm that prices below its cost appears to be acting irrationally unless one assumes that the present sacrifice of profits will result in supracompetitive profits once rivals are excluded. Conduct like this that makes no economic sense apart

---

[4] 540 U.S. at 407.

from an exclusionary motive would be condemned. This proposed test has been criticized on various grounds, including the observation that some exclusionary acts (such as lying about one's rival or blowing up its factory) cost virtually nothing to perform and hence involve no sacrifice of profits.

A similar test, proposed by Judge Posner, would condemn as exclusionary those acts capable of excluding an *equally efficient competitor*. This test would permit dominant firms to exploit their efficiency advantages, such as economies of scale or scope, to exclude less efficient rivals, but condemn them for undertaking acts such as predatory pricing that could drive out equally efficient firms. This test has the appeal of protecting efficiency and preventing less efficient firms from complaining about "exclusionary" practices that actually benefit consumers. As we shall see in the following chapter, an "as efficient" component has worked its way into the legal tests for some species of exclusionary conduct.

Judge Posner's test has its critics, too. For example, suppose that a dominant firm engages in conduct that excludes new entrants who are operating at a small scale, and hence less efficiently, but who could have grown to a more efficient scale absent the exclusionary conduct. There seems to be some bootstrapping in the monopolist's claim that the conduct should be lawful since the excluded firms weren't as efficient. Or suppose that the excluded firm is perpetually 10 percent less efficient than the monopolist. However, the less efficient competitor's entry forces the monopolist to lower its price from one that is 20 percent above competitive levels to one 10 percent above competitive levels (where *competitive* assumes competition from equally efficient firms). In that scenario, exclusion of the less efficient rival may still negatively affect consumer welfare.

The quest for a unifying theory of Section 2 liability is a rather metaphysical undertaking. The courts have largely avoided the metaphysics and come up with concrete tests for particular types of business behavior, as we shall see in Chapter 8. However, background academic discussions often influence the way that the courts come up with the doctrinal tests and ultimately decide the cases.

To recap: *Monopolize* under Section 2 is an active verb that requires an exclusionary act. Monopolies obtained through historical accident or "superior skill, foresight, or industry" are not illegal. Monopolies obtained through the use of other devices are illegal. The line of theoretic demarcation between the two categories is blurry. The best way to understand the dividing line is to observe courts in practice on particular forms of alleged misconduct — the subject of the next chapter.

3.   Competition, Not Competitors

We have already seen that much of the lawyers' play around monopolization offenses consists of deploying legal axioms. Here is another very important principle — one that has taken off in the last 20 years: "It is axiomatic that the antitrust laws were passed for 'the protection of competition, not competitors.' "[5] This distinction between (a) competition as a process protected for the benefit of consumers and (b) injury to individual competitors has become increasingly emphasized in the cases. Consider the following from the Supreme Court's *Spectrum Sports* opinion.

> The purpose of the [Sherman] Act is not to protect businesses from the working of the market; it is to protect the public from the failure of the market. The law directs itself not against conduct which is competitive, even severely so, but against conduct which unfairly tends to destroy competition itself. It does so not out of solicitude for private concerns but out of concern for the public interest.[6]

The "competition, not competitors" theme is not limited to monopolization cases but may be asserted any time that a firm complains that its rival's business tactics are unfair or predatory. The Supreme Court has increasingly held that even aggressive competitive behavior that may be unethical or tortious and harms a competitor does not give rise to an antitrust violation unless it disrupts the market's competitive functioning. Thus, "[e]ven an act of pure malice by one business competitor against another does not, without more, state a claim under the federal antitrust laws."[7]

A case in point: Discon, Inc., sold call-switching equipment removal services to telephone companies, in competition with AT&T Technologies. NYNEX, the local exchange carrier in New York and Connecticut, purchased removal services. At the time of the events giving rise to the case, NYNEX was rate regulated. Discon alleged that NYNEX and AT&T Technologies entered into a corrupt deal whereby AT&T Technologies would get all NYNEX's removal business and charge NYNEX an inflated price, which would then allow NYNEX to claim a higher cost basis and thus induce the rate regulators to approve higher rates, after which AT&T would give secret rebates to NYNEX. The effect, alleged Discon, was to cut out Discon as a supplier of removal services to NYNEX. The Supreme Court, however, unanimously ruled

[5] *Brooke Group, Ltd. v. Brown & Williamson Tobacco Corp.*, 509 U.S. 209, 224 (1993).
[6] *Spectrum Sports, Inc. v. McQuillan*, 506 U.S. 447, 458 (1993).
[7] *Brooke Group*, 525 U.S. at 225.

that Discon had not stated a claim under either Section 1 or Section 2 of the Sherman Act.[8] While Discon alleged the commission of illegal and fraudulent acts by a competitor that caused Discon to lose business, it omitted the crucial component — a showing that the alleged fraud perpetrated on the rate regulators would diminish the competitiveness of the call-switching equipment removal services market. Allowing such claims of "regulatory fraud would transform cases involving business behavior that is improper for various reasons, say, cases involving nepotism or personal pique, into treble-damages antitrust cases."

The upshot is that in all antitrust cases involving competitor complaints, but particularly in Section 2 cases, the plaintiff must carefully articulate a theory of how the challenged behavior was not merely unethical or tortious or harmful to the plaintiff or other competitors, but also how the alleged misconduct impaired the competitiveness of the market itself. Anything short of that will bring the "competition, not competitors" maxim quickly into play.

4. The *Microsoft* Principles

The D.C. Circuit's 2001 unanimous en banc decision in *Microsoft*[9] is many things to many people. Like Judge Hand's *Alcoa* and Judge Taft's *Addyston Pipe* opinions before it, *Microsoft* has the status of a transformative lower court opinion that is almost equal in authority to a Supreme Court decision. We will not be able to do it justice here. However, one aspect of the case that is useful pedagogically is the court's efforts to distill five general principles "from a century of case law on monopolization under §2." We have already seen some of these principles in play.

The first two principles are really one principle with a specification about the burden of proof. "First, to be condemned as exclusionary, a monopolist's act must have an 'anticompetitive effect.' That is, it must harm the competitive *process* and thereby harm consumers. In contrast, harm to one or more *competitors* will not suffice." And "[s]econd, the plaintiff, on whom the burden of proof of course rests, . . . must demonstrate that the monopolist's conduct indeed has the requisite anticompetitive effect." These two principles pick up on the "competition, not competitors" theme just discussed and make clear that the plaintiff bears the burden of proving the injurious effect on competition.

[8]*NYNEX Corp. v. Discon, Inc.*, 525 U.S. 128 (1998).
[9]*United States v. Microsoft Corp.*, 253 U.S. 34 (2001).

Moving on: "Third, if a plaintiff successfully establishes a *prima facie* case under §2 by demonstrating anticompetitive effect, then the monopolist may proffer a 'procompetitive justification' for its conduct. . . . If the monopolist asserts a procompetitive justification — a nonpretextual claim that its conduct is indeed a form of competition on the merits because it involves, for example, greater efficiency or enhanced consumer appeal — then the burden shifts back to the plaintiff to rebut that claim." This principle should be familiar by now, because it is effectively the second-to-last stage of rule-of-reason analysis under Section 1. It underlines the fact that there are no per se offenses under Section 2 — that procompetitive justifications are always admissible to justify an allegedly monopolizing act.

The next principle is more controversial: "Fourth, if the monopolist's procompetitive justification stands unrebutted, then the plaintiff must demonstrate that the anticompetitive harm of the conduct outweighs the procompetitive benefit." This suggests that the elusive *Alcoa* question — what is an unlawfully exclusionary act — might be answered by balancing an act's procompetitive benefits against its anticompetitive harms. But even if this principle is sound in theory, it is hard to find actual examples of courts engaging in such balancing. As many commentators have pointed out, the *Microsoft* court itself did not do so. There were certainly occasions when Microsoft argued that a particular kind of conduct was justified by procompetitive justifications and the court disagreed, but one cannot find significant examples where the court held that Microsoft had shown conduct to have procompetitive justifications and yet held those were outweighed by anticompetitive effects. In most monopolization cases, if a court holds that the defendant has proven that its conduct has procompetitive benefits, it finds that conduct not illegal under Section 2 without undertaking any balancing. Indeed, going back to the metaphysical discussion about what is an exclusionary act, one could argue that only acts with *no* efficiency justification should be condemned under Section 2.

And as for principle 5: "Finally, in considering whether the monopolist's conduct on balance harms competition and is therefore condemned as exclusionary for purposes of §2, our focus is upon the effect of that conduct, not upon the intent behind it. Evidence of the intent behind the conduct of a monopolist is relevant only to the extent it helps us understand the likely effect of the monopolist's conduct." This principle is also somewhat controversial, although probably more in line with the mainstream of current antitrust practice. The idea is that litigating antitrust cases with reference to the subjective intentions of the accused, often gleaned from internal memoranda or e-mails, is not a way to make rational antitrust policy. Many business people employ aggressive language — often involving sports or war metaphors — when speaking about their competitors: Let's crush them! Let's cut their throats!!! When read in the calm air of the jury room, that language may sound frightful, but is that a basis for concluding that the conduct is anticompetitive? What if the firm was going to "crush" the competitors by building a better mousetrap or "cut their throats" by reducing prices to competitive but nonpredatory levels? The question, many judges and commentators say, is whether the conduct was objectively anticompetitive, not whether the defendant took pleasure in the demise of a competitor. As Judge Posner has written, "[e]specially misleading is the inveterate tendency of sales executives to brag to their superiors about their competitive prowess, often using metaphors of coercion that are compelling evidence of predatory intent to the naïve."[10]

The *Microsoft* principles provide a useful, if incomplete and in part controversial, checklist for thinking through general Section 2 issues. Recite them liberally, but pay due attention to their nuances.

5.   Attempted Monopolization

Attempted monopolization is an unsuccessful attempt to obtain a monopoly. It is illegal under Section 2. The elements of the offense are "(1) that the defendant has engaged in predatory or anticompetitive conduct with (2) a specific intent to monopolize and (3) a dangerous probability of achieving monopoly power."[11]

The first element is "simply" the anticompetitive conduct element of *Alcoa* and *Grinnell*. Whatever conduct counts as unlawfully exclusionary for purposes of actual monopolization also counts as exclusionary for purposes of attempted monopolization. So, for example, pricing below an appropriate measure of cost — which we will examine in the next chapter as a prerequisite for predatory pricing liability — can equally serve as the second element of actual monopolization under *Grinnell* and the first element of attempted monopolization under *Spectrum Sports*.

The second element is specific intent. We just saw how, in *Microsoft*, the D.C. Circuit debunked the notion that specific intent is a helpful tool for identifying when conduct is anticompetitive. However, since attempted crimes at common law always required specific intent and attempted monopolization is modeled on the common law attempted crimes, specific intent is an additional element in attempted monopolization cases. Observe that, in theory at least, the specific intent

---

[10]Richard A. Posner, *Antitrust Law* 215 (2d ed. 2001).
[11]*Spectrum Sports*, 506 U.S. at 456.

analysis under prong 2 should be independent of the anticompetitive element of prong 1. Just because there is specific intent to harm a rival does not mean that the harm is objectively anticompetitive under the first prong.

That leaves the "dangerous probability" prong. The test goes back *Swift & Co. v. United States*,[12] where Justice Oliver Wendell Holmes explained:

> Where acts are not sufficient in themselves to produce a result which the law seeks to prevent,—for instance, the monopoly,—but require further acts in addition to the mere forces of nature to bring that result to pass, an intent to bring it to pass is necessary in order to produce a dangerous probability that it will happen .... But when that intent and the consequent dangerous probability exist, this statute, like many others, and like the common law in some cases, directs itself against that dangerous probability as well as against the completed result.

The question, then, is how close to obtaining a monopoly the defendant must have come for the monopoly to have been "dangerously probable." The leading Supreme Court opinions on attempted monopolization—*Spectrum Sports* and *Lorraine Journal*—have little of use to contribute on this third, distinctive element of attempted monopolization. There is no single leading lower court opinion, but some observations can be gleaned from the outcomes of litigated attempted monopolization cases.

First and foremost, by far the most important factor in determining dangerous probability is the defendant's market share. This shouldn't come as a surprise, since in Chapter 3 we saw that the defendant's market share is also the most important factor in determining whether the defendant has monopoly power. If, following *Alcoa*, a market share above 60 percent is generally required for a finding of monopoly (although some courts say 50 percent), a market share somewhat less than actual monopoly will generally be required for a finding of dangerous probability. Courts tend to follow something like a 10 percent rule. If a court says that a defendant can't be a monopolist unless it has at least a 60 percent market share, then it will probably also say that a defendant with less than a 50 percent share does not create a dangerous probability of monopolizing if it engages in anticompetitive acts.

Of course, these market share numbers are all quite arbitrary (although not as much as my 10 percent rule). What may be more

---

[12] 196 U.S. 375, 396 (1905).

telling than just the defendant's market share are changes to the defendant's and its competitors' market shares during the period of alleged anticompetitive behavior. Courts frequently point to a defendant's declining market share during the relevant period and say, "There was no dangerous probability since the defendant was actually losing share—going in the opposite direction from the monopoly position." Conversely, if the defendant was gaining share during the period, a court might use that fact as evidence of dangerous probability, particularly if the share numbers are in the 50 to 60 percent gray zone. So pay special attention to trends in share during the relevant period.

Apart from market share, there is no universally agreed-upon set of relevant secondary factors, although the following list is characteristic: "the strength of the competition, the probable development of the industry, the barriers to entry, the nature of the anticompetitive conduct and the elasticity of consumer demand."[13] Most of these are the same sorts of factors that one examines in determining whether the defendant had an actual monopoly for purposes of Section 2. However, the first factor—the strength of competition—deserves special mention because it often plays out distinctively in attempted monopolization cases.

Most attempted monopolization cases are private lawsuits in which a smaller firm that is still a rival in the relevant market claims that the defendant's conduct has so threatened its existence that but for the grace of God or the Honorable U.S. District Judge Before Whom We Now Appear, it will shortly have to exit, leaving the market in the sole possession of its ruthless competitor. One of the defendant's major lines of defense will be to show that the plaintiff isn't doing so poorly after all—that its existence in the market is hardly threatened. Evidence of the plaintiff's market share, market share growth, investments in new products or services, profitability, signing up of new customers, and the like will be in focus. In other words, the attempted monopolization case will turn into a referendum on whether the plaintiff is or was at one time facing a dangerous probability of having to exit

[13]*International Distribution Centers, Inc. v. Walsh Trucking Co.*, 812 F.2d 786, 792 (2d Cir. 1987). *See also Broadcom Corp. v. Qualcomm Inc.*, 501 F.3d 297, 318 (3d Cir. 2007) (listing the relevant factors as "significant market share coupled with anticompetitive practices, barriers to entry, the strength of competition, the probable development of the industry, and the elasticity of consumer demand"); *Multistate Legal Studies, Inc. v. Harcourt Brace Jovanovich*, 63 F.3d 1540, 1554 (10th Cir. 1995) ("Factors relevant to determining dangerous probability include, but are not limited to, a defendant's market share, whether the defendant is a multimarket firm, the number and strength of other competitors, market trends, and entry barriers.").

the market. Even if the plaintiff was or is in danger of forced exiting, if there are other significant firms in the market (particularly ones that entered during the period of alleged attempted monopolization), the defendant may deploy the "competition, not competitors" maxim and claim that the plaintiff is just whining about her own frailties when the market is perfectly robust.

Chapter 8

Exclusionary Practices

In the preceding chapter we saw the general principles applicable to monopolization cases. Over time the courts have developed more specific principles addressing particular forms of allegedly exclusionary behavior. These practices are often challenged under Section 2 of the Sherman Act, but some of them may also be challenged under Section 1, Section 3 of the Clayton Act, the Robinson-Patman Act, or Section 5 of the FTC Act (but only by the FTC). With a few exceptions, which this chapter won't cover, it doesn't matter which statutory section a plaintiff invokes in challenging the practice. For example, predatory pricing can be challenged either under Section 2 of the Sherman Act or as an instance of primary line price discrimination under the Robinson-Patman Act; the Supreme Court has held that claims in the two cases are functionally identical.[1] Hence, in studying exclusionary practices in this chapter, we shall not be concerned with fine differences between legal theories but will instead try to understand the principal legal standards and economic theories applicable to the behaviors.

The list that follows is not exhaustive or exclusive. A favorite maxim of lower courts is that "'[a]nticompetitive conduct' can come in too many different forms and is too dependent upon context, for any court or commentator ever to have enumerated all the verities."[2] Some courts have also invoked "monopoly broth" theories, in which exclusionary effect is assessed from an aggregate of disparate forms of conduct.[3] One of the contested questions in many exclusionary conduct cases is whether the facts alleged by the plaintiff fall within one of the established patterns subject to developed legal rules (such as the requirement of proving below-cost pricing in predatory pricing cases) or

---

[1]*Brooke Group, Ltd. v. Brown & Williamson Tobacco Corp.*, 509 U.S. 209, 222 (1993) ("the essence of the claim under either statute is the same").

[2]*Caribbean Broadcast Sys., Ltd. v. Cable & Wireless PLC*, 148 F.3d 1080, 1087 (D.C. Cir. 1998).

[3]*See* Daniel A. Crane, *Does Monopoly Broth Make Bad Soup?*, 76 Antitrust L.J. 663 (2010).

whether the alleged misconduct is different enough from established patterns to be free from the constraints of the legal rules. With those considerations, let us dive into the leading categories of anticompetitive conduct.

1.   Refusals to Deal

A monopolization case often arises when a dominant firm refuses to cooperate in some way with its smaller rivals. In such cases, the smaller firm may claim that the larger one has monopolistically refused to deal. The defendant's standard answer is that there is no "duty to deal" and hence that the plaintiff's claim is not cognizable, even if the alleged refusal had an exclusionary effect. Two important contemporary Supreme Court decisions supply the essential doctrinal tools to address such questions.

Aspen, Colorado, is a beautiful place full of beautiful — and very rich — people. It has four beautiful skiing mountains. The rest of this story is not so beautiful. Through a confluence of events a company we'll call Ski Co. acquired control of three of the mountains. The fourth was owned by Highlands. Between 1967 and 1977 Ski Co. and Highlands jointly offered a four-mountain pass so that skiers could sample all four mountains at their pleasure. In 1978 Highlands and Ski Co. had a falling out over continuation of the arrangement, with Ski Co. demanding a considerably higher percentage of shared revenues than Highlands would accept. Eventually, Highlands brought a Section 2 lawsuit, claiming that Ski Co. had discontinued the four-mountain pass relationship in order to disadvantage Highlands as a rival.

The Supreme Court upheld Highlands' claim.[4] It began with the conventional observation that "even a firm with monopoly power has no general duty to engage in a joint marketing program with a competitor."[5] However, held the Court, Ski Co. had not simply refused to deal with a competitor. Rather, it had cut off a previously profitable business relationship solely for the purpose of disadvantaging Highlands. Further, it had refused to sell its lift tickets to Highlands at their ordinary retail price so that Highlands could cobble together its own version of a four-mountain pass. The Supreme Court found this evidence sufficient to sustain liability under Section 2.

Those interested in the sordid backstory of the case should buy my book *Antitrust Stories* and read the chapter on *Aspen Skiing* by George

---

[4] *Aspen Skiing Co. v. Aspen Highlands Skiing Co.*, 472 U.S. 585 (1985).
[5] 472 U.S. at 600.

Priest and Jonathan Lewinsohn.[6] According to their research, Highlands was a "beaten down resort" that did fun things like covering up lift chair derailments, hiring "scruffy college students" with poor "appearance, deportment, [and] attitude," and paying locals to "pack the lines on days when joint-ticket surveys were taken." Naughty behavior, but not part of the Supreme Court's decision.

Aspen Skiing appeared to open the door to a limited duty to deal for dominant firms, albeit under narrow circumstances. Almost 20 years later, in *Trinko*,[7] the Supreme Court sharply limited the reach of any such duty. Verizon Communications was the incumbent local exchange carrier (ILEC)—or telephone company—serving New York State. The 1996 Telecommunications Act required ILECs such as Verizon to share their networks with competitors on terms established by state regulators and the Federal Communications Commission (FCC). Verizon dragged its feet in filling orders by its competitors to access Verizon's network, which delayed the competitors from establishing a competitive service. After the competitors complained, the New York Public Service Commission and the FCC investigated and ultimately entered into consent decrees with Verizon that required Verizon to pay millions of dollars to the federal government and to competitors.

None of that involved antitrust law. What happened next did. A customer of AT&T brought suit alleging that Verizon had monopolized the local telephone market by its delay in complying with its statutory obligations. The Supreme Court unanimously rejected the customer's claim (although three justices would have denied standing and not reached the merits). Its analysis is complex and reflects an effort to cobble together a coalition of perspectives, so at times the opinion can seem inconsistent.

The Court's Section 2 analysis began with a recitation of reasons not to impose a duty to deal on monopolists. Forced sharing of infrastructure could enable free riding and hence diminish the incentives to invest. "Enforced sharing also requires courts to act as central planners, identifying proper price, quantity, and other terms of dealing—a role for which they are ill suited."[8] Moreover, forcing negotiations between rivals could lead to "the supreme evil of antitrust: collusion."[9]

---

[6] George L. Priest & Jonathan Lewinsohn, *Aspen Skiing: Product Differentiation and Thwarting Free Riding as Monopolization*, in ANTITRUST STORIES 229-255 (Eleanor M. Fox & Daniel A. Crane, eds, 2007).

[7] *Verizon Commuc'ns. Inc. v. Law Offices of Curtis V. Trinko LLP*, 540 U.S. 398 (2004).

[8] 540 U.S. at 408.

[9] *Id.*

What about *Aspen Skiing*? The Court found *Aspen Skiing* to lie "at or near the outer boundary of §2 liability," a polite way of limiting *Aspen Skiing* to its facts. The Court noted that, unlike in *Aspen Skiing*, Verizon had not discontinued a previously profitable relationship, nor had it refused to sell at retail a good or service it sold to regular customers. This also distinguished the facts of *Trinko* from those in *Otter Tail*,[10] in which the Court upheld Section 2 liability where the defendant was already in the business of providing transmission of power over its lines to some customers but refused that service to other customers who wanted to compete with the supplier.

The Court then considered the relevance of the Telecommunications Act in determining whether Verizon had an antitrust duty to deal. An important concept coming out of *Trinko* is the distinction between a general duty to deal—for example, one imposed by a regulatory scheme—and an *antitrust* duty to deal. General Section 2 principles do not impose a duty to deal, and the Court found that the presence of the Telecom Act's regulatory scheme cut against imposing such a duty. Since the regulators were capable of enforcing the statutory obligation to deal, there was no reason for antitrust courts to do so. Reflecting a theme repeated in many recent Section 2 cases, the Court worried about the costs of false positives—erroneous condemnations of pro-competitive behavior.

Finally, the Court rejected the argument that an essential facilities type obligation—discussed in Chapter 5—could support the imposition of a duty to deal in *Trinko*. The Court observed that it had never actually recognized such a doctrine, but in any event the doctrine would not be availing since regulators had the power to order access for rivals.

In light of *Trinko*, any antitrust duty to deal seems to be very sharply limited. A fair reading of *Trinko* suggests that a plaintiff would have to be able to fit into one of three exceptions to the general rule of no duty to deal in order to establish a violation:

1. Discontinuance of a previous business relationship for anticompetitive purposes (*Aspen Skiing*)
2. Refusal to deal on the same terms with rivals as with ordinary customers (*Aspen Skiing* and *Otter Tail*)
3. Refusal of access to the facilities of a joint venture that creates market power

The last category is reflected in a footnote in *Trinko* where the Court distinguished the earlier *Terminal Railway* and *Associated Press* cases as ones where "concerted action" was involved.

[10] *Otter Tail Power Co. v. United States*, 410 U.S. 366 (1973).

Is there any rhyme or reason to this list of exceptions? Whether or not so intended by the Court, there is. As we have seen, one of the most compelling justifications for rejecting an antitrust duty to deal is a concern over administrability—the feasibility of having generalist courts mandate compulsory terms of dealing between two parties. In each of the exceptions listed above, terms of dealing have already been contractually established, so it is less difficult for courts to impose the same or similar terms of dealing between the litigants. Apart from these exceptional cases, there seems to be little call for an antitrust duty to deal in present U.S. law.

2. Predatory Pricing

Predatory pricing involves a tale of two times. In time 1, a dominant firm prices below cost. Smaller rivals are driven out of the market or so marginalized that they are no longer effective competitors. In time 2, the dominant firm enjoys monopoly power and raises its prices above competitive levels. So predatory pricing is a story that involves both prices that are too low and prices that are too high.

For many years, predatory pricing was considered a strategy commonly chosen by monopolists. Standard Oil was considered a classic example of a predator—dramatically underpricing independent refiners and petroleum distributors to drive them into financial ruin and then buying up their assets. The Chicago School, however, disparaged the idea that predatory pricing was occurring often, if at all. In several decisions in the 1980s and 1990s, the Supreme Court accepted the key tenets of the Chicago School attack.[11] Predatory pricing schemes would rarely be attempted, wrote the Court, because they would be exceedingly expensive and risky. The predator would have to sacrifice short-run profits in the hopes of driving out rivals, preventing entry by new rivals, and recovering the costs of predation through future recoupment.

There was a second prong to the Chicago School attack on predation theories—an argument that legal rules encouraging predatory pricing lawsuits could chill lawful and pro-consumer price discounting:

[T]he mechanism by which a firm engages in predatory pricing—lowering prices—is the same mechanism by which a firm stimulates competition; because "cutting prices in order to increase business often is the

---

[11] *See Brooke Group, Ltd. v. Brown & Williamson Tobacco Corp.*, 509 U.S. 209 (1993); *Matsushita Elec. Indus. Co. v. Zenith Radio Corp.*, 475 U.S. 574 (1986).

very essence of competition . . . [;] mistaken inferences . . . are especially costly, because they chill the very conduct the antitrust laws are designed to protect."[12]

Despite accepting the Chicago School views almost wholesale, the Supreme Court did not jettison the cause of action for predatory pricing altogether. Instead, it announced standards for predatory pricing cases that have made predation difficult to prove.

As noted in the introduction to this chapter, predatory pricing can be attacked under either the Robinson-Patman Act or under Section 2 of the Sherman Act, and the legal elements are essentially identical. In order to make out a claim of monopolization through predatory pricing, the plaintiff must prove two elements under the *Brooke Group* test: (1) the defendant priced below an "appropriate measure of cost," and (2) the predatory pricing created a dangerous probability that the defendant would obtain monopoly power and recoup the costs of predation through supracompetitive pricing. Let's consider each of these elements in turn.

2.1.   The Appropriate Measure of Cost

As the Supreme Court has made clear on several occasions, sharp price discounts are not illegal unless the prices offered fall below an appropriate measure of cost. The Supreme Court has not yet decided what constitutes an appropriate measure of cost; however, there is a vast body of lower court precedent. For the sake of relative simplicity, let's focus on the test adopted by a majority of the lower courts: the average variable cost (AVC) test.

The AVC test goes back to a pathbreaking 1975 *Harvard Law Review* article by Phillip Areeda and Donald Turner, both professors at Harvard.[13] Areeda and Turner began by noting that under classical economic assumptions, competition should drive prices down toward *marginal cost* — the cost of producing the next unit of output. Faced with competition, it is rational for a firm to lower its cost to the marginal cost rather than lose a sale. For example, if making another widget would cost a manufacturer $2 in labor costs and $2 in materials costs, it is rational for the manufacturer to make the widget so long as it can charge at least $4. On the other hand, it would not be rational for a manufacturer to incur $4 in marginal costs to make the widget

---

[12]*Brooke Group*, 509 U.S. at 226.

[13]Phillip Areeda & Donald F. Turner, *Predatory Pricing and Related Practices Under Section 2 of the Sherman Act*, 88 Harv. L. Rev. 697 (1975).

and then sell it for $3.95. At that point, the manufacturer would have been better off not making the widget at all. Thus, argued Areeda and Turner, prices at or above marginal cost are presumptively lawful since they reflect ordinary competitive pressures, but prices below marginal cost cannot be explained by ordinary business logic. Hence, marginal cost is the theoretically appropriate measure of cost for deciding whether the defendant's prices were predatory or legitimate.

However, noted Areeda and Turner, marginal cost is largely an economist's construct; it isn't a measure of cost used by business people in the ordinary course of business. To be workable as a legal test, they argued, the predatory pricing measure of cost would need to draw on the kind of accounting that business people ordinarily do. Areeda and Turner noted that business people tend to divide the world of costs into two buckets: variable costs, which change with the level of output; and fixed costs, which do not change with the level of output. Examples of variable costs are labor and raw materials. When a factory produces more widgets, these costs tend to rise. By contrast, the cost of building the factory, the salaries of senior managers, and research and development costs typically stay constant whether the firm builds one widget or a thousand.

Areeda and Turner argued that variable costs are very similar to marginal costs and can serve as a good proxy for marginal costs in the formulation of the legal rule. Hence, with a few qualifications beyond the scope of this discussion, Areeda and Turner proposed that the legal test for predatory pricing be *average variable cost*, "the sum of all variable costs divided by output."[14] Unless the defendant's price is below the average of all costs that fluctuate with changes in the level of output, the defendant cannot have engaged in predatory pricing. Application of the AVC test requires sorting the defendant's costs into the fixed and variable costs buckets and then asking whether the price was above or below the variable costs.

The AVC test tends to be very conservative, particularly in industries with very high fixed costs. In an industry like software, there are virtually no marginal or variable costs, which means that it is virtually impossible to prove predatory pricing. Nonetheless, the D.C. Circuit in *Microsoft* stuck to the view that predatory pricing requires a showing of pricing below marginal cost even in high-fixed-cost industries.[15] Other courts have adopted rules allowing for consideration of total costs (fixed and variable) under some circumstances.[16] Still other

[14] 88 Harv. L. Rev. at 700.

[15] *United States v. Microsoft*, 253 F.3d 34, 75 (D.C. Cir. 2001) (rejecting "condemnation of low but non-predatory pricing" by Microsoft).

[16] *See, e.g., Morgan v. Ponder*, 892 F.2d 1355 (8th Cir. 1989).

courts have accepted that marginal or incremental cost (basically syn-
onymous) is the appropriate level, but have adopted a "long-run incremental cost" approach that asks about the relationship between costs
and output levels over quite a long period, with the effect of making
incremental or marginal some costs that would appear as fixed under
the AVC test.[17]

2.2. Recoupment

The second prong of the *Brooke Group* test is a dangerous probability
that the below-cost pricing would result in a market structure that
would allow the defendant to *recoup* the costs of predation through
supracompetitive pricing. Note at the outset that the "dangerous probability" formulation in the *Brooke Group* test assumes that predatory
pricing cases will be attempted, rather than actual, monopolization
cases. If the defendant has successfully excluded its competitors and
recouped, then a showing of actual recoupment suffices. However,
most predatory pricing cases do fall in the attempted monopoly category: the plaintiff alleges that even if the defendant never quite
acquired monopoly power and recouped, its below-cost pricing led to
the dangerous probability that it would.

The recoupment prong is the place where the Supreme Court has
done most of its cutting back on predatory pricing theories.
In *Matsushita*[18] the Court rejected a claim by U.S. television manufacturers that Japanese television manufacturers had conspired over a
two-decade period to dump below-cost TVs on the U.S. market for
the purpose of displacing U.S. competitors. The Supreme Court
found this allegation inherently implausible, noting that engaging in
below-cost pricing for such a long period would be excessively expensive and the prospects of recouping all of this predatory investment
with interest in the future excessively remote.

In *Brooke Group*, Liggett — a relatively small cigarette manufacturer — alleged that Brown & Williamson had engaged in a predatory
pricing campaign designed to punish Liggett for lowering its prices in
black and white (or generic) cigarettes. Liggett alleged that Brown &
Williamson's objective was to force Liggett back into a pattern of consciously parallel price setting in the cigarette industry. The Supreme
Court took the unusual step of engaging in sufficiency-of-the-evidence
review (the Court usually decides abstract legal questions) and found
that the jury did not have sufficient evidence to reach a finding of

---

[17]*MCI Commc'ns Corp. v. AT&T*, 708 F.2d 1081 (7th Cir. 1982).
[18]*Matsushita Elec. Indus. Co. v. Zenith Radio Corp.*, 475 U.S. 574 (1986).

predatory pricing because the market was not conducive to recoupment. The Court noted that Brown & Williamson had a market share of 12 percent; hence, for every dollar that Brown & Williamson invested in predatory pricing it would need to generate $9 in excess profits in the market as a whole to recoup its investment, of which competitors would reap $8 without having taken any risk.

In light of *Matsushita* and *Brooke Group*, a predatory pricing plaintiff must have strong evidence that the market is structurally conducive to recoupment if rivals are driven from the market or marginalized. The factors are generally the same as those used for assessing market power: the presence of high entry barriers, weak competitors, a small or disorganized customer base, and low demand elasticity.

3. Predatory Overbidding and Price Squeezes

In a several recent cases the Supreme Court has extended the logic of its predatory pricing rulings to circumstances that did not involve claims that a dominant firm simply lowered its price to drive out competitors. These cases involved different patterns of commercial behavior that the Court thought should be captured by the broad principles of its predation cases. Let us consider two such cases.

Weyerhaeuser is a diversified conglomerate that operated hardwood lumber sawmills in the Pacific Northwest.[19] A competitor sawmill brought a Section 2 suit alleging that Weyerhaeuser had deliberately driven up the price of alder logs by paying too high a price and buying more logs than it needed, simply so its competitors would go out of business, leaving Weyerhaeuser with a monopsony over alder log purchasing in the relevant geographic region. The problem with this claim was that Weyerhaeuser faced vigorous competition in the downstream market for finished hardwood lumber. Hence, even if Weyerhaeuser were successful in excluding competitors from the purchase of alder logs in the particular region where its sawmills were located, it would not be able to recoup by charging its own customers supracompetitive prices in the much broader market for finished lumber. The Court found predatory overbidding to be theoretically similar to predatory pricing, and hence applied the two-part *Brooke Group* test for predatory pricing (below-cost pricing and recoupment) to predatory overbidding claims. The Supreme Court rejected the sawmill's claim, noting that there was no evidence that the alleged overbidding on the

---

[19]*Weyerhaeuser Co. v. Ross-Simmons Hardwood Lumber Co.*, 549 U.S. 312 (2007).

input side led Weyerhaeuser to price below cost when selling to its
customers.

The second case illustrating the extension of the Supreme Court's
predatory pricing jurisprudence, as well as its duty-to-deal jurisprudence, concerns the so-called price squeeze. A *price squeeze* occurs
when a vertically integrated firm supplies a competitor with an
input at wholesale and then markets its own good or service at retail
at a price that the competitor could not match given the wholesale price
of the input. Consider the facts of *linkLine*.[20] AT&T was the incumbent
local phone service company in California and thus controlled the "last
mile," the lines that connect homes and businesses to telephone networks. As a condition of a merger, AT&T was required to provide digital subscriber line (DSL) transport services to its competitors so that
they could compete with AT&T by offering their own retail DSL services. Four competitors sued AT&T, alleging that it had "squeezed"
them by charging them too high a wholesale price and then lowering
its own retail prices. The combination of AT&T's high wholesale and
low retail prices allegedly left competitors without a sufficient margin
to compete profitably.

The Supreme Court unanimously rejected the competitors' claim.
First, it found that "a straightforward application" of *Trinko* foreclosed
any challenge to AT&T's wholesale prices.[21] Since AT&T had no antitrust duty to deal, it had no antitrust duty to charge reasonable
wholesale prices. Second, *Brooke Group* foreclosed a challenge to
AT&T's low retail prices. Since the competitors made no allegation
that AT&T was charging a price below an appropriate measure of
cost, it could not mount a challenge to AT&T's retail prices. Calling
the claim a "price squeeze" rather than predatory pricing was imma-
terial. Quoting its earlier decision in *Atlantic Richfield*,[22] the Court
observed that "[l]ow prices benefit consumers regardless of how
those prices are set, and so long as they are above predatory levels,
they do not threaten competition."[23] Since the claim alleged an excessively low price, it had to meet the *Brooke Group* test.

An important lesson from *Weyerhaeuser* and *linkLine* is that plaintiffs cannot escape the strictures of the *Brooke Group* test by labeling
their claim something other than predatory pricing. If the essence of
the claim involves a unilateral pricing decision, *Brooke Group* applies.

---

[20] *Pacific Bell Telephone Co. v. linkLine Commc'ns, Inc.*, 555 U.S. 438 (2009).
[21] *Id.* at 459.
[22] *Atlantic Richfield Co. v. USA Petroleum Co.*, 495 U.S. 328, 340 (1990).
[23] 555 U.S. at 451.

4. Tying

Tying is one of the most complicated and contested issues of exclusionary practices law. In a delightful turn of fortune, one of the leading tying cases involves shoes,[24] so all sorts of "funny" jokes can be told about tying shoes. (Some years ago I worked on a merger in the diaper industry, which produced all sorts of even funnier jokes about "elasticities.") A tying arrangement occurs when a firm with a monopoly or strong market position in a "tying" market forces its customers to purchase a complementary product in a second market (the "tied" market). It is closely related to *bundling*, where a seller chooses not to sell two items individually but only in a package. Tying is governed by a multipart legal test that disguises most of the interesting and contested economic issues. As an introduction to the topic (because it would be impossible to do it full justice here), let us begin with the legal elements and then consider some highlights of economic theory and the related policy discussion.

4.1. Legal Doctrine

Alas, the doctrine governing tying arrangements is a muddle, reflecting perhaps some of the underlying economic controversies. For one thing, the Supreme Court has curiously continued to affirm in present times that tying arrangements meeting certain criteria are per se illegal under Section 1 of the Sherman Act. In *Jefferson Parish*[25] four justices, led by Justice O'Connor, argued that the Court should get rid of the per se label in tying cases since it no longer bears any relation to the substance of the legal doctrine. Justice Stevens's majority opinion rejected this suggestion, asserting that it is "far too late in the history of our antitrust jurisprudence to question the proposition that certain tying arrangements pose an unacceptable risk of stifling competition and therefore are unreasonable 'per se.'"[26] As with horizontal group boycotts (discussed in Chapter 5), it makes little difference whether we call certain tying arrangements per se illegal or not; what matters is satisfaction of the various elements of the applicable test. If the test is satisfied, the arrangement is illegal, and if it is not satisfied, the arrangement is legal.

Tying arrangements can be challenged under Section 1 or 2 of the Sherman Act or Section 3 of the Clayton Act. While some courts may

[24]*United States v. United Shoe Mach. Co.*, 110 F. Supp. 295, 343-45 (D. Mass. 1953
[25]*Jefferson Parish Hosp. Dist. No. 2 v. Hyde*, 466 U.S. 2 (1984).
[26]*Id.* at 10.

insist that there are fine differences in the required proofs under Section 1 and Section 3, and all courts would insist that a Section 2 tying claim involve proof that the tying led to the creation of a monopoly (or dangerous probability in an attempt case) in the tied market, the essential standards for tying cases are the same whichever statutory section the plaintiff invokes.

What are the elements of a tying claim? The Supreme Court has never given the lawyer class the satisfaction of a neat list. Take a quick journey through the third edition of *Federal Reporter* and you will be dismayed to note that the courts of appeal list anywhere from three to four elements, in different orders and with different emphases. Nonetheless, it is possible to construct a fairly coherent list of factors from overlaps in the majority and concurring opinions in *Jefferson Parish* and other cases. The elements (in Crane's most logical order) are (1) two distinct products, (2) market power in the tying market, (3) anticompetitive effects in the tied market, and (4) the absence of efficiency justifications.[27] Let's consider each element.

First, a tying arrangement requires proof of tying and tied products that are separate products from the perspective of the consumer. A moment's reflection will show that it is possible to break down any product into various subcomponents and fault the seller for refusing to sell them individually. For example, one could complain about a manufacturer who insists on selling cars with engines on the theory that the manufacturer is "tying" the engine to the body of the car. But that would be a silly argument, since most customers obviously expect to buy cars with engines and understand the engine to be an essential part of a car.

Whether the first element is satisfied usually comes down to evidence about whether a substantial number of customers want a choice about whether to buy two complementary products from the same producer. In *Jefferson Parish* Justices Stevens and O'Connor clashed over whether surgery and anesthesia should be considered separate services. Justice O'Connor pointed out the obvious fact that patients (except for a few masochists whose interests judges don't honor) always want to buy anesthesia services when buying surgery services. Justice Stevens rejoined that while all patients buy both products, a substantial number of patients would like to choose their anesthesiologist separately from their surgeon.

The next element is market power in the tying market. Unless the seller has power in the tying market, it cannot force the customer to

---

[27] Many courts also list the jurisdictional element — an effect on a not insubstantial volume of commerce. However, this is not unique to tying cases and therefore is not discussed here.

purchase the tied product. Customers would simply choose another seller in the tying market.

Two notes are in order on the second element, one historical and one doctrinal. The historical note is that for many years the law was that if the seller had a patent or copyright on the tying product (one court said even a trademark),[28] there was a conclusive presumption that market power existed in the tying market. In *Independent Ink*[29] the Supreme Court unanimously jettisoned this long-standing presumption at least as to patents (although its holding logically applies to copyrights and trademarks as well) and held that a plaintiff must prove market power in the tying market whether or not there are patent rights in that market. It is important to flag this fairly recent change in doctrine, because there are many older cases that largely ignore the market power element as a result of the now-jettisoned presumption as to intellectual property.

The doctrinal note concerns the degree of market power necessary to sustain the plaintiff's case. Most lower courts hold that the firm engaging in tying must have at least a 30 percent share in the tying market for there to be sufficient market power.[30] This number may be arbitrary, but it is at least a useful marker for law students.

The third element requires a showing of harmful effects in the tied market. Exactly what this showing must be remains unclear doctrinally. Justice Stevens's majority opinion in *Jefferson Parish* stated that "the essential characteristic of an invalid tying arrangement lies in the seller's exploitation of its control over the tying product to force the buyer into the purchase of a tied product that the buyer either did not want at all, or might have preferred to purchase elsewhere on different terms."[31] This identification of "forcing" in the tied market as the essential ingredient suggests that a plaintiff need not show that the tying arrangement reduces the competitiveness of the tied market, so long as the tie forces some consumers to make choices other than those they would prefer to make. On the other hand, Justice O'Connor's concurring opinion argued that "there must be a substantial threat that the tying seller will acquire market power in the tied-product market."[32]

One way to understand the difference in emphasis between the majority and concurring opinions in *Jefferson Parish* is to draw a distinction between the creation, preservation, and enlargement of

[28] *Siegel v. Chicken Delight, Inc.*, 448 F.2d 43 (1971).
[29] *Illinois Tool Works Inc. v. Independent Ink, Inc.*, 547 U.S. 28 (2006).
[30] *See, e.g.*, *Breaux Bros. Farms, Inc. v. Teche Sugar Co.*, 21 F.3d 83, 87 (5th Cir. 1994).
[31] 466 U.S. at 12.
[32] 466 U.S. at 38.

117

market power and the exploitation of market power. Justice O'Connor, whose views might command a majority of the Supreme Court today, seems to believe that the antitrust laws should reach only conduct that creates, preserves, or enlarges market power—in the tied market in a tying case. Justice Stevens would certainly agree that such conduct should be condemned; his *Jefferson Parish* majority decision discusses ways in which tying arrangements could exclude competitors in the tied market or create entry barriers. But he also seems to believe that tying arrangements should be unlawful if they exploit existing market power to the detriment of consumers—for example, by forcing consumers to make purchases they would prefer not to make. Whether tying should be considered condemned only when it is exclusionary or also when it is exploitive remains contested in the academy, in the courts, and in antitrust enforcement.[33]

The fourth element—the absence of efficiencies—is arguably not an element at all, since the burden of proof probably lies with the defendant, as it does in any rule-of-reason case. Both the majority and concurrence in *Jefferson Parish* would allow efficiencies as an offset against any anticompetitive effects—which again prompts the question of what sense there is in continuing to employ the per se label.

4.2.   Economics and Policy

The economics of tying arrangements are considerably more complex than the legal doctrine suggests. Let us survey the key movements, beginning with a gem of economic wisdom announced by the Supreme Court in 1949 and repeated on numerous occasions. According to Justice Frankfurter, "[t]ying agreements serve hardly any purpose beyond the suppression of competition."[34] Well, true or false? By now you should not be surprised to learn that the Chicago School shouted out "false!" As usual, the Chicago School proceeded with a one-two punch, knocking out the ostensibly anticompetitive explanation for the challenged practice and offering an ostensibly procompetitive explanation in its place.

The core of the Chicago School observation is that a seller with a monopoly in the tying market could not extract a second monopoly from the tied market without eating away at its profits in the tying market, and hence would have no incentive to leverage market

---

[33] *See, e.g., Brantley v. NBC Universal, Inc.*, 675 F.3d 1192 (9th Cir. 2012) (rejecting claim that cable television programmers unlawfully tied valued channels to less-valued channels on grounds that plaintiffs failed to allege harm to market competitiveness).

[34] *Standard Oil Co. v. United States*, 337 U.S. 293, 305 (1949).

power into the tied market. To understand this *one-monopoly profit theory*, consider the facts of *International Salt*.[35] International Salt leased patented machines that canning companies used to inject salt into their canned goods. It essentially required its licensees to agree contractually to buy their salt requirements from International Salt. The government successfully challenged the lease restrictions as unlawful tying.

How was competition harmed? Going back to Justice Frankfurter's observation, the theory would seem to be that International Salt was using its power in the tying market (salt injection machines) to force customers to make purchases in the tied market (salt) so that International Salt could charge its customers a higher than competitive price for salt. Isn't it obvious that a seller would prefer to earn two monopoly rents over one? Not really, said the Chicago School. At least not if the second monopoly profit comes out of the first one.

The problem is that salt injection machines and salt are complements, meaning that they are joint inputs in the production of something else — canned foods in this case. The demand for a commodity and the demand for its complements are interdependent. If people always eat mustard with hot dogs and the price of mustard increases, they will purchase fewer hot dogs, since the joint price of consuming mustard-smeared hot dogs has increased (the opposite occurs if the price of mustard decreases). If International Salt is already charging the profit-maximizing monopoly price for its salt injection machines and then raises the price of salt, what will happen to the demand for its machines? It will fall. By leveraging its monopoly power in the tying market into the tied market, International Salt will have encroached on its tying market monopoly profits. Since, argued the Chicago School, there is only one monopoly profit to be had from complementary goods, Justice Frankfurter's pronouncement is economically ignorant. The explanation for tying arrangements must lie elsewhere.

Of course, the Chicago School was eager to supply the elsewhere. Tying, argued Chicago, was often explicable as a means of *price discrimination* through *metering*. The classic example is IBM mainframe computers and punch cards. In the old days, IBM sold mainframe computers and insisted that its customers buy their punch cards from IBM as well. What IBM was trying to do, argued the economists, was not to prevent competition, but to charge different effective prices for the mainframe–punch card combination based on the different demand elasticities of different customers. Like every other seller, IBM would like to charge each customer that customer's reservation price, the maximum price the customer is willing to pay. Unfortunately,

---

[35] *International Salt Co. v. United States*, 332 U.S. 392 (1947).

customers don't walk around with their reservation prices printed on their foreheads. So IBM would use the customer's intensity of use as a proxy for the customer's willingness to pay. It would assume that more intensive users, those who used more punch cards, valued their computer systems more and were therefore willing to pay more for them. In order to price-discriminate, IBM might lower the price of its main-frame computers slightly below their monopoly price but then insist that all customers buy their punch cards from IBM. IBM would then raise the price of punch cards somewhat above the competitive price. Non-intensive customers who bought fewer punch cards would pay somewhat less for the computer–punch card combination than they would without the tie, and intensive customers would pay somewhat more. Through this means, IBM could vary the effective price for using its systems based on the customer's willingness to pay and thereby increase its profits.

There is one final piece to the argument. Many (although not all) Chicago School proponents believe that price discrimination is socially beneficial because it may lower the social cost of monopoly. This argument is based on the observation that the perfect price discrimination scenario—in which each customer is charged precisely its reservation price—is one without any deadweight loss, since every customer willing to pay at least marginal cost will make a purchase. In *Jefferson Parish* Justice O'Connor noted that "[p]rice discrimination may . . . *decrease* rather than increase the economic costs of a seller's market power."[36]

In sum, the Chicago School argued that tying was unlikely to involve monopoly leverage because of the one-monopoly profit theory and that it was likely to involve price discrimination, which was all for the good. While widely influential, those views never received quite the vindication in the courts that Chicago School doctrines have received in other areas, such as intrabrand vertical restraints and predatory pricing. Post-Chicago theorists and some court decisions have pushed back on the Chicago arguments with several counter-arguments.

First, post-Chicagoans argue that the one-monopoly profit theory holds only under limited circumstances. Among other things, they argue that the theory assumes that the tying and tied products are used in fixed ratios and, if that assumption is relaxed, charging a monopoly profit in the tied market may actually be profitable. They also argue that a seller may leverage into the tied market not to generate a second monopoly rent in the tied market but to create an entry barrier into the tying market. This was one of the government's successful theories in *Microsoft*. Microsoft allegedly thwarted competition

---

[36] 466 U.S. at 36 n.4.

in the browser market not to charge a monopoly price for browsers (which it was basically giving away for free) but to impede entry in the operating systems market.

Post-Chicagoans also challenge the assumption that price discrimination—if this is what tying is all about—is socially desirable. In *Jefferson Parish* Justice Stevens argued that price discrimination "can increase the social cost of market power."[37] Supporting this view, post-Chicagoans note that the argument that price discrimination is output expanding assumes perfect or "first-degree" price discrimination and that when price discrimination is less than perfect (when the seller doesn't know individual reservation prices but uses proxies), price discrimination may actually be output decreasing. They also argue that allocative efficiency isn't the only measure of social welfare and that antitrust policy should be independently concerned about the wealth transfers caused by price discrimination.

We will not attempt to solve these cutting-edge disagreements here. Suffice it to say that underneath the murky doctrine of tying lies much murky economic and policy disputation.

4.3. *Kodak* and the Single-Brand Issue

A final tying issue that merits some attention is antitrust treatment of post-contract lock-in. The leading case on point is *Kodak*,[38] a controversial 5-4 decision of the Supreme Court in which the Chicago camp suffered a rare defeat. Kodak sells photocopiers and micrographic equipment, which tend to require a large sunk investment for most buyers. Over time, users of Kodak equipment need replacement parts and service. Kodak developed a policy of not selling its parts to independent service organizations (ISOs), who would have competed with Kodak for servicing Kodak equipment. The ISOs sued, alleging that Kodak was using its market power in Kodak branded parts to tie in service for Kodak machines. The Supreme Court majority held that the ISOs had sufficient evidence to take their case to a jury.

Kodak is interesting in part because the majority of the justices were willing to accept arguments that relied on informational asymmetries and other market failures. Kodak's principal argument was that since the primary market (copies and other durable equipment) was concededly highly competitive, Kodak could not have market power in the aftermarket for parts or service, which would be necessary to state a tying claim. Under Kodak's reasoning, customers would

---

[37] 466 U.S. at 14-15.
[38] *Eastman Kodak Co. v. Image Tech. Servs., Inc.*, 504 U.S. 451 (1992).

not choose Kodak copiers over the copiers of competitors like Xerox or Canon if they knew that they were going to be exploited by high prices in the aftermarkets for parts and service. The Court rejected this reasoning as a complete bar to the possibility of coercive tying. It might be the case, the Court reasoned, that customers would fail to take into account information about the costs of the aftermarket parts and services and make their purchasing decisions based only on the initial cost of the copier. The majority's openness to considering market failures based on shortcomings in consumer decision making has led many commentators to brand *Kodak* the leading (or only!) example of a post-Chicago Supreme Court decision.

Kodak has been criticized on many grounds, one of which deserves special mention. Herbert Hovenkamp, the senior author of the highly influential Areeda-Turner treatise,[39] argues that the *Kodak* majority erred by allowing a single brand to serve as a relevant market definition (i.e., "Kodak parts"). Hovenkamp worries that allowing power in an aftermarket to become market power within the meaning of antitrust law would dangerously expand the antitrust domain by making "antitrust the vehicle for fixing contracts that we might think unfair or, worse yet, for protecting people from their own carelessly made bargains."[40] Perhaps reflecting some of these concerns, lower courts since *Kodak* have been reluctant to allow relevant markets to be defined by reference to a single brand except in cases that closely mirror the facts of *Kodak*.[41]

5.   Exclusive Dealing

You have now earned a break and will get one with exclusive dealing. Compared to most other exclusionary practices, the legal test and at least some of the economics governing exclusive dealing contracts

[39]The student of antitrust law should become acquainted with the multivolume Areeda treatise, which is one of the most influential legal treatises of all time. Justice Breyer once quipped that every Supreme Court advocate knows that it's better to have "two paragraphs of Areeda's treatise on their side than three Courts of Appeals or four Supreme Court Justices." Justice Stephen Breyer, *In Memoriam: Phillip E. Areeda*, 109 Harv. L. Rev. 889 (1996).

[40]Herbert Hovenkamp, *The Antitrust Enterprise: Principle and Execution* 101 (2005).

[41]*See, e.g., PSKS, Inc. v. Leegin Creative Leather Prods., Inc.*, 615 F.3d 412, 418 (5th Cir. 2010) (stating that single-brand relevant markets may be defined only in "rare circumstances"); *In re ATM Fee Antitrust Litig*, No. C 04-2676 CRB., 2010 WL 2557519, at *6-7 (N.D. Cal. June 21, 2010) (explaining restrictive circumstances necessary for single-brand relevant market to be allowed).

are straightforward. An exclusive dealing contract is one where a buyer agrees to buy all of its requirements from a particular seller, or a seller agrees to sell all of its output to a particular buyer. The alert law student may recall such agreements from the Uniform Commercial Code,[42] where they were labeled requirements or output contracts and raised issues of consideration, mutuality of obligation, and indefiniteness. In antitrust law, exclusive dealing contracts come down to two words — substantial foreclosure.

The leading Supreme Court case on exclusive dealing is *Tampa Electric*.[43] A public utility in Tampa, Florida, had entered into a contract with a coal supplier from the Appalachian coal region, agreeing to purchase all of its coal requirements for 20 years from the supplier. When the market price of coal rose considerably above the contract price, the coal supplier wanted out of the deal and sued to invalidate it, arguing that the contract was anticompetitive. The Supreme Court articulated a three-part test for exclusive dealing under Section 3 of the Clayton Act (and courts typically apply the same rules for Sherman Act Section 1 or 2 claims): (1) What is the line of commerce affected? (2) What is the area of effective competition? (3) Is the competition foreclosed by the contract "a substantial share of the relevant market"?[44]

The good news is that elements (1) and (2) are none other than the definitions of a relevant product and geographic market. Thus, the only unique element of exclusive dealing comes down to the third element: substantial foreclosure. If the exclusive dealing arrangement substantially forecloses the opportunities of rivals to participate in the relevant market, it is illegal.

In *Tampa Electric*, the Supreme Court gave relatively little guidance on how to apply the substantial foreclosure test. Since the challenged contract covered less than 1 percent of the coal sold from the Appalachian region, it would hardly foreclose the ability of rival coal sellers to find customers. In addition to its decision upholding the legality of the contract, the Court offered the following description of the substantial foreclosure test:

> [I]t is necessary to weigh the probable effect of the contract on the relevant area of effective competition, taking into account the relative strength of the parties, the proportionate volume of commerce involved in relation to the total volume of commerce in the relevant market area,

[42]U.C.C. §2-306.
[43]365 U.S. 320 (1961).
[44]365 U.S. at 328.

and the probable immediate and future effects which pre-emption of that share of the market might have on effective competition therein.[45]

Unfortunately, these words provide little guidance to courts addressing exclusive dealing claims, because they contain no suggestion about the magnitude of any of the effects listed necessary for foreclosure to be considered substantial. Lower courts since *Tampa Electric* have developed some rules of thumb. Most courts will not allow an exclusive dealing claim unless the contract or contracts at issue foreclose at least 30 percent of the relevant market.[46]

Three points are worthy of note. First, many students confuse the defendant's market share and the percentage of the relevant market foreclosed. Don't do this. If the defendant has a 75 percent market share and has ten contracts with exclusive dealing provisions that cover 17 percent of the market, the substantial foreclosure analysis looks to the 17 percent, which is the portion of the market foreclosed to rivals. The defendant's market share might be relevant in a case where the plaintiff alleged monopolization through exclusive dealing. If the defendant's exclusive dealing contracts amounted to 45 percent of the relevant market, a court might say, "that's substantial foreclosure" and hence an exclusionary act; if the defendant's overall market share was 75 percent, a court might say, "and this exclusionary act has allowed you to maintain your monopoly power, which is evidenced by your 75 percent share of the relevant market."

Second, sometimes multiple sellers will have exclusive dealing contracts in the same relevant market, and the question arises whether the foreclosure percentages attributable to different sellers can be aggregated to conduct a substantial foreclosure analysis. In *Standard Stations*,[47] Standard Oil of California's exclusive dealing arrangements with gasoline retailers were condemned even though Standard's contracts covered only 6.7 percent of the market. As the Supreme Court saw it, the problem was that the seven largest oil companies had exclusive dealing contracts that collectively covered 65 percent of all retail sales. When all the biggies' contracts were put together, the foreclosure looked substantial.

Finally, exclusive dealing contracts do not necessarily have to be long-term to be anticompetitive. Although some courts have held

[45]365 U.S. at 329.

[46]*See, e.g., Sterling Merchandise, Inc. v. Nestle, S.A.*, 656 F.3d 112, 124 (1st Cir. 2011) ("[A]s a practical matter, in applying the rule of reason calculus to exclusive dealing arrangements, 'foreclosure levels are unlikely to be of concern where they are less than 30 or 40 percent . . . .'").

[47]*Standard Oil Co. v. United States*, 337 U.S. 293 (1949).

that short-term exclusive dealing contracts do not foreclose competition at all since competitors will soon have the opportunity to compete for that business, in *Dentsply*[48] the Third Circuit held that even exclusive dealing contracts terminable at will could be anticompetitive. The issue remains an open one.

6. Bundled and Loyalty Discounting

We close our examination of exclusionary practices with some issues that the Supreme Court has not yet addressed but that are actively percolating in the lower courts. Although there are many different kinds of arrangements at issue, we can group them for convenience under the broad heading "loyalty discounting." Loyalty discounts are those that reward customers for being loyal to a seller. The two most common forms are bundled discounts, where the customer receives a better price for buying products in different categories, and market share discounts, where the customer receives a better price for buying a specified percentage of its requirements from the seller.

As of the writing of this book, there is a circuit split over how to address bundled discounting. The leading decisions are the Third Circuit's en banc decision in *LePage's*[49] and the Ninth Circuit's subsequent decision in *Peacehealth*.[50] In *LePage's* the conglomerate manufacturer 3M offered rebates to retailers who purchased 3M's full line of health care, home care, home improvement, stationery, retail auto, and "Leisure Time" products. To qualify for 3M's best rebates, a retailer would have to make specified levels of purchases in multiple product categories. LePage's made just transparent tape, in competition with 3M's Scotch brand and private label tape. LePage's alleged that 3M's bundled rebate structure impaired LePage's ability to compete for business, since LePage's could not offer its own discounts on product lines that it did not sell. 3M argued that LePage's claim failed under *Brooke Group*, since LePage's could not show that the rebates resulted in 3M's pricing below an appropriate measure of cost. In a contentious decision, the Third Circuit majority held that *Brooke Group* did not apply to multiproduct discounting, that tying and exclusive dealing were better analogies to bundled discounting than predatory pricing, and that 3M had sufficient evidence to sustain a monopolization case.

---

[48] *United States v. Dentsply Intern., Inc.*, 399 U.S. 181 (3d Cir. 2005).
[49] *LePage's, Inc. v. 3M*, 324 F.3d 141 (3d Cir. 2003) (en banc).
[50] *Cascade Health Solutions v. Peacehealth*, 515 F.3d 883 (9th Cir. 2008).

By the time the Ninth Circuit decided *Peacehealth* five years later, there had been a steady drumbeat of criticism over *LePage's* from many sources, including the Solicitor General of the United States, the Justice Department, the Antitrust Modernization Commission, several district court opinions, and many academics. The chief criticisms were that the Third Circuit too quickly jettisoned the *Brooke Group* test and failed to give adequate guidance on when bundled discounts could exclude equally efficient competitors. In *Peacehealth*, the Ninth Circuit rejected *LePage's* and applied a modified version of *Brooke Group* to bundled discounts. Reading the tea leaves from *Weyerhaeuser*, the Ninth Circuit expressed reluctance to abandon a cost-price test in deciding the legality of unilaterally set price discounts. Instead, the court adopted a "discount attribution test:" Under this test

> the full amount of the discounts given by the defendant on the bundle are allocated to the competitive product or products. If the resulting price of the competitive product or products is below the defendant's incremental cost to produce them, the trier of fact may find that the bundled discount is exclusionary for the purpose of §2.[51]

The basic logic of the discount attribution test is to see whether the bundled discount would have excluded a competitor as efficient as the defendant if that firm had to offer the entire package discount just on the competitive product. If the equally efficient competitor could have given the entire bundled discount on just the competitive product without pricing below marginal or variable cost, then the discount is not exclusionary under *Peacehealth* and is per se lawful under *Brooke Group*.

The discount attribution test has both supporters and detractors, and there are many complexities in applying it. For purposes of this snapshot, the essential point is that courts and commentators disagree vigorously over whether predatory pricing rules, modified or not, have much usefulness in addressing discounts or rebates that span multiple products.

The final word on exclusionary practices applies to market share discounts. A market share discount is conditional upon the customer's purchasing some minimum percentage of her requirements from the seller. Thus, in *Concord Boat*,[52] perhaps the leading lower court case, a boat engine manufacturer with a 75 percent market share adopted a program whereby customers would receive a 3 percent discount if they purchased at least 70 percent of their requirements from the

---

[51]515 F.3d at 906.
[52]*Concord Boat Corp. v. Brunswick Corp.*, 207 F.3d 1039 (2000).

manufacturer, a 2 percent discount for buying 65 percent of their requirements, and a 1 percent % discount for buying at least 60 percent of their requirements. Rival engine manufacturers challenged these discounts as exclusionary on the theory that they provided strong incentives for customers to give a large share of their business to the dominant defendant. The Eighth Circuit disagreed, finding that the loyalty discounts had violated neither Section 1 nor Section 2 of the Sherman Act. They did not violate Section 1, because there was no evidence that the discounts required exclusive dealing with the defendant. They did not violate Section 2, because the loyalty discounts did not result in pricing below an appropriate measure of cost.

Given the recent trajectory of Supreme Court cases extending the *Brooke Group* framework to pricing practices such as alleged overbidding and price squeezes, it would not be surprising if the *Concord Boat* approach eventually wins out in the Supreme Court. But there are alternatives. In challenges to Intel's loyalty discounts for computer microprocessors sold to original equipment manufacturers (OEMs), the FTC and European Commission argued that even above-cost market share discounts could foreclose competitors. In their view, if a dominant seller like Intel had effective control over an incontestable portion of the market — an amount of business that OEMs would allot to Intel without considering competitive alternatives — and offered loyalty rebates that spanned the contestable and incontestable segments of the market, rival sellers like Advanced Micro Devices (AMD) might be foreclosed from selling to those customers because they could not compete with the discounts on the incontestable segment. In this view, loyalty discounts may function similarly to bundled discounts where the defendant can discount across a broad product line but the rival can respond only by offering discounts on the single product she sells.[53]

Legal and economic wrangling over bundled and loyalty discounts is likely to persist for some time, at least until the Supreme Court weighs in. And, if the history of monopolization law is any predictor of the future, new forms of allegedly exclusionary conduct will arise to offer new challenges to the next generation of economists, lawyers, antitrust enforcers, and judges.

---

[53]*See also ZF Meritor, LLC v. Eaton Corp.*, 698 F.3d 254 (3d Cir. 2012) (analyzing loyalty discounts as creating a form of "de facto partial exclusive dealing").

Chapter 9

The Robinson-Patman Act

The Robinson-Patman Act (RPA) is unpopular among antitrust elites. In 2007 the presidentially appointed, bipartisan Antitrust Modernization Commission recommended its repeal, echoing a refrain that has been repeated often over the decades. The FTC and Justice Department haven't enforced the statute in decades, basically treating it like a crazy old uncle that one calls on his birthday but doesn't invite to dinner. Still, the Act remains good law and there is little if any political momentum for repeal. This may be due in part to the fact that in the Chicago School era, the Supreme Court rolled back many of the RPA's most controversial applications, bringing the act more in line with Sherman Act jurisprudence. Despite these assaults, the RPA remains an important statute in some areas of economic activity, particularly in franchising and distribution. We shall consider it here, but briefly.

Congress passed the RPA in 1936 essentially as an amendment to Section 2 of the original Clayton Act, which contained a prohibition on price discrimination in commodities that had the effect of substantially lessening competition or tending to create a monopoly. Like every other statute, the RPA was a product of its times, and its times were unhappy ones for small retailers. Large chain stores such as A&P were using their economic clout during the Depression to bargain for large quantity discounts, special advertising and promotional allowances, and brokerage commissions. Small retailers and wholesalers were feeling squeezed.

Congress responded to the cry of the small dealers and retailers by significantly strengthening Section 2 of the Clayton Act. One important change was that the price discrimination prohibition would now apply not only to sellers that gave discriminatory prices but to the buyers (like A&P) that received them. The RPA was popularly known as the "Anti-A&P Act." The RPA also differed from the original Clayton Act insofar as it prohibited not only discriminatory prices that threatened competition as a whole, but also those that might "injure, destroy, or prevent competition with any person." The essential text of the RPA reads as follows:

[I]t shall be unlawful for any person engaged in commerce . . . to discriminate in price between different purchasers of commodities or like grade and quality . . . and where the effect of such discrimination may be substantially to lessen competition or tend to create a monopoly in any line of commerce, or to injure, destroy, or prevent competition with any person who either grants or knowingly receives the benefit of such discrimination, or with customers of them.

The RPA is unpopular among the antitrust elite in contemporary times for reasons that we discussed in Chapter 8 with respect to tying arrangements. Since many economists and other academics believe that price discrimination is often output expanding and therefore socially beneficial, a statute that strikes directly against price discrimination — and particularly price discrimination that does not necessarily harm competition as a whole — seems allocatively inefficient and protectionist of inefficient firms. However, the RPA retains some defenders, particularly people who believe that antitrust law should guarantee a level playing field among competitors and who worry that Chicago School–style notions of efficiency are overly narrow.

1. Jurisdictional and Technical Limitations

The RPA is a rare antitrust statute insofar as its scope and coverage are limited in some technical ways that may seem quaint or incomprehensible by modern standards and serve the noble purpose of enriching lawyers. Let us consider some of the statutory quirks.

Interstate commerce. Unlike the Sherman Act, which applies jurisdictionally to any activity that affects interstate commerce, the RPA applies only to sales *in* interstate commerce. Hence, one of the two sales at issue in an RPA case — either the high sale or the low one — must cross a state line in order for the statute to apply.[1] Watch this one — sneaky law professors like to work it into exams. Be alert to the fact that Albuquerque and Santa Fe are in the same state.

Sales. Unlike the Sherman Act, which applies to all kinds of economic dealing, the RPA applies only to sales. Leases, licenses, and bartering are not covered.

Two sales. Discrimination requires that two different people be treated differently; hence, the RPA applies only where goods have been sold to two different purchasers. Thus, if the seller gives a sweetheart deal

---

[1] *See Gulf Oil Corp. v. Copp Paving Co.*, 419 U.S. 186 (1974).

to an advantaged buyer and then refuses to sell to another, or offers to sell at a discriminatory price that the second buyer refuses, the statute does not apply.[2]

Commodities. The RPA applies only to the sale of commodities, which generally means tangible products. Services are not covered.

Like grade and quality. A whole set of RPA questions arise around the question of whether the goods sold to the different buyers were of "like grade and quality," as required for the Act to apply. Essentially, this means that the goods sold at discriminatory prices must be fungible.

Discrimination. One question that often arises in RPA cases is whether there has been discrimination within the meaning of the statute. All relevant terms of dealing — including price, discounts, rebates, credit terms, and charges — need to be assessed.

2. Lines of Price Discrimination

Courts have classified RPA theories into three "lines" of price discrimination, conveniently named primary, secondary, and tertiary. The reader will be delighted to know that we can immediately get rid of the first and third.

Primary line price discrimination occurs when the alleged discrimination harms competition or competitors at the level of the firm giving the discount. Thus, if a dominant seller gives discriminatory discounts to selected customers for the purpose of driving its rival out of business, we may have primary line price discrimination. Conveniently, as we saw in Chapter 8, in *Brooke Group*[3] the Supreme Court ruled that primary line price discrimination under the RPA and predatory pricing under Section 2 of the Sherman Act are functionally identical — so we have already learned everything we need to know about primary line price discrimination.

Secondary line price discrimination occurs when the alleged discrimination harms competition or competitors at the level of the firm receiving the discount. Thus, if Walmart procures a favorable deal from Nike that makes it difficult for Target to sell athletic shoes, we may have a secondary line price discrimination issue. Most of what is relevant about the RPA today occurs in the field of secondary line price discrimination.

[2]*In re Matter of Bird & Son, Inc.*, 25 F.T.C. 548 (1937); *Crossroads Cogeneration Corp. v. Orange & Rockland Util., Inc.*, 159 F.3d 129 (3d Cir. 1998).
[3]*Brooke Group, Ltd. v. Brown & Williamson Tobacco Corp.*, 509 U.S. 209, 222 (1993).

Tertiary line price discrimination occurs when the alleged discrimination harms competition or competitors at a level removed from the level of the firm receiving the discount. Thus, if Nike gives a discriminatory price to a wholesaler and the wholesaler passes on the discriminatory price to Walmart to the detriment of Target, there may be a tertiary line price discrimination claim. Such claims are cognizable,[4] but they are sufficiently infrequent and similar to secondary line claims not to warrant further discussion here.

3.   Elements of Secondary Line Price Discrimination

The elements of a secondary line claim are (1) sales in interstate commerce, (2) two sales of like grade and quality, (3) discrimination by the seller between the plaintiff and another purchaser, and (4) that the effect of such discrimination may be to injure, destroy, or prevent competition to the advantage of the favored purchaser.[5] The core of a secondary line case is a disadvantaged buyer's claim that its rival got superior terms from the seller, which caused the plaintiff to be at a competitive disadvantage when making sales to its own customers. One issue that often arises in secondary line cases is whether there is discrimination at all, particularly when the seller offers all customers an identical menu of options. If equal terms are offered and realistically available to all customers and the complaining customer simply chooses a less advantageous offering from the menu, there is probably not price discrimination within the meaning of the statute.[6] On the other hand, a seller may discriminate between buyers if it offers all buyers an identical menu of options but some buyers are not realistically able to take advantage of the best offers. In *Morton Salt*[7] a salt manufacturer offered its best price to any buyer who would purchase at least 50,000 cases of salt in any consecutive 12-month period. Large chain stores often purchased in this bulk, but not a single independent retail grocery store purchased 50,000 cases in a single year. The Supreme Court ruled that the discount was discriminatory in effect and therefore violated the RPA. Students of constitutional law may recognize this distinction between formal and substantive equality. Under the RPA, it is substantive equality that counts.

---

[4] *Perkins v. Standard Oil Co.*, 395 U.S. 642 (1969).

[5] *Volvo Trucks of North America, Inc. v. Reeder-Simco GMC, Inc.*, 546 U.S. 164, 176 (2006).

[6] *See, e.g., Metro Ford Truck Sales v. Ford Motor Co.*, 145 F.3d 320 (5th Cir. 1998).

[7] *FTC v. Morton Salt Co.*, 334 U.S. 37 (1948).

3. Elements of Secondary Line Price Discrimination

Another issue in proving the existence of discrimination arises when a vertically integrated purchaser acts as both a wholesaler and a retailer and receives a better price than firms that act only as retailers. In *Texaco v. Hasbrouck*[8] Texaco argued that the allegedly advantaged firm had not received a discriminatory price at all, but rather had received a "functional discount" because it saved Texaco money by performing a wholesale function that Texaco would otherwise have had to pay another company to perform. The Supreme Court rejected functional discounting as a categorical defense, effectively requiring the defendant to show that the discounts were cost justified (an issue addressed below).

An important restriction on secondary line cases concerns proof of damages. When a retailer complains that his rival received a lower price from the manufacturer, he would naturally like to take the difference between the price charged to his competitor and the price charged to him as his recoverable damages. In *J. Truett Payne v. Chrysler Motors Corp.*,[9] the Supreme Court foreclosed this possibility, ruling that the disadvantaged dealer would have to prove lost profits from sales he lost to the advantaged rival because of the discriminatory wholesale price. This ruling has made it considerably more challenging to bring secondary line cases.

A final notable question about the existence of discrimination arises when multiple buyers are competing for the seller's favor, but not in order to make sales to the same buyers. In *Reeder-Simco*[10] the plaintiff was a heavy-duty truck retailer franchised by Volvo Trucks. It claimed that Volvo was trying to eliminate some of its dealers, including Reeder-Simco, by offering superior prices to the favored dealers it wanted to maintain. Reeder-Simco's legal problem was that it was not generally competing against other Volvo dealers for any particular customer's sale. Customers generally selected only one Volvo dealer to offer them a bid, and the dealer then negotiated a wholesale price with Volvo before submitting its own bid to customers. The Supreme Court held that Reeder-Simco had not been the victim of price discrimination within the meaning of the RPA, since it was not competing on price with other Volvo dealers.

That much of *Reeder-Simco* may be relatively technical and uninteresting. At the end of the opinion, however, Justice Ginsburg's majority opinion veered to a much more general direction. Citing *Sylvania* (see Chapter 6), she noted that "interbrand competition . . . is the primary

---

[8]*Texaco, Inc. v. Hasbrouck*, 496 U.S. 543 (1990).
[9]451 U.S. 557 (1981).
[10]*Volvo Trucks of North America, Inc. v. Reeder-Simco GMC, Inc.*, 546 U.S. 164 (2006).

concern of antitrust law."[11] She further noted that the RPA "signals no large departure from that main concern," that the Court would "resist interpretation geared more to the protection of existing *competitors* than to the stimulation of *competition*," and that it would seek to interpret the RPA "consistently with the broader policies of the antitrust laws."[12]

These moves are jarring in light of the RPA's legislative history and traditional interpretation, which made the RPA an outlier in the modern era insofar as it tended to protect competitors rather than competition. Many commentators read *Reeder-Simco* as signaling an intention by the Supreme Court to do with secondary line price discrimination what *Brooke Group* definitively accomplished with primary line price discrimination—bring it into conformity with modern Section 2 analysis. If that occurs, the RPA may cease to be a target of antitrust elites—simply because it has become irrelevant. The crazy old uncle will no longer be merely ignored; he will have passed onto greener pastures.

4. The Meeting Competition and Cost Justification Defenses

We close with the two statutory defenses available in RPA cases: meeting competition and cost justification. Section 2(b) allows a seller to rebut a prima facie case of price discrimination "by showing that his lower price or the furnishing of services or facilities to any purchaser or purchasers was made in good faith to meet an equally low price of a competitor." This meeting competition defense is designed to allow sellers some competitive flexibility. The Supreme Court has held that a good faith belief rather than absolute certainty that a competitor was offering a particular price is sufficient to sustain the defense, although casual reliance on uncorroborated reports is insufficient.[13] The meeting competition defense has been successfully invoked in a number of RPA cases.

By contrast, the cost justification defense has been a dead letter. The RPA provides that "nothing herein contained shall prevent differentials which make only due allowance for differences in the cost of manufacture, sale, or delivery resulting from the differing methods or quantities in which such commodities are to such purchasers sold

---

[11] 546 U.S. at 180.
[12] *Id.* at 181.
[13] *United States v. United States Gypsum Co.*, 438 U.S. 422 (1978).

4. The Meeting Competition and Cost Justification Defenses

or delivered." This sounds like a promising opportunity to uphold the lawfulness of price discounting by proving that it was simply cheaper to sell to the favored customer — for example, because that customer was more convenient to deliver to, provided warehousing services, or (as in *Hasbrouck*) performed wholesale functions. However, the courts have given the defense a construction that makes it very difficult to prove. The price differential cannot exceed the magnitude of the cost savings, which the seller bears the burden of proving. Practitioners who have litigated RPA cases warn against relying on the cost justification defense.

This could change, of course, if the courts get serious about bringing the RPA into conformity with the rest of the antitrust laws. Reducing the stringency of the cost justification defense would be another way to defang the statute's more protectionist elements.

PART IV

MERGERS

Chapter 10

Merger Law: The Old School

Through the Sherman Act, the Supreme Court revolutionized anti-trust law of the last 30 years. However, the Court has not decided a merger case on its substantive merits since the mid-1970s. Thus, Supreme Court merger law remains largely frozen in its pre–Chicago School state, except for one tantalizing case that appeared right before the long period of silence. On the other hand, the learning regarding mergers has changed dramatically in the intervening years. The anti-trust agencies have taken the leading role in defining and updating merger law, with occasional interaction with the lower courts.

The result is an odd state of affairs wherein the Supreme Court law on mergers is wildly out of date with the practice of merger policy. Still, the older Supreme Court cases have not been overruled, and we must consider them as potential precedents in deciding merger cases. In this chapter we shall briefly consider the "old school" of merger law — the developments that led to a period of hyperactivity on mergers in the Supreme Court during the 1950s, 1960s, and early 1970s — and then look at the freezing of the Supreme Court canon in the mid-1970s. In the next chapter we shall survey in greater detail modern merger practice, with special emphasis on the FTC and Justice Department's Horizontal Merger Guidelines, but also with reference to some lower court decisions in more recent times.

1. Celler-Kefauver, Structuralism, and the "Government Always Wins" Period

Since 1914 we have been subject to Section 7 of the Clayton Act, the section of the antitrust laws applicable to mergers.[1] In 1950 Congress

---

[1]Prior to the passage of the Clayton Act, there was some question about whether Sections 1 and 2 of the Sherman Act could apply to various forms of merger. The Clayton Act resolved those questions with a statutory section explicitly devoted to mergers and acquisitions.

passed the Celler-Kefauver Act with the intention of strengthening Section 7. The Robinson-Patman Act amended the Clayton Act and came to be known as the "relevant act." Similarly, people continue to refer to Section 7 of the Clayton Act (as modified by Celler-Kefauver) as the "relevant statute." (Referring to Section 7 as the Celler-Kefauver Act would be as big a faux pas as hyphenating "antitrust.")

Celler-Kefauver was intended to effect two principal textual changes to Section 7. First, the original Section 7 applied only to stock acquisitions and thus had an "asset loophole." To avoid application of Section 7, an acquiring firm could simply agree to buy the acquired firm's assets rather than its shares. Celler-Kefauver amended Section 7 so that the statute applies to stock and asset acquisitions.

Second, the original text of Section 7 prohibited mergers that would affect competition between the acquiring and acquired firms, which suggested that only horizontal mergers were covered. Celler-Kefauver amended the text to make clear that any merger affecting competition — whether horizontal, vertical, or conglomerate — could be covered. The current text of Section 7 reads as follows:

> No person engaged in commerce or in any activity affecting commerce shall acquire, directly or indirectly, the whole or any part of the stock or other share capital and no person subject to the jurisdiction of the Federal Trade Commission shall acquire the whole or any part of the assets of another person engaged also in commerce or in any activity affecting commerce, where in any line of commerce or in any activity affecting commerce in any section of the country, the effect of such acquisition may be substantially to lessen competition, or to tend to create a monopoly.

In its *Brown Shoe* decision[2] the Supreme Court read the congressional intent in amending the Clayton Act as reaching beyond these textual changes. The Court saw congressional concern over the "rising tide of economic concentration" in the U.S. economy and a desire to arrest "mergers at a time when the trend to a lessening of competition in a line of commerce was still in its incipiency."[3] This formulation — a mandate to strike at mergers before markets became excessively concentrated — provided impetus for a broad attack on merger activity in the postwar era.

Two important factors, one historical and one intellectual, contributed significantly to this movement against economic concentration

[2]*Brown Shoe Co. v. United States*, 370 U.S. 294 (1962).
[3]*Id.* at 317.

140

through merger or acquisition. One was the experience of World War II. Many American politicians viewed excessive concentrations of economic power in Germany and Japan as having facilitated the rise of fascism. The perception that the U.S. economy was undergoing rapid concentration during the postwar (and post-Depression) industrial boom fed this fear.

The second factor arose from the dominant intellectual school in U.S. antitrust theory during the 1950s and 1960s — *structuralism* or the *Harvard School*. Structuralism was heavily associated with Harvard-trained economists Joe Bain and Carl Kaysen and Harvard professor Donald Turner. Its essential claim was that there is a deterministic linkage between a market's structure, conduct, and performance. Under the *S-C-P paradigm*, a concentrated market (structure) would inevitably lead firms in the market to engage in certain behaviors (conduct) such as collusive information exchange, which would inevitably lead to higher prices or reduced quality (performance). Given that this relationship is deterministic, the reasoning goes, antitrust policy makers need not attack anticompetitive conduct in order to ensure better market performance. Since the root of all antitrust evil is structure, the best policy is to prevent the formation of concentrated markets.

Merger law was the natural repository for this policy prescription.[4] And the Supreme Court took it to heart. During the 1950s, 1960s, and early 1970s, the Supreme Court decided many merger cases brought by the FTC or Justice Department and decided almost all of them for the government. In *Von's Grocery*[5] a frustrated Justice Stewart complained that "[t]he sole consistency that I can find is that in litigation under §7, the Government always wins."[6] *Von's Grocery* involved a merger between two Los Angeles area grocery chains that resulted in a company with a combined share of 7.5 percent in a market with many competitive firms — a pattern that would not raise any interest today.

The leading structuralist merger case is *Philadelphia National Bank*[7] an opinion that, oddly, in light of subsequent history, was written by Richard Posner, who was a law clerk to Justice Brennan. The second and third largest of 42 commercial banks in the Philadelphia area proposed a merger. The combined bank would have become the

---

[4]Structuralists also proposed amendments to Section 2 of the Sherman Act that would create no-fault monopolization offenses and allow the Justice Department to "deconcentrate" markets by seeking the breakup of monopolies without a showing of any anticompetitive conduct. These proposals never gained traction.

[5]*United States v. Von's Grocery Co.*, 384 U.S. 270 (1966).

[6]*Id.* at 301.

[7]*United States v. Philadelphia Nat'l Bank*, 374 U.S. 321 (1963).

largest in the region, with a market share of approximately 34 to 36 percent (depending on how one defined market share). Postmerger, the two largest banks would have had a combined share of 59 percent and the four largest banks would have had a combined share of 77 to 78 percent. The overall increase in market concentration would have been 33 percent.

Based on these numbers, the Supreme Court found it easy to condemn the merger. Important to structuralists was the *four-firm concentration ratio*, the percentage of the market controlled by the four largest firms after the merger. Mergers in which the four largest firms controlled more than 75 percent of the market postmerger should be challenged automatically, according to structuralist assumptions. Also important was the change in concentration resulting from the merger (or delta). In a market deemed concentrated, like the Philadelphia banking market, even a small increase in concentration was perceived as furthering the dangerous "rising tide of economic concentration."

The firms argued that their merger would actually be procompetitive because it would increase the capitalization of the bank, allowing the merged bank to make larger business loans and hence compete with banks in larger cities such as New York. The Court rejected this argument, holding that procompetitive effects in one market should not be allowed to overcome anticompetitive effects in another one. The merger was enjoined.

2. The Chicago School Assault on Structuralism

One of the Chicago School's first attacks was on structuralism. Although Chicago School scholars did not deny that concentrated markets *could* behave less competitively than less concentrated markets, they strenuously argued that the relationship between structure, conduct, and performance was not nearly as deterministic as the Harvard School structuralists had asserted. In particular, the Chicago School debunked the empirical claims that underlay the Harvard School policy prescriptions, showing, for example, that the relationship between concentration and firm profits was not nearly as strong as claimed. By the mid-1970s structuralism was in decline in the academy, with even early structuralists like Harvard's Don Turner confessing that some of structuralism's claims had been overstated.

As noted throughout this book, the mid- to late 1970s was the period of the Chicago School's ascendancy on the Supreme Court. The clarion call came in 1977 with *Sylvania* (see Chapter 6). For reasons we shall consider momentarily, the mid-1970s was also when the Supreme

Court got out of the business of deciding merger cases. But before it did so, it decided one merger case — *General Dynamics*[8] — that suggested a softening of structural presumptions and an inclination in the Chicago School's direction.

General Dynamics acquired the stock of United Electric Coal Companies. The deal was horizontal, since the acquiring and acquired firms both were involved in coal mining. Various regions were at issue and the relevant geographic market definitions in dispute. Under some sets of assumptions, the merger resulted in a two-firm concentration ratio of 52.9 percent in the Illinois region, a top-four concentration ratio of 75.2 percent, and a concentration increase of 20.2 percent. Under a straightforward application of *Philadelphia National Bank*'s structuralist presumptions, the merger looked anticompetitive.

But the Supreme Court looked past the structural presumptions. It noted that the coal industry (as we saw in *Tampa Electric* in Chapter 8) was characterized by long-term contracts at predetermined prices. Most of United Electric's coal reserves were already locked up under such contracts. Excluding the coal already committed to customers, United Electric was actually an insignificant coal company. Its acquisition by General Dynamics would have very little effect on the overall competitive landscape.

General Dynamics invited a less mechanistic form of economic reasoning than the one deployed in *Philadelphia National Bank*. It invited courts to look at the realities of competition in the relevant industry, the true economic positions of the merging parties, and the actual economic effects likely to result from a merger. Deployed on a larger scale, *General Dynamics* could have signaled a dramatic shift in Supreme Court merger jurisprudence. But, for better or worse, the Court got out of the merger business almost immediately after deciding *General Dynamics*, leaving largely intact the preexisting structuralist case law.

3. Hart-Scott-Rodino and the Era of Silence

While causal stories are never simple, and a variety of factors contributed to the Supreme Court's exit from the mergers and acquisitions business, the most important part of the story is the passage of the Hart-Scott-Rodino Antitrust Improvements Act in 1976.

The key feature of Hart-Scott was the creation of a premerger notification system. Prior to Hart-Scott, companies that wanted to merge

---

[8]*United States v. General Dynamics Corp.*, 415 U.S. 486 (1974).

could simply do so without informing the government. Antitrust enforcement officials often learned about deals by reading about them in the *Wall Street Journal* after they closed. If the merger was objectionable, the government had to sue to dissolve it. This was a cumbersome and ineffective way to run a merger control system. Breaking apart consummated mergers was costly and inefficient.

Hart-Scott requires any party meeting a certain statutory threshold (based on the value of the transaction and the size of the parties involved) to file a premerger notification with the Justice Department and the FTC. After filing, the parties must wait 30 days to close their merger, unless the agencies grant them early termination. During the 30-day waiting period, the government may sue to block the merger. Or, if the government needs more time to assess the merger's competitive impact, it may issue the dreaded *second request for information*. The second request prolongs the waiting period for the parties to close the transaction until they have substantially supplied the requested information. Since the information requested is often voluminous and can take up to six months to compile, the government has an effective veto over many mergers. Since mergers are often highly time-sensitive, the mere fact of a second request induces many parties to abandon the merger.

The upshot is that the agencies rarely have to fight mergers in court. Since Hart-Scott provides a great deal of leverage, when the agencies are concerned about a merger, the parties will usually seek to negotiate with the agencies to restructure the deal or else abandon the merger. Today there are few litigated merger cases — often no more than two or three a year between the two agencies.

In light of the procedural shift brought about by Hart-Scott, the most important source of substantive legal guidance on merger policy today is not the older Supreme Court cases or even the relatively sparse lower court cases, but the agencies' guidelines and other policy statements. The Supreme Court has not weighed in for decades because it has not been asked to. Merger control has become a largely administrative practice where the parties seek to assuage the agencies' concerns or offer up-front remedies. With this background, we turn in the next chapter to modern merger practice as influenced by the Merger Guidelines and a few lower court opinions.

Chapter 11

Merger Law: Modern Practice

Oliver Wendell Holmes famously defined law as a prediction of what courts will do.[1] Since courts decide relatively few merger cases today, it may be accurate to say that merger law is a prediction of what the antitrust agencies will do. True, the agencies operate in the shadow of their own predictions of what courts would do if push came to shove, but given the dynamics of merger review discussed in the previous chapter, the agencies have a good bit of discretion in formulating and enforcing the relevant norms. Since 1968 the agencies have helpfully disclosed their enforcement perspectives in merger guidelines. These do not constitute "law" in a formal sense, because the agencies have no statutory authority to adopt regulations fleshing out Section 7 of the Clayton Act. In a Holmesian sense, however, they are the best predictions of what will happen to a proposed merger and, hence, the best evidence of current merger law. Further, although courts are not bound to follow the merger guidelines, they often cite them as persuasive authority.

The guidelines have undergone significant revision since their adoption. The 1968 guidelines were the brainchild of then Assistant Attorney General Donald Turner, a leading Harvard Schooler, and reflected a strongly structuralist bent. The Reagan administration substantially revised the guidelines in 1982 and 1984, not surprisingly showing a more favorable disposition toward mergers. In 1992 the FTC and Justice Department announced new guidelines applicable only to horizontal mergers; thus were born the Horizontal Merger Guidelines (HMG). There were relatively modest revisions in 1997, but the core of the 1992 HMG persisted until 2010, when they were completely rewritten. The 2010 HMG are the brainchild of two Berkeley economists and co-authors, Carl Shapiro and Joe Farrell, who "just coincidentally" happened to be the chief economists at the Antitrust Division and FTC,

---

[1] Oliver Wendell Holmes, *The Path of the Law*, 10 Harv. L. Rev. 457, 457-461 (1897).

respectively, during the first years of the Obama administration and were thus able to implement a part of their academic vision for merger policy through wholesale revisions of the HMG.

This chapter focuses primarily on the HMG, because horizontal mergers are the core concern of Section 7 enforcement. Where they may be helpful in illustrating modern merger concepts, judicial decisions will be discussed. At the end of the chapter we will briefly discuss vertical mergers. Purely conglomerate mergers are virtually never challenged today and therefore are not addressed in this chapter.

1. Overview

The HMG differ from most of the sources of antitrust law addressed in this book insofar as they present a systematic, regulatory approach to addressing questions of market power. The student of antitrust is well advised to read the HMG carefully, familiarize herself with their sometimes idiosyncratic jargon, and apply them methodologically to merger problems. This is not to say that merger cases come down to a mechanical application of the HMG. One of the reasons for the 2010 revisions was a perception that the 1992 and 1997 guidelines were no longer good predictors of what the agencies were actually doing in merger cases. Still, for pedagogical (*hint:* exam) purposes, a systematic deployment of the HMG is advisable.

The 2010 HMG are presented in 13 sections, which are not of equal importance. The headings in this chapter largely track the section headings, although some of sections are collapsed to emphasize important organizational features.

Section 1 provides an overview of what the HMG attempt to do. Some important themes quickly emerge. "The unifying theme of these Guidelines is that mergers should not be permitted to create, enhance, or entrench market power or to facilitate its exercise." In other words, modern merger control is concerned with the same things that Sections 1 and 2 of the Sherman Act are concerned with—the acquisition, maintenance, and exercise of market power. Also, Section 1 makes clear that consumer welfare is the primary goal of merger policy. As discussed in greater detail below, producer efficiencies are not considered a reason to allow a merger that creates market power unless those efficiencies are passed on to consumers. Modern merger policy is distinctly focused on protecting the welfare of consumers, to the exclusion of other values such as stimulating productive efficiency, protecting smaller firms from rapacious takeovers, or maintaining a "level playing field" for its own sake.

Another important theme flagged in the HMG introduction is that theories of anticompetitive harm from mergers come in two basic flavors: *unilateral effects* and *coordinated effects* theories. Much more on this to follow.

2. Evidence of Adverse Competitive Effects and Price Discrimination

The major story behind the 2010 HMG is the continuing demise of both structuralism and formalism. The core of a structuralist approach to merger control is to define a relevant market, identify the market shares of the firms in the market, reach a conclusion as to the concentration of the market, and then apply strong presumptions based on the concentration figures before and after the merger. As we saw in *Philadelphia National Bank* in Chapter 10, the structuralists employed presumptions based on the two-firm or four-firm concentration ratio. The 1982 guidelines introduced a more sophisticated economic tool, the *Herfindahl-Hirschman Index* (HHI), which is still in effect in Section 5 of the 2010 HMG. However, the major announcement in Section 2 (and repeated in various ways throughout the guidelines) is that structural evidence is *only one* of the many available tools for deciding whether a market is likely to create or enhance market power or facilitate its exercise. Indeed, market structure is often not the best evidence. Turning to structural evidence in Section 4, the HMG announces: "The Agencies' analysis need not start with market definition. Some of the analytical tools used by the Agencies to assess competitive effects do not rely on market definition, although evaluation of competitive alternatives available to customers is always necessary at some point in the analysis."

One thing to keep in mind as we consider the HMG's deemphasis of structural considerations is that courts still play some role in merger cases, and it is far from clear whether courts have yet caught up to the view that merger review can proceed without traditional structural analysis. It is hornbook law that a plaintiff in a Section 7 case must prove the presence of a relevant market in which competition will be affected.[2] Almost every recent litigated merger case has risen or fallen on controversies about the scope of the relevant market. In deemphasizing market structure, the 2010 HMG are pushing hard on the boundaries of current legal doctrine although, as noted, the agencies

[2] *See, e.g., United States v. Oracle Corp.*, 331 F. Supp. 2d 1098, 1123 (N.D. Cal. 2004).

are far less reliant on courts to back up their views in merger cases than in others.

Section 2 of the HMG provides a non-exhaustive catalog of five types of evidence the agencies consider probative of anticompetitive effects. Four of the five could be categorized as "direct" evidence insofar as they don't rely on inferences from market structure. The third in the list, Section 2.1.3, provides traditional market definition and concentration measures, the bulk of most traditional merger analysis. We will come back to traditional market definition when we examine Section 4.

The first of the four direct evidence categories, Section 2.1.1, identifies actual effects in consummated mergers as especially probative. Although most merger decisions are made before a merger closes because of Hart-Scott's premerger notification system (see Chapter 10), in a few cases the antitrust review may happen after a merger has closed and there are actual data about what happened to prices or output after the merger. Section 2.1.1 states that "[e]vidence of observed post-merger price increases or other changes adverse to customers is given substantial weight."

It may seem intuitive that a sharp increase in prices following a merger is evidence that the merger created market power, but it would be risky for the agencies to place excessive weight on postmerger price increases without presenting a convincing story based on market definition and structure. Consider the stunning facts of *Lundbeck*.[3] At the time the FTC brought the case, there were two FDA-approved drugs (Indocin and NeoProfen) for patent ductus arteriosus, a life-threatening heart condition affecting low-weight newborn babies. Lundbeck purchased the rights to Indocin from Merck in 2005 and the rights to NeoProfen in 2006. Immediately after buying NeoProfen, Lundbeck raised the price 1300 percent! Under Section 2.1.1, that would seem compelling evidence that the merger created vast market power. Nonetheless, the Eighth Circuit held that FTC had failed to prove the illegality of the merger because it had failed to prove that Indocin and NeoProfen were in the same relevant market. Structuralism may be shrinking in influence in the guidelines, but its vestiges die hard in the courts.

Section 2.1.2 lists direct comparisons based on experience as another important source of information regarding potential anticompetitive effects. A recent merger in the same market or a similar one may provide a good basis for predicting the effects of the merger under review.

Section 2.1.4, concerning substantial head-to-head competition between the merging firms, is largely a preview of what follows in Section 6, on unilateral effects theories.

---

[3] *FTC v. Lundbeck, Inc.*, 650 F.3d 1236 (8th Cir. 2011).

2. Evidence of Adverse Competitive Effects

Finally, Section 2.1.5 introduces the idea of *mavericks*. A maverick is a competitor that plays a disruptive role in a market disproportionate to its size or market share. For example, in *Brooke Group* (discussed in Chapter 8), Liggett alleged that it was a maverick in the cigarette market because it refused to play along with the oligopolistic, conscious parallelism game played by the industry's "big boys" like Brown & Williamson, R.J. Reynolds, and Philip Morris. A larger firm may desire to acquire a maverick to stamp out a gadfly that is keeping prices too low. The concentration increase may not look significant, but the agencies consider the loss of an independent maverick a serious blow to the market's competitive dynamics.

After listing types of evidence the agencies consider significant, Section 2 discusses the importance of various sources of evidence. Obviously, the parties themselves often provide much of the relevant information. Customers are often a good source of information, and the agencies pay special attention to whether customers support or oppose the merger. However, Section 2.2.2 flags the concern that some customers may not be harmed or may even benefit by postmerger price increases, and hence urges some restraint in relying on customer evidence. Finally, competitors of the merging firms are regarded as often dubious sources of information because they have mixed or conflicting motivations with respect to mergers by their rivals. A competitor may (1) oppose the merger on the ground that it will create a stronger rival; (2) support a merger on the ground that it will increase market concentration and hence make collusion or conscious parallelism easier; (3) oppose the merger because it will result in an increase in concentration that will make the competitor's own merger plans harder to carry out in the future; or (4) support the merger in order to establish a favorable precedent that will enable the development of its own merger plans in the future. None of the possibilities aligns the competitor with the interests of consumers.

Section 3 of the HMG concerns targeted customers and price discrimination. Like much of Section 2, Section 3 is included largely to foreshadow themes discussed in greater detail later. The key point takes us back to *Grinnell* in Chapter 3. A merger may create no market power with respect to most customers but allow the merging parties or other market participants to charge a higher price to targeted customers. We saw in Chapter 8 that the social welfare effects of price discrimination are ambiguous and contested. The HMG have a consumer welfare orientation and hence take the view that a merger that facilitates price discrimination is problematic: "When discrimination is reasonably likely, the Agencies may evaluate competitive effects separately by type of customer."

Section 3 then repeats economic theory that the alert reader of this book already knows. For price discrimination to be feasible, two conditions must be satisfied. First, sellers must have mechanisms for separating customers by their differential willingness to pay; and second, arbitrage must not be widely available. For greater detail on these points, refer back to the discussion of *Grinnell* in Chapter 3.

3. Vestiges of Structuralism: Market Definition, Shares, and Concentration

Sections 4 and 5 of the HMG are the guts of the older guidelines — the roadmap for considering structural factors. Structural analysis in these sections essentially breaks down into four steps: (1) define the relevant markets, (2) identify the firms in the markets, (3) identify each firm's market share, and (4) calculate the HHI resulting from the merger and the delta (or change) from the previous concentration level. The resulting HHI and delta are then plugged into a concentration table, and presto — we know whether the merger is concerning or not under structural assumptions.

3.1. Defining a Relevant Market

The first step in this process is defining a relevant market. The process will be largely familiar, since it is a modified version of *du Pont* with splashes of *Grinnell* and *Brown Shoe*. One important initial point distinguishes the HMG from nonmerger market definition: we are told in Section 4 that "[m]arket definition focuses solely on demand substitution factors." Recall that in Chapter 3 we noted that in *Grinnell* the Supreme Court allowed both demand-side (customer response) and supply-side (supplier response) considerations to be factors in defining relevant markets. The HMG certainly deem the responses of suppliers important in merger analysis, but they do so by considering who is "in" the market and who might enter the market in response to a price increase, not what the market is.

The key concept in HMG market definition is the *hypothetical monopolist* or *SSNIP test*. Unfortunately, we need to quote the technical definition of the test, so prepare for a mouthful: "the test requires that a hypothetical profit-maximizing firm, not subject to price regulation, that was the only present and future seller of those products ('hypothetical monopolist') likely would impose at least a small but significant and non-transitory increase in price ('SSNIP') on at least one product in the market, including at least one product sold by one of the merging firms."

Here's what all this means. As with nonmerger market definition, the essential task is to decide what products consumers find reasonably interchangeable. The HMG ask us to start with a small grouping of products based on some intuitions about the narrowest possible market definition. Say that one or both of the merging firms make widgets, and we want to know what relevant market widgets are part of. We start by asking whether a single seller who controlled the sale of all widgets would raise its price by a small but significant amount (generally defined in the HMG as 5 percent) for the foreseeable future. If the answer is yes, then widgets are a relevant market. We know this because customers wouldn't substitute away in response to a price increase. But if the answer is no — if an SSNIP wouldn't be profitable — that must mean that demand is elastic, because buyers would substitute another good or service in response to an SSNIP.

In that case, the HMG instruct us to ask our question again, adding to widgets the next best substitute — the product that would receive the most demand diversion in the event of an SSNIP on widgets. Let's call the next product fidgets. Now we ask whether a hypothetical monopolist with control of all widgets and fidgets would find it profitable to raise the price of widgets and fidgets 5 percent. Again, the answer can be yes or no. If it's yes, such a price increase would be profitable, and we have our relevant market. It's widgets and fidgets. But if the answer is no, meaning that a price increase wouldn't be possible, then there's still some third product out there that customers would easily substitute in the event of a price increase. That product also belongs in the relevant market. So we add that next product — let's call it gidgets — and ask our question again. After however many rounds of this game are necessary, we finally come to a point where the answer is yes! A hypothetical monopolist with control of all sales of widgets, fidgets, gidgets, and midgets would find it profitable to increase prices by 5 percent. Now we slam closed the doors of the Ark and claim victory. We have defined our relevant market.

Having completed this task for the relevant product market, we then have the pleasure of doing it all over again for the relevant geographic market. Under Section 4.2, we take the relevant product and identify the smallest plausible geographic market — say the neighborhood in which a grocery store is located — and ask whether a hypothetical monopolist controlling all grocery sales in that neighborhood could profitably impose an SSNIP. If yes, the neighborhood is the relevant market. If no, then we have to add another neighborhood into the mix and ask the question again — and continue the process until we have the satisfaction of a "yes" answer (yes, an SSNIP would be profitable) and hence our relevant geographic market.

At this point, the alert reader may protest that the Merger Guidelines are subject to the *Cellophane* fallacy. The very alert reader will rejoin that the explanation for why this is not the case was offered in Chapter 3. In the vast majority of cases, the merger has not yet closed when the antitrust agencies and courts scrutinize it, so there cannot yet be price increases attributable to the merger.

The SSNIP approach to market definition suggests a level of mathematical precision that can never occur in the real world of market definition. It is best understood as a mental exercise to illustrate ideal market definition. The HMG are down to earth and describe implementation of the SSNIP test with a list of the kinds of evidence the agencies typically look for. This is all done in Section 4.1.3, which includes such information as how customers have shifted purchases in the past in response to price changes, buyer surveys or other information, the conduct of industry participants, objective information about product characteristics, evidence about a product's lost sales when its price has gone up, evidence from sellers of complementary products, legal or regulatory requirements, and the influence of downstream competition. A comparable list for performing SSNIP analysis to calculate geographic markets appears in Section 4.2.1.

To get a sense of the kinds of evidence that are often determinative of market definition (and hence often of the outcome of the entire case) in modern merger litigation, consider the following examples of litigated merger cases:

Staples / Office Depot.[4] The question was whether there was a separate relevant market for office superstores or whether the superstores competed with other mass retailers, such as Walmart, K-Mart, and Target, that also sell office goods. The major hurdle for the FTC was that nearly every product sold in an office superstore can also be found at some other retailer. But a study commissioned by the FTC showed that Staples's prices were 13 percent lower in markets where it faced competition from one of the other two superstores — Office Depot or Office Max — than in markets where it was the only superstore. Based on this and similar evidence, the district court found that office superstores were a distinct relevant market. (As of this writing, Office Depot and Office Max are trying to merge. Which part of "office superstores are a distinct relevant market" did they not understand?)

Whole Foods / Wild Oats.[5] In a case that raised themes similar to those in *Staples*, the FTC prevailed in the D.C. Circuit in its argument that premium, natural, and organic superstores ("PNOS" in the trade or "granola yuppie stores" to the rest of us) were in a different relevant market from other grocery stores, including those that sold a large number of premium, natural, and organic products. The evidence

[4] *FTC v. Staples, Inc.*, 970 F. Supp. 1066 (D.D.C. 1997).
[5] *FTC v. Whole Foods Market, Inc.*, 548 F.3d 1028 (D.C. Cir. 2008).

was sharply contested, but the court accepted the FTC's claim that there is a group of core customers who would strongly prefer PNOS to other superstores and would not switch to a conventional grocery retailer in response to an SSNIP.

TurboTax.[6] H&R Block proposed the acquisition of TaxAct, a competitor in the digital tax software business. If digital tax software was the relevant market, then the merger would create a duopoly between H&R Block and Intuit's TurboTax software, with the two firms having a share over 90 percent. H&R Block protested that there are many ways to prepare taxes other than using digital tax software. One could hire an accountant or, as many Americans do, prepare the tax forms personally using pen and paper or not pay taxes and hope no one notices. The Justice Department prevailed, largely on evidence from internal documents by the merging parties and other tax preparation software companies showing that these firms considered tax preparation software a separate line of business from tax preparation assistance more generally. The evidence showed that the prices of digital software products and accountant services were very different, with software packages priced around $44 and accountant services falling in the $150 to $200 range.

Beyond these conventional sources of evidence for defining relevant markets, the HMG recognize a somewhat controversial tool: *critical loss analysis* (CRA). CRA, which differs somewhat from conventional SSNIP analysis, asks whether imposing at least an SSNIP on a product in a candidate market would raise or lower the hypothetical monopolist's profits. To undertake a CRA calculation, one needs to calculate the predicted loss, which is to say the number of unit sales that the hypothetical monopolist is predicted to lose due to an SSNIP, and also the critical loss, the number of lost unit sales that would leave profits unchanged. If the predicted loss is greater than the critical loss, then the hypothetical monopolist would not have an incentive to raise its price since that would result in lower profits. Conversely, if the predicted loss is smaller than the critical loss, then a price increase would be profitable.

What makes CRA controversial is its use of the premerger profit margins of the merging firms in performing the calculations. Section 4.1.3 states that high premerger profit margins are normally associated with inelastic demand. The upshot is that "[t]he higher the premerger margin, the smaller the recapture percentage necessary for the candidate market to satisfy the hypothetical monopolist test." The reason this is potentially troubling is that many firms in differentiated goods markets have relatively high profit margins, at least on an

---

[6] *United States v. H&R Block, Inc.*, 2011 WL 5438955 (D.D.C. Nov. 10, 2011).

incremental or marginal cost basis. Use of profit margins to predict postmerger market power could potentially sweep many more mergers, particularly those in differentiated goods markets, into the antitrust danger zone by defining narrower relevant markets. We will see this theme arise again in connection with the discussion of unilateral effects theories in differentiated goods markets.

Section 4.1.4 picks up on the theme raised in Section 3: price discrimination. Consistent with *Grinnell* and *Brown Shoe* (see Chapter 3), the agencies will define "price discrimination markets," really what *Brown Shoe* referred to as submarkets, around groups of customers who could be the victims of price discrimination as a result of the merger.

3.2.   Identifying the Market Participants

Once relevant product and geographic markets are established, the next step is to identify the participants in the market, which takes us into Section 5 of the HMG. Here it is important to pay attention to "HMG-speak," the peculiar use of vocabulary and concepts in the HMG. Obviously, all firms that currently sell or earn revenues in the market are considered "in" the market. Also, "[v]ertically integrated firms are also included to the extent that their inclusion accurately reflects their competitive significance" (Section 5.1). Thus, for example, if a steel producer has its own truck fleet and a relevant market is defined in trucking for transportation of steel in the Great Lakes region, the producer's fleet might be included in the relevant market because the trucker can service its own transportation needs and could even carry steel for other producers if trucking prices rose.

The odd aspect to the HMG's definitions is that *rapid entrants* are included as already "in" the market and hence count for purposes of concentration analysis, even though these are firms that do not currently, and may never, participate in the market. Under Section 5.1, a rapid participant is defined as a firm that could "likely provide rapid supply responses ... without incurring significant sunk costs" in response to an SSNIP. The 2010 HMG do not quantify "rapid" or "significant," but by way of reference the 1992 version defined rapid as "within a year" of the SSNIP and stated that sunk costs would not be considered significant if the rapid entrant could recover them within a year of its entry. The HMG provide the example of a milk producer that has bid to supply milk to a school district many times and has never won a contract, but is currently supplying milk in adjacent school districts and could easily serve the relevant market if prices rose.

It is important at this point to underline a distinction between classes of potential entrants. As noted, the HMG do not consider the responses of suppliers to price increases (supply elasticity) in defining the relevant market. Supply-side considerations show up in two other places in the guidelines. The first is here, where the objective is identifying the firms in the market. Rapid entrants are considered already in the market. Later, in Section 9, the HMG consider the relevance of possible entrants who are not yet in the market under Section 5.1 because their entry would be slow and they would have to incur significant sunk costs, but might still be relevant to a consideration of whether the merged firms would have the power to raise prices or reduce output because of the merger. For analytical purposes on an exam, it is crucial to decide whether a potential new entrant would enter "rapidly," and hence belongs in the market, or whether it would enter more sedulously, and hence should be evaluated much later in the analysis.

3.3. Calculating Market Shares

The next step in the structural part of HMG analysis is to define the market share of each firm in the relevant market (Section 5.2). The guiding principle is to choose a measure of market share "based on the best available indicator of firms' future competitive significance in the relevant market." In most cases historical revenues in the market are used. However, there are cases when another measure is preferable. For example, suppose that the market includes both high-priced and low-priced products, and a unit of the low-priced product can substitute for a unit of the high-priced product. In that case, units rather than revenues may be used to define shares. Also, as we saw in *General Dynamics* (Chapter 10), in some cases (particularly in homogeneous goods markets) future capacity or reserves rather than current revenues or units will be a better indication of future share. In assigning shares in a market that includes rapid entrants, neither current units nor revenues can be used since there are firms not presently selling in the market; therefore, some other estimate of future competitive significance, such as manufacturing capacity, factory size, or the scale of other productive or distributive assets, has to be used.

3.4. Calculating the HHI

At long last we come to market concentration — the point of the market definition and market participant identification steps that came before. Having identified all the market shares in the relevant market, we can now follow *Philadelphia National Bank* (Chapter 10) in calculating the market's concentration before and after the merger.

However, unlike the practice during the structuralist period, the HMG no longer call for use of two-firm or four-firm concentration ratios. Instead, they ask for use of the *Herfindahl-Hirschman Index* (HHI), which is intended to provide a snapshot of the entire market rather than just of some arbitrary number of firms.

Despite its fancy name, the HHI is simple to calculate. It is just the sum of the squares of the shares of the individual market participants.[7] Suppose that the market has ten sellers, each with a market share of 10 percent. Two of them propose to merge. Prior to the merger, the HHI is 10^2 times 10, or 1,000. After the merger, the HHI is 10^2 times 8 plus 20^2, or 1,200. The merger has resulted in a market with an HHI of 1,200 and a delta (difference in concentration before and after) of 200.

Once we have the resulting HHI and the delta, we look at the classifications in Section 5.3 to see whether the merger is a matter of concern from a structural perspective. The guidelines break markets into three categories:

- Unconcentrated markets, which have an HHI below 1,500
- Moderately concentrated markets, which have an HHI between 1,500 and 2,500
- Highly concentrated markets, which have an HHI above 2,500

Regardless of the concentration of the market, mergers with a delta of less than 100 ordinarily do not raise competitive concerns; the change in concentration is just too trivial to matter. Similarly, mergers that result in unconcentrated markets ordinarily raise no concerns. Structural concerns arise only when the resulting market concentration figure is 1,500 or higher. If the resulting concentration figure is moderate (i.e., 1,500 to 2,500) and the delta is more than 100, then the merger "potentially raise[s] significant competitive concerns and often warrant[s] scrutiny." Finally, if the merger results in a highly concentrated market, everything comes down to the delta. If the delta is under 100, no worries. If it's between 100 and 200, then the merger "potentially raise[s] significant competitive concerns and often warrant[s] scrutiny," the same words used to describe any delta above 100 in a moderately concentrated market. It's time to call a good lawyer. If the delta is above 200, the merger will "be presumed to be likely to enhance market power." Call a priest. The merger may need last rites.

These numbers are significantly higher in the 2010 HMG than they were in the previous guidelines. One of the reasons for the change is that the more restrictive numbers did not accord with actual agency

---

[7] For all the Illyrian Renaissance Sheepherding Fiction majors, "sum" means "add" and "square" means "multiply by itself, as in through asexual reproduction."

practice. Many mergers that should have looked troubling from a structural perspective under the old numbers were easily cleared. Time will tell whether the new numbers bear a closer relationship to the enforcement reality.

4. Unilateral Effects Theories

Theories of anticompetitive harm from mergers fall into two categories: *unilateral effects* and *coordinated effects*. This is true whether one pursues a highly structuralist approach or a direct evidence approach, although coordinated effects theories are more highly correlated with a structuralist approach and the unilateral effects theories are increasingly used to justify non-structuralist approaches. Unilateral approaches are in many ways a method of compensating for weaknesses in the process of market definition.

A unilateral effects approach to merger review, the subject of Section 6 of the HMG, asks whether the merging parties will, postmerger, have the power to raise price or reduce output regardless of any tacit or explicit coordination with competitors. Section 6 lists four market conditions under which unilateral effects are possible. The first of these, differentiated products markets, is the most important. As a general matter, unilateral effects theories are associated with *differentiated products* markets, whereas coordinated effects theories are associated with *homogeneous products* markets. The theory of unilateral effects in differentiated goods markets is often called an *upward pricing pressure* (UPP) model because it posits that mergers can create pressures for firms unilaterally to increase their prices to consumers.

Imagine that the reviewing agency has conducted relevant market definition in a proposed merger between BMW and Audi, and has concluded that the market consists of luxury sedans, including Mercedes-Benz, Lexus, Audi, Infiniti, BMW, Acura, Cadillac, Lincoln, and Jaguar. In this nine-firm market, a merger between two firms with relatively modest market shares might not seem problematic under ordinary structuralist assumptions. Plenty of competition remains from the other seven firms. But what if it turns out that a substantial number of BMW buyers view Audi as their next best choice and vice versa? In that case, the merged company might have an incentive to increase its prices in order to capture more profits from the customers who really want one of the sporty German choices (Mercedes is a little stuffier, and what potential buyer of a German sports sedan would buy a Lincoln instead?).

Section 6.1 suggests that three criteria are important to UPP theory. First, the goods or services must be *differentiated* (see Chapter 1).

Second, the goods sold by the merging parties must be close substitutes. The primary analytical means used to determine this are the *diversion ratios* of the products sold by the merging firms. The diversion ratio is the fraction of unit sales lost by the product due to an increase in its price that would be diverted to the second product. For example, if an increase in the price of BMWs leads to $100 of lost sales and $30 of those dollars are spent on Audis, the diversion ratio is roughly 1/3. A high diversion ratio like this tells us that Audi and BMW are close substitutes within the market for luxury sedans.

Finally, reiterating a controversial point raised in the discussion of market definition, Section 6.1 says that the larger the premerger profit margins on an incremental cost basis, the stronger the concern over unilateral effects, on the theory that the merging firms already have a good bit of pricing discretion and will find it profitable to exercise that discretion postmerger.

The UPP model could potentially serve as a device for proving the existence of anticompetitive effects even when the agencies have trouble defining a robust relevant market and demonstrating troubling levels of concentration. Section 6.1 notes that "[t]he Agencies rely much more on the value of diverted sales than on the level of the HHI for diagnosing unilateral price effects in markets with differentiated products." In some litigated cases in which the agencies lost on market definition grounds, the UPP model — *if approved by the courts* — could have come in handy. In *Oracle/PeopleSoft*[8] the question was whether there was a separate market for high-end human relations management (HRM) software enterprise application software, or whether there was a much larger market for all HRM and financial management enterprise resource planning (ERP) software systems. Oracle prevailed by showing that there was significant substitution between high-end HRM and general ERP systems and hence that a high-end HRM market definition would be inappropriate. Under a unilateral effects analysis that did not depend on conventional market definition, the government might have had an easier time proving that the merger would likely result in price increases to some customers. Software products are clearly differentiated rather than fungible, and Oracle and PeopleSoft were close competitors. The government did not attempt to calculate diversion ratios or incremental cost margins, but such evidence might have shown that Oracle and PeopleSoft were each other's closest competitors and operated with substantial incremental cost margins, and that the merger would therefore enable the merging firms unilaterally to raise their prices to some customers.

---

[8] *United States v. Oracle Corp.*, 331 F. Supp. 2d 1098 (N.D. Cal. 2004).

Beyond the UPP model of Section 6.1, the HMG list three additional scenarios that may give rise to unilateral effects concerns. First, when goods or services are sold through an auction process and a merging firm has frequently been the runner up to the other firm in the auction, there is a concern that the diminution in competition between the firms will increase prices (Section 6.2). Second, Section 6.3 outlines concerns over unilateral effects even in homogeneous goods markets. The second paragraph of Section 6.3 lists five criteria that students may want to note, but the essential point is that unilateral effects can occur in homogeneous goods markets when the merger would result in a single firm with a very large market share and competitors would be unable to supply customer demand in response to a price increase. Finally, Section 6.4 raises the concern that the merger will lead to diminished innovation. If one of the merging firms was previously engaging in research and development toward a new product that would have primarily cannibalized revenues from the second merging firm, the incentive to continue innovating postmerger may diminish.

5. Coordinated Effects Theories

The other major category of anticompetitive effects theories is coordinated effects, the subject of Section 7 of the HMG. Good news! Coordinated effects theories call for the application of principles that you have already learned by this point. The question in a coordinated effects case is whether the merger will create or encourage a market structure that is conducive to tacit or explicit collusion. In discussing cartel and facilitating practices theory in Chapter 5, we spent a good bit of time on the kinds of market conditions necessary for price fixing to work, and Section 7 of the HMG is largely a reprisal of those themes. It is important to note that a coordinated effects theory does not depend on a showing that postmerger, the firms in the relevant market will likely engage in conduct that would meet the *Interstate Circuit/Theater Enterprises* definition of agreement under Section 1 of the Sherman Act and hence constitute per se illegal price fixing. While that would certainly be a reason to disapprove a merger under Section 7 of the Clayton Act, if the merger would even facilitate "mere conscious parallelism" (see Chapter 5), that alone could be a sufficient reason to condemn it. Thus, coordinated interaction theories are essentially facilitating practices theories applied to mergers—the merger is the practice that facilitates conscious parallelism (or worse).

Coordinated effects theories are thus good opportunities (on an exam, for example) to re-deploy your great depth of learning on proof of agreement and facilitating practices. Under Section 7, the following are some of the factors that are considered relevant:

- Market concentration, particularly where the resulting market is moderately or highly concentrated (see prior HHI discussion).
- A history of prior collusion in the market or in a similar market.
- Product homogeneity. The more fungible or homogeneous the products, the easier it is to set collusive terms and police them.
- Pricing transparency. When prices aren't transparent, it's hard for the colluding firms to monitor cheating on a tacit or explicit price-fixing agreement. (You may want to refer back to Chapter 6, on pricing transparency and resale price maintenance as a method to stabilize a manufacturers' cartel.)
- Rivals can effectively punish defection from the collusive agreement.
- Sales are small and frequent rather than occasional and large. If sales are primarily made to a few large customers, the incentive to cheat in order to lock in a big customer for a long time is great.
- Low demand elasticity.
- Buyer characteristics. Large, powerful buyers may undermine collusive behavior by sellers.
- The acquired firm is a maverick.

Coordinated effects theories, which tend to rely heavily on structural presumptions, have fallen out of favor with the agencies, and also to some extent with the courts. In *Arch Coal*[9] the FTC lost an action to enjoin a coal merger where the commission's theory of anti-competitive harm was that after the merger, the coal companies would have an incentive to engage in coordinated output reductions. The merger resulted in an HHI of 2,365, with a delta of 163 if current production totals (rather than reserves as in *General Dynamic*) were considered the appropriate measure of market share. After review of the factual record, the D.C. District Court found coordinated interaction to reduce output postmerger feasible but unlikely, and held that the FTC had failed to meet its burden of proof.

6. Mitigating Factors and Defenses

We now have seen the major working parts of the HMG — the identification of theories of harm, sources of evidence, and structural

---

[9]*FTC v. Arch Coal, Inc.*, 329 F. Supp. 2d 109 (D.D.C. 2004).

presumptions. In Sections 8 to 11, the guidelines present mitigating factors or defenses that may overcome a conclusion that the merger is prima facie anticompetitive. Those factors or defenses include powerful buyers (Section 8), entry (Section 9), efficiencies (Section 10), and the failing firm defense (Section 11).

6.1. Entry

Section 8 states that the agencies "consider the possibility that powerful buyers may constrain the ability of the merging parties to raise prices." However, the presence of powerful buyers is not an automatic pass for mergers that are otherwise of concern. If the presence of one of the merging parties contributed significantly to a buyer's leverage, the elimination of that party as an independent force will diminish the buyer's leverage.

Section 9 concerns new entry, and thus requires a cross-reference back to Section 5.1 on market participants. Even though a firm may have been disqualified as a rapid entrant currently "in" the market under Section 5.1 because its potential entry was not sufficiently speedy or free of sunk costs, that firm may still be considered a potential entrant whose presence on the outskirts of the market would reduce the incentive of the firms in the market to raise prices. In order to qualify, a potential new entrant must satisfy three criteria.

First, its entry in response to an SSNIP would have to be timely — "rapid enough to make unprofitable overall the actions causing those effects and thus leading to entry." Recall that timeliness is also a criterion for being "in" the market, so this timeliness is probably a little less stringent than under Section 5.1. Although the 2010 HMG do not give numbers, their 1992 predecessor said that a firm was in the market if it could enter within a year of an SSNIP and could generally be counted as *not* in the market but still a potentially disciplining force if it could enter within two years.

Second, entry must be sufficiently likely to occur. Relevant factors include the output level the new entrant would need to reach in order to make its entry sustainable, the price it could charge upon entry (keeping in mind that its own entry could depress prices), and the new entrant's per-unit costs (keeping in mind that the new entrant might not be able to reach an efficient scale very quickly).

Finally, the new entry must be on a sufficiently large scale to counteract the anticompetitive effects of the merger. If the new entrant merely comes in to skim off a few select customers at the high prices facilitated by the merger, the new entry does not address the core concerns of antitrust law.

6.2.   Efficiencies

The next mitigating factor, efficiencies (Section 10), is merger law's bête noire. It deserves considerably more time than we can give it here. In a nutshell, during structuralism's high-water mark, efficiencies resulting from a merger were sometimes seen as a reason to *oppose* rather than allow a merger, on the theory that efficiencies would create dominant firms. Slowly, the view changed to the point where efficiencies were not a reason to condemn mergers, but they could also not be used to offset concerns about anticompetitive steps. Then, even more slowly, the view emerged that efficiencies could sometimes be used to justify otherwise anticompetitive mergers, but only under very narrow circumstances. And that is largely the view reflected in Section 10.

To qualify as potentially offsetting anticompetitive concerns, efficiencies must meet a rigorous litmus test. They must be merger-specific, meaning that they could not reasonably have been accomplished without the merger. They also must be concretely verified; vague, speculative, or otherwise wishful claims will not be allowed. They have to be sufficient to offset the harms created by the merger. Reflecting the HMG's consumer welfare orientation, this means that the efficiencies must be sufficiently passed on to consumers to offset any price increases that would otherwise occur because of the creation or exercise of market power. In other words, efficiencies that benefit only the merging firms (and hence society under a total social welfare perspective) do not count.

The agencies also give us some hints about the kinds of efficiencies claims they are more likely to favor and disfavor. Moving from most to least favored, efficiencies that arise from shifting production among facilities formerly owned separately (for example, by consolidating production in a single modern plant) are likely to reduce the incremental cost of production to the benefit of consumers. Research and development efficiencies are "potentially substantial" but are often speculative. Finally, efficiencies from procurement, management, or capital cost reductions are less likely to be merger-specific or substantial.

6.3.   The Failing Firm Defense

The last of the mitigating factors or defenses, covered in Section 11, is the failing firm defense. This defense is even narrower and harder to prove than the efficiencies defense. The idea is that if the acquired firm is on the brink of bankruptcy and but for this acquisition would go out of business, then an otherwise anticompetitive merger should be allowed on the theory that it doesn't worsen competition and makes things a little easier for shareholders, employees, creditors, and others affected by the potential bankruptcy. In order for the defense to apply, however, the merging firms must prove three things: (1) the allegedly failing firm is insolvent, and can't meet its financial obligations in the near future; (2) the firm couldn't successfully reorganize under Chapter 11 of the Bankruptcy Act; and (3) the firm has made unsuccessful good faith efforts to be acquired by another entity that would keep the failing firm's assets in the relevant market and raise fewer competitive concerns than the acquiring firm.

7. Mergers of Competing Buyers and Partial Acquisitions

The final two sections, which are new to the 2010 HMG, concern two circumstances in which antitrust scrutiny of mergers or acquisitions has not traditionally come to bear but could raise competitive concerns.

The first, reflected in Section 12, concerns mergers of competing buyers. The alert reader may recall that questions of monopsony or oligopsony power arose in connection with buyer price fixing (Chapter 5) and predatory overbidding (Chapter 8). The HMG treat mergers between buyers that create buyer market power as essentially the flip side of mergers that create seller market power. If a merger creates buyer power that allows the merging parties to drive input prices below competitive levels, the merger may be condemned as anticompetitive. However, it is important to distinguish mergers that create monopsony or oligopsony power from mergers that allow the merging firms to pay lower prices because they qualify for volume discounts or realize transactions costs savings.

Section 13 relates to partial acquisitions. Acquisitions of just a portion of the acquired firm's shares require fairly conventional merger analysis if the acquiring firm has gained effective control over the acquired firm. Even when the acquisition does not result in effective control by the acquiring firm, concerns may arise in three circumstances. First, a minority voting interest or governance right, such as the right to appoint board members, can enable the acquiring firm to influence competitive behavior and thereby induce the acquired firm to compete less aggressively. Second, a partial acquisition can blunt the acquiring firm's incentives to compete because it would share in any losses inflicted on the acquired firm. Finally, a partial acquisition can give the acquiring firm access to sensitive competitive information and thus enable pricing coordination. This is a good place to cross-reference Chapter 5, on information exchange among competitors.

8. Vertical Mergers

The antitrust agencies scrutinize vertical mergers far less aggressively than they do horizontal mergers. The currently applicable vertical merger guidelines are the vertical portion of the 1984 Merger Guidelines promulgated by the Justice Department. That the guidelines have not been revised in so long a time is less a reflection of contentment with the 1984 text than one of general indifference toward vertical mergers. It has been many years since there has been a litigated vertical merger case, although the agencies have imposed conditions on some vertical mergers, such as Google's acquisition of the ITA travel software company, Ticketmaster's acquisition of the Live Nation concert promotion service, and Comcast's acquisition of NBC.

As usual, Chicago School economics played a significant role in demoting vertical mergers as an antitrust concern. Chicago School scholars first argued that concerns about the potential of vertical mergers to foreclose competitors were overstated. They then argued that vertical integration was often efficient and good for consumer welfare. In particular, the Chicago School argued that vertical integration was desirable because it reduced the social costs of *double marginalization* — successive monopoly markups by vertically related firms capable of exercising market power. Economic theory shows that a vertically integrated firm will sometimes maximize profits by charging a lower price than if the same good were produced and distributed through a chain of vertical contracts by multiple firms with market power.

Under the vertical merger section of the 1984 guidelines, the agencies' primary concern is that vertical mergers could create entry barriers for rivals by foreclosing their opportunity to access a needed input in either an upstream or downstream market. Three conditions must be satisfied for a vertical merger to create foreclosure concerns.

First, the degree of vertical integration between the two markets must be so extensive that entrants to one market (the "primary market") would have to enter the other market (the "secondary market") simultaneously. Second, the requirement of entry at the secondary level must make entry at the primary level significantly more difficult and less likely to occur. Finally, the structure and other characteristics of the primary market must be otherwise so conducive to noncompetitive performance that the increased difficulty of entry is likely to affect its performance. To illustrate these elements, consider a merger between a shoe manufacturer and a shoe retailer. Postmerger, the integrated firm might distribute its shoes solely through its own retail outlets, and the retail outlets might refuse to carry other brands.[10] This could cause competitive harm to other shoe retailers, who would lose a source of shoes, and to rival manufacturers, who would have fewer retail outlets to distribute their wares. For the merger to be a concern, it would have to be the case under criterion 1 that manufacturers would have to enter retailing or retailers would have to enter manufacturing if the merged firm began to deal exclusively with itself. However, if there are at least "two [unintegrated] *minimum-efficient-scale* plants" in the "primary market"—the market in which the agency identifies competitive concerns—the merger is not problematic. For example, if there are at least two other independent shoe manufacturers operating at an efficient scale, the agencies would not be concerned that retailers will be unable to find shoes to stock their stores.

The second factor requires that forcing competitors to enter both markets makes entering the primary market more expensive. For example, if a small shoe retailer would have to build a big factory—disproportionate to its needs—in order to reach an efficient scale, then the second factor might be satisfied.

Finally, even if the first two conditions are satisfied, the guidelines state that the Justice Department will not be concerned unless the primary market is structurally susceptible to monopolization or collusion. Under the 1984 guidelines, the Justice Department is unlikely to challenge a vertical merger in a market with an HHI of 1,800 or less.

---

[10]This hypothetical is based on *Brown Shoe Co. v. United States*, 370 U.S. 294 (1962), a case decided in favor of the government during a period when vertical mergers were scrutinized in the courts and agencies with much more suspicion than they are today.

PART V

PROCEDURAL HURDLES AND IMMUNITIES

Chapter 12

Antitrust Injury, Standing, and Jurisdiction

This book has focused primarily on the substance of antitrust law rather than the methods and procedures by which it is implemented. However, nine out of every ten antitrust cases litigated today are brought by private plaintiffs, and private cases are governed by threshold rules that often consume as much energy as the substantive issues. This chapter provides a brief introduction to three important threshold issues that often arise in private antitrust litigation: antitrust injury, standing, and jurisdiction. Many other trans-substantive issues are also important to private antitrust litigation, including pleading requirements, class certification, discovery, statutes of limitation, and damages. This chapter is limited to the three categories mentioned because those are areas in which antitrust cases raise unique issues.

1. Antitrust Injury

Section 4 of the Clayton Act provides a private right of action for treble damages to "any person who shall be injured in his business or property by reason of anything forbidden by the antitrust laws."[1] However, this right is subject to two significant limitations. The private plaintiff must have suffered *antitrust injury* and she must have standing.[2] We discuss each limitation in turn.

The antitrust injury requirement originated in *Brunswick*.[3] Pueblo Bowl-O-Mat operated ten bowling alleys. Brunswick was one of the

---

[1] The statute also permits a prevailing plaintiff to recover her costs and attorney's fees from the defendant.

[2] The antitrust injury and standing requirements are inapplicable in a case brought by the government. *See In re High Tech Employee Antitrust Litig.*, 2012 WL 1353057 *19 n.2 (N.D. Cal. April 18, 2012); *FTC v. Cephalon, Inc.*, 551 F. Supp. 2d 21, 29 (D.D.C. 2008).

[3] *Brunswick Corp. v. Pueblo Bowl-O-Mat, Inc.*, 429 U.S. 477 (1977).

largest manufacturers of bowling equipment in the United States.
During the 1960s a large number of bowling center operators began
to default on their obligations to Brunswick, and Brunswick began
to buy up many of the defaulting centers. During the seven years preceding the trial in the case, Brunswick had purchased 222 centers.
Three of the centers it acquired were in markets where Pueblo also
had centers. Unhappy that a big national company had bought up
failing bowling centers in its markets, Pueblo brought a lawsuit alleging that the acquisitions violated Section 7 of the Clayton Act and
caused harm to Pueblo.

The Supreme Court rejected the lawsuit. Writing for a unanimous
Court, Justice Thurgood Marshall (not one to mollycoddle antitrust
defendants) observed that "[a]t base, [Pueblo] complain[s] that by
acquiring the failing centers [Brunswick] preserved competition,
thereby depriving [Pueblo] of the benefits of increased concentration."[4]
While this act might have been unlawful, and it might have caused
Brunswick damage, that was not enough to sustain a treble damages
action:

> [Plaintiffs] must prove more than injury causally linked to an illegal
> presence in the market. Plaintiffs must prove antitrust injury, which
> is to say injury of the type the antitrust laws were intended to prevent
> and that flows from that which makes defendants' acts unlawful. The
> injury should reflect the anticompetitive effect either of the violation
> or of anticompetitive acts made possible by the violation.[5]

Brunswick led to a cottage industry of new cases in which the
defendant argued that the plaintiff's claimed injury, although purport-
edly flowing from an illegal act, was not an antitrust injury — an injury
of the kind that the antitrust laws were intended to prevent. Defendants have usually prevailed in these arguments when plaintiffs
sought recovery for injuries that reflected an intensification, rather
than a diminution, of competition.

Often the antitrust injury analysis seems to bolster the judge's con-
viction that the conduct probably isn't anticompetitive anyway. In
Atlantic Richfield (ARCO)[6] an oil company sued its competitor, alleging that the defendant violated Section 1 of the Sherman Act by engaging in maximum resale price setting. This allegedly harmed USA
Petroleum, the plaintiff, since it lost market share due to lower
ARCO prices. However, the Supreme Court held that USA Petroleum

---

[4] *Id.* at 488.
[5] *Id.* at 489.
[6] *Atlantic Richfield Co. v. USA Petroleum Co.*, 495 U.S. 328 (1990).

had not suffered antitrust injury as a result of the nonpredatory maximum pricing. Even if the conduct was illegal under *Dr. Miles* and *Albrecht* (see Chapter 6) as a restraint on the freedom of ARCO dealers to set their own prices, the injury to USA Petroleum from lower prices was not of the kind that the antitrust laws were intended to deter.

Seven years later, in *State Oil v. Khan*, the Supreme Court unanimously overruled *Albrecht* and held that maximum resale price setting is subject to rule-of-reason rather than per se analysis (see Chapter 6). With hindsight, it seems that the Court's unwillingness to allow the competitor suit in *ARCO* on antitrust injury grounds may have been influenced in part by a rising doubt as to whether maximum resale price maintenance should have been illegal at all. Similarly, it is doubtful that in 1977 the Court would have found illegal the acquisitions in *Brunswick*, which resulted in a national market share of only 2 percent. Often the antitrust injury analysis seems to be a way of signaling that conduct isn't really illegal while conceding the possibility that it could be.

2. Standing

2.1. Purchaser Standing

In applying the standing limitation to purchasers, the federal story is a play in three acts. In *Hanover Shoe*[7] in 1968, the Supreme Court held that a private plaintiff who is a direct purchaser from a defendant who is able to raise the price of goods because of unlawfully obtained market power has a right of action to recover the full extent of the overcharge, even if the plaintiff passes on the entire overcharge downstream and therefore suffers no economic damage. Thus, for example, if a wholesaler purchases goods from a manufacturer who is involved in a price-fixing cartel but then simply raises the price of the goods when he sells them to retailers and sees no decline in volume (because downstream demand is inelastic), the wholesaler can still recover the full extent of the overcharge. Then, in *Illinois Brick*[8] in 1977, the Court held that an indirect purchaser bearing the real economic brunt may recover nothing. Thus, in the previous example, the retailer who buys from the wholesaler or the customer who buys from the retailer and ultimately pays the passed-on overcharge does not have standing to sue under federal antitrust law under the *direct purchaser rule*.

[7] *Hanover Shoe Inc. v. United Shoe Machinery Corp.*, 392 U.S. 481 (1968).
[8] *Illinois Brick Co. v. Illinois*, 431 U.S. 720 (1977).

The Supreme Court's vision in the *Hanover Shoe–Illinois Brick* tandem of creating a uniform, administrable national rule was quickly shattered as state policy makers began to react. Particularly unpalatable to many state officials was the possibility that large corporate middlemen — whether wholesalers or retailers — would receive huge windfall damages awards while consumers, who paid the ultimate price, could recover nothing. The states began to rebel against *Illinois Brick*'s prohibition of direct purchaser suits, which led to the third act of the play, *ARC America*.[9]

ARC America was an antitrust suit brought by four states — Alabama, Arizona, California, and Minnesota — against cement producers that the states accused of price fixing. The states purchased cement but often did so through middlemen and hence counted as indirect purchasers. Nonetheless, the states asserted claims under state antitrust statutes as well as under the Sherman Act. The Supreme Court had to decide whether the state laws were preempted by federal law. Nothing in Section 4 of the Clayton Act suggested an intention to displace state indirect purchaser suits, since, indeed, nothing in the text of the Clayton Act predetermined the results in *Hanover Shoe* or *Illinois Brick*. Furthermore, the Court noted that the purpose of the Sherman Act was to supplement state antitrust laws rather than to displace them. Thus, the only question was whether "state laws permitting indirect purchaser recoveries pose[d] an obstacle to the accomplishment of the purposes and objectives of Congress."[10] The Court concluded that *Hanover Shoe* and *Illinois Brick* found no general congressional policy about private antitrust claims, but only about private *federal* antitrust claims. Those cases, the Court reasoned, had been about the management of only the federal system. How the states wanted to run their private litigation systems was their own business. If the federal courts did not want to hear the state law indirect purchaser claims because they were too complicated or burdensome, they could simply decline to exercise supplemental jurisdiction over those claims.[11] Indirect purchaser claims under state law simply were not a federal problem.

Since *ARC America*, the trend toward state allowance of indirect purchaser litigation has continued. About half of the states and the District of Columbia have adopted "*Illinois Brick* repealer statutes," permitting either their own consumers or their attorneys general as parens patriae to bring indirect purchaser claims. Additionally, courts in Massachusetts, Nebraska, Vermont, Florida, and New Jersey have

---

[9]*California v. ARC America Corp.*, 490 U.S. 93 (1989).
[10]*Id.* at 102.
[11]*Id.* at 103-104.

ruled that indirect purchasers can sue under their consumer protection statutes; and Arizona, Iowa, North Carolina, and Tennessee courts have ruled that their citizens can sue under their state antitrust statutes. Thus, a majority of states have rejected *Illinois Brick* and allow some form of indirect purchaser suits.

The upshot is that consumer antitrust cases are often a muddle. Typically, there is a federal direct purchaser class action brought by large corporate middlemen and then one or more indirect purchaser class actions under the crazy quilt of applicable state law provisions. Since both the direct and indirect purchasers are theoretically able to recover for the full overcharge under many states' laws regardless of pass-on, it is at least theoretically possible that plaintiffs can recover the same overcharge multiple times, all before trebling.

Relatively few people in the antitrust community are satisfied with this state of affairs. Many proposals for reform have been raised. For example, in 2007 the bipartisan Antitrust Modernization Commission (AMC) called for legislative reform that would overrule both *Illinois Brick* and *Hanover Shoe* and hence allow both indirect and direct purchasers to bring antitrust claims. The statute would then provide that damages in such actions could not exceed the overcharges (trebled) incurred by the direct purchasers. Defendants would pay a treble-damages award for the direct purchaser overcharge into the court's coffers, and the direct and indirect purchasers could then seek an apportioned share of the damages pot, up to their actual damages. The AMC declined to recommend legislative overruling of *ARC America* and preemption of state indirect purchaser laws. Citing considerations of "federalism and political pragmatism," the commission instead endorsed legislation that would allow removal of state indirect purchaser actions to federal court to the full extent permitted by Article III of the Constitution. Under a multidistrict litigation process, all the federal and state direct and indirect claims would be consolidated in a single district court for all purposes, including discovery and trial.

It remains to be seen whether any reform proposals will gain political traction. In the meantime, antitrust lawyers are blessed with a good deal of business related to working through the litigation muddle created by the *Hanover Shoe–Illinois Brick–ARC America* trifecta.

2.2. Standing of Competitors and Other Affected Parties

Antitrust violations have ripple effects that can harm many different classes of people in addition to buyers. Imagine that Goliath Corp. knocks David Co. out of business and monopolizes the widget market. Widget customers pay higher prices, of course, but many other interests also suffer adverse consequences. David's shareholders see their investment value liquidated, its suppliers lose a customer, its employees have to find new work, and its creditors may not be able to recover the loans they have made. Which, if any, of these other interests can sue?

The easy case is David, the rival. Subject to the antitrust injury requirement previously discussed, a rival who is injured by an antitrust violation usually has standing to seek recovery of its damages. The difficult competitor standing cases arise in circumstances where a firm claims that it was excluded from entering the market at all. The courts tend to be concerned that such claims could be highly speculative and attract fortune hunters (imagine all the tech companies that might claim that but for exclusionary conduct by Microsoft, they would have entered the PC-compatible operating systems market and earned a fortune). Hence, a potential rival that claims it was anticompetitively excluded from a market must prove that it had the "intention and preparedness" to enter, meaning that it would have entered but for the antitrust violation and that it took actual, concrete steps toward entry such as securing financing, hiring employees, and leasing office space.[12]

The harder case is the "all others" category — suppliers, employees, shareholders, creditors, and so forth. Standing is generally denied on the theory that expanding the circle of plaintiffs would allow duplicative recoveries and would overly complicate antitrust litigation. In *Associated General Contractors*[13] the Supreme Court announced a number (four, five, or six depending on which circuit court opinion you consult) of factors that determine standing. Borrowing from the Fifth Circuit's distillation, they are as follows:[14]

> (1) the nature of the plaintiff's alleged injury: Is the injury "of a type that Congress sought to redress in providing a private remedy for violations of the antitrust laws"?; (2) the directness or indirectness of the asserted injury; (3) the proximity or remoteness of the party to the alleged injurious conduct; (4) the speculativeness of the damages claim; and (5) the risk of duplicative damages or complexity in apportioning damages.

The first factor is just the antitrust injury requirement. Many courts break factor 5 into two factors (risk of duplication and complexity of

---

[12] *See, e.g., Ashley Creek Phosphate Co. v. Chevron USA, Inc.*, 315 F.3d 1245 (10th Cir. 2003).

[13] *Associated General Contractors of California v. California State Council of Carpenters*, 459 U.S. 519 (1983).

[14] *Procter & Gamble Co. v. Amway Corp.*, 242 F.3d 539, 562-563 (5th Cir. 2001).

apportionment) and add two additional factors: whether the defendant intended harm to the plaintiff and whether there are other plaintiffs better able and motivated to vindicate the interests of the antitrust laws.

3. Jurisdiction

Our last topic — jurisdiction — is not limited to private enforcement; however, private cases raise unique jurisdictional questions. Most of the antitrust-related conduct that occurs within the United States easily falls within the jurisdictional reach of the Sherman Act and Clayton Act under the modern, expansive reading of Congress's Commerce Clause powers (but recall the narrower jurisdictional reach of the Robinson-Patman Act; see Chapter 9). The interesting action is with respect to conduct that occurs outside the United States, which raises important questions about the extraterritorial reach of the U.S. antitrust laws.

A quick historical sketch will illustrate. In the first decade of the twentieth century, two American fruit producers staged an industrial war in Central America. A predecessor to the plaintiff, American Banana, had started a banana plantation in Panama, at that time part of Colombia. This made the defendant, United Fruit, very unhappy and it began to cash in on its political favors with the governments of Costa Rica and Colombia to hassle American Banana. After Panama became an independent country (with a little, ahem, help from Teddy Roosevelt), United Fruit persuaded the Costa Rican army to take over American Banana's plantation in Panama, seize its supplies, and stop construction of the plantation and a railroad. This obviously made it difficult for American Banana to produce bananas and ship them to the United States. The company brought suit against United Fruit under the Sherman Act.

The Supreme Court held that the suit could not be pursued in the United States.[15] "[T]he general and almost universal rule," Justice Holmes explained, "is that the character of an act as lawful or unlawful must be determined wholly by the law of the country where the act is done."[16] Since the allegedly bad acts had taken place in Panama, it was up to the laws and courts of Panama to determine their legality.

This territorial approach to jurisdiction is associated with some major difficulties. Suppose that the CEOs of two U.S. companies

[15] *American Banana Co. v. United Fruit Co.*, 213 U.S. 347 (1909).
[16] *Id.* at 356.

happen to run into each other at a tiki bar in Bermuda, start chatting over a margarita, and end up fixing prices in the United States. Under *American Banana*, since the bad conduct took place in the Bermuda, it should be judged under Bermuda law and in Bermuda courts. But that would be a very silly proposition, since Bermuda has no interest in the controversy and won't feel the effects of the price-fixing agreement. Although the bad acts occurred in Bermuda, they have nothing to do with Bermuda.

Once again, Judge Learned Hand rode to the rescue in *Alcoa*.[17] The proper test, Judge Hand explained, is whether the conduct in the foreign market was meant to and did produce a substantial effect in the United States. Hence, instead of focusing on territorial sovereignty, courts should employ an *effects test* that asks where the effects of the conduct were felt. The situs of the conduct's effects should determine the entity that asserts jurisdiction over the conduct.

A broad interpretation of the effects test would be problematic. In an increasingly interconnected world, the ripple effects of conduct are often felt far from their origin. Seeking to place some limits on the extraterritorial reach of U.S. antitrust law, Congress enacted a version of the *Alcoa* effects test in the Foreign Trade Antitrust Improvements Act (FTAIA) in 1982. The FTAIA is an awkwardly worded statute, but its key components include a statutory adoption of the effects test with limitations. Only foreign conduct that has a "direct, substantial, and reasonably foreseeable effect" on U.S. commerce falls within the reach of the U.S. antitrust laws.

The FTAIA contains an additional condition requiring that the effect giving rise to the plaintiff's claim be the same as the effect giving rise to jurisdiction. This little proviso has turned out to be of multi-billion-dollar importance to global antitrust litigation. In *Empagran*[18] a class of plaintiffs who had purchased vitamins in foreign markets sued in federal court, arguing that there was jurisdiction under the FTAIA because the same price-fixing conspiracy that had raised the prices of their vitamins had raised the prices of vitamins sold in the United States as well. If the Supreme Court had allowed such claims, U.S. courts would have become open to the claims of all purchasers from global cartels that made sales into the United States. But the Court unanimously rejected this claim, holding that plaintiffs could not bring suit in U.S. court unless the effect giving rise to their claim — an anticompetitive effect in a foreign market — was the same as the "direct, substantial, and reasonably foreseeable effect" on U.S. commerce required under the FTAIA.

[17]*United States v. Aluminum Co. of America*, 148 F.2d 416, 444 (2d Cir. 1945).
[18]*F. Hoffman-La Roche, Ltd. v. Empagran, S.A.*, 542 U.S. 155 (2004).

The effect of *Empagran* (and a remand decision in the D.C. Circuit that closed a tiny window the Supreme Court had left open) is to confine purchaser litigation to U.S. purchasers. (*Important point*: When I, like many other lazy commentators, say "U.S. purchasers," I'm making a shorthand reference to where the purchaser made her purchase, not to her nationality. If a U.S. citizen goes to India and buys a rug whose price has been fixed, she cannot bring a claim in the United States. Conversely, if an Indian citizen travels to the United States and buys a computer that has been price-fixed, she can sue in the United States. The jurisdictional question for *Empagran* purposes is where the transaction took place. Of course, there are many complex transactions that take place over the phone and Internet on a global basis, and figuring out where the transaction "took place" is tough work. Fortunately, those difficult questions are beyond the scope of this chapter.)

Chapter 13

Antitrust Immunities

One of the great disappointments for plaintiffs' lawyers is uncovering a juicy set of antitrust facts only to discover that the defendants are subject to some immunity from suit. Antitrust immunities come in two varieties. First, over the years Congress has occasionally passed statutes immunizing particular industries from suit. The most famous of these is the baseball exemption, which started as a judicial decision that baseball isn't interstate commerce and hence is unreachable under the federal commerce power.[1] It then (once it became obvious that baseball is a multi-billion dollar interstate racket even without accounting for performance-enhancing drugs) morphed into a weird, quasi-statutory immunity after the Commerce Clause jurisprudence underpinning the original decision had eroded. A more conventional, and commercially important, immunity is the McCarran-Ferguson Act's immunity for certain aspects of insurance. The federal code is littered with additional immunities for a wide variety of industries. These immunities are rarely studied in antitrust courses, although it is fun to peruse them to see which industries have the best lobbyists.

This chapter focuses on immunities of the second kind, which are more general than the statutory, industry-specific immunities and much more commonly studied in antitrust courses. These are judicially created immunities for certain kinds of behavior that the antitrust laws cannot penalize without impinging on democratic values. These immunities come in two flavors. *Noerr-Pennington* immunity insulates from antitrust challenge the act of "petitioning" the government to take action that disadvantages competitors or otherwise disrupts the competitive process. *Parker* immunity insulates from antitrust challenge actions taken by state or local governments that may disadvantage competitors or suppress ordinary competitive processes. Together these two doctrines immunize from suit a vast array of potentially anti-competitive practices.

---

[1] *Federal Baseball Club of Baltimore, Inc. v. National League of Professional Baseball Clubs, Inc.*, 259 U.S. 200 (1922).

Here's an encouraging note to students who may be feeling that antitrust is too heavy on economics and a little beyond their zone of comparative advantage. The antitrust immunities are traditional lawyer work. The doctrines tend to be straightforward, testable, and tested. Now is the time to make up lost ground!

1. *Noerr-Pennington* Immunity

Noerr-Pennington immunity arises from two cases, surprisingly called *Noerr*[2] and *Pennington*.[3] Both cases involved allegedly nefarious efforts by private parties to influence government officials to take anticompetitive action against rivals. *Noerr* involved a political grudge match between long-distance trucking companies and 24 major railroads. The truckers brought an antitrust complaint under Sections 1 and 2 of the Sherman Act. "The gist of the conspiracy alleged," explained the Court, was that the railroads had retained a third party "to conduct a publicity campaign against the truckers designed to foster the adoption and retention of laws and law enforcement practices destructive of the trucking business, to create an atmosphere of distaste for the truckers among the general public, and to impair the relationships existing between the truckers and their customers."[4] The railroads allegedly used sleazy methods to obtain support for anti-trucker legislation, such as a "third party technique" where surrogates for the railroads were retained to make anti-trucker statements that seemed to come from independent citizens or civic groups.

In *Pennington* a group of small, non-union coal mine owners alleged that the unions and larger mines had conspired to lobby the Secretary of Labor to establish minimum wages for companies selling coal to the Tennessee Valley Authority. This conspiracy was allegedly designed to put the smaller, non-union mines out of business.

In both cases, the Supreme Court held that even if all the events alleged were true, they did not give rise to antitrust violations. The antitrust laws, the Court explained in *Noerr*, do "not prohibit two or more persons from associating together in an attempt to persuade the legislature or the executive to take particular action with respect to a law that would produce a restraint or a monopoly."[5] A construction of

---

[2] *Eastern R.R. Presidents Conference v. Noerr Motor Freight, Inc.*, 365 U.S. 127 (1961).
[3] *United Mine Workers of America v. Pennington*, 381 U.S. 657 (1965).
[4] 365 U.S. at 129.
[5] *Id.* at 136.

the antitrust laws that reached such petitioning of the government would raise First Amendment concerns, but the Court did not have to address the constitutional question given its construction of the Sherman Act. Under the *Noerr-Pennington* doctrine, efforts to influence the government to adopt anticompetitive rules do not fall within the ambit of the antitrust laws.

In *Noerr* the Court left a possible loophole. It recognized that there may be situations where an act of ostensible petitioning of the government "is a mere sham to cover what is actually nothing more than an attempt to interfere directly with the business relationships of a competitor and the application of the Sherman Act would be justified."[6] However, that was not the case in *Noerr*, since the railroads were trying to achieve their allegedly anticompetitive goals *through* the instrumentality of governmental restrictions on truckers.

As later cases explained, the *sham exception* is not satisfied merely by a showing that the defendant's lobbying of the government was unethical or dishonest. Rather, as the Court explained in *Omni*,[7] a sham occurs only when "persons use the governmental *process* — as opposed to the *outcome* of that process — as an anticompetitive weapon." A case in which the Court found the existence of a sham was *California Motor*,[8] where a group of trucking companies sued another group of trucking companies, claiming that the defendants had mounted a series of frivolous objections to the plaintiffs' license applications with no expectation of achieving denial of the licenses but simply to cause expense and delay. The crucial attribute of a sham is that the defendant could have achieved its anticompetitive objective whether or not the government took action in the defendant's favor. If the government takes anticompetitive action in favor of the defendant, that's just icing on the cake. An anticompetitive scheme that could work only if the defendant is successful in persuading the government to take action favorable to it is, by definition, not a sham.[9]

---

[6]*Id.* at 144.

[7]*City of Columbia v. Omni Outdoor Advertising, Inc.*, 499 U.S. 365, 380 (1991).

[8]*California Motor Transport Co. v. Trucking Unlimited*, 404 U.S. 508 (1972).

[9]There may be a narrow exception to the sham exception rules for fraudulent statements in an adjudicatory context. If a litigant commits fraud on a court or administrative body and induces that court or agency to take anticompetitive action, that fraud may serve as a sham under *Noerr-Pennington*, even though the anticompetitive effect occurs solely as a consequence of the governmental decision. *See Mercatus Group, LLC v. Lake Forest Hosp.*, 641 F.3d 834 (7th Cir. 2011). However, this possible exception applies only to adjudicative proceedings. Fraud on legislators or the executive is not a sham if it results in the executive or legislative body taking anticompetitive action.

Noerr-Pennington immunity applies to efforts to persuade any branch of the government—legislative, executive, judicial, or administrative—to take anticompetitive action. In recent years much of the most significant *Noerr-Pennington* action has transpired with respect to allegations that the plaintiff in a prior litigated case attempted to use litigation to stifle competitors. Such claims have become disfavored because they raise the possibility that much litigation among competitors will inevitably slip into round 2—an antitrust case challenging the bringing of the first case.

Seeking to stem the tide of such litigation, the Supreme Court adopted a two-part test to govern anticompetitive litigation claims in *Professional Real Estate Investors* (*PREI*).[10] PREI operated a resort hotel that rented video disks to its patrons for in-room viewing. A consortium of seven major Hollywood studios brought a copyright infringement case against PREI. PREI counterclaimed on an antitrust theory, alleging that the very filing of the lawsuit was an attempt to eliminate PREI as a competitor. PREI won its copyright case, but not its antitrust counterclaim. The Supreme Court ruled that to establish that the filing of a lawsuit is a sham, the claimant must show two things. First, she must show that the prior lawsuit was "objectively baseless in the sense that no reasonable litigant could realistically expect success on the merits." Only if she shows this first element may she proceed to the second: a showing that the lawsuit was subjectively motivated by a desire to interfere directly with the competitor.

Proof of the objective and subjective elements merely shows that the lawsuit was a sham and therefore strips away *Noerr-Pennington* immunity. It does not affirmatively establish the plaintiff's antitrust case. For that, the plaintiff must pick a legal theory and establish whatever affirmative elements that entails (e.g., a relevant market, market power, anticompetitive effects, etc.).

2. *Parker* Immunity

Noerr-Pennington immunity covers efforts to persuade the government to take anticompetitive action, involving the inputs to governmental decision making. *Parker*[11] immunity covers the other end of the spectrum: the outputs of governmental decision making. When a government initiates actions that harm competition, the

---

[10] *Professional Real Estate Investors, Inc. v. Columbia Pictures Indus., Inc.*, 508 U.S. 49 (1993).

[11] *Parker v. Brown*, 317 U.S. 341 (1943).

question arises whether those actions are illegal under the Sherman Act. *Parker* and its progeny give an answer: generally not, with some qualifications.

Parker arose from the California Agricultural Prorate Act, an act of the California legislature designed to prevent "excessive" and "wasteful" agricultural production by limiting competition among California farmers. The act established a commission tasked with instituting programs to limit wasteful production "without permitting unreasonable profits to producers" — essentially a state-run commission to set sail on Justice Taft's "sea of doubt" (see *Addyston Pipe*, discussed in Chapter 4) by determining "reasonable" production levels, and hence reasonable prices, for California farmers. The commission would select a program committee to formulate a marketing program, which would then be adopted as law if assented to by a requisite percentage of affected farmers. The raisin producers voted to accept a marketing plan that prorated raisin production and substantially limited raisin output. The plan worked pretty much as its framers intended: production fell and prices rose.

Inconveniently, one raisin farmer exceeded his quota and challenged the entire proration system as an anticompetitive scheme in violation of the Sherman Act and the "dormant" Commerce Clause of Article I, Section 8 of the Constitution. The Supreme Court rejected both arguments; we will consider just the antitrust argument. The Court began with the assumption that the raisin proration scheme would have been illegal under the Sherman Act if adopted by a private contract among raisin growers. However, the Court found in the Sherman Act's legislative history "no suggestion of a purpose to restrain state action."[12] Since the state was exercising its legislative judgment in authorizing the anticompetitive regulation, the suppression of competition was an act of a sovereign state and hence beyond the reach of the Sherman Act.

The *Parker* doctrine is also called the state action doctrine (not to be confused with the state action doctrine for purposes of Fourteenth Amendment analysis).[13] It reflects a principle of federalism that states are sovereign actors and may choose to regulate competitive behavior, with the necessary implication that the states will sometimes suppress competition in pursuit of wider social objectives.

---

[12] *Id.* at 313.

[13] Although *Parker* immunity does not technically extend to agencies of the federal government, the courts have held that the Sherman Act does not apply to the federal government. *U.S. Postal Service v. Flamingo Industries (USA) Ltd.*, 540 U.S. 736 (2004); *United States v. Cooper Corp.*, 312 U.S. 600 (1941).

Chapter 13. Antitrust Immunities

The *Parker* opinion left us with the germ of a principle rather than a doctrinal structure for assessing anticompetitive state regulation. That task fell to the Court in *Midcal*.[14] *Midcal* articulated a two-part test for determining whether *Parker* immunity applies. To qualify, an anticompetitive scheme must be (1) "clearly articulated and affirmatively expressed as state policy," and (2) "actively supervised by the state itself."[15] It is this two-part test that you should use in analyzing *Parker* immunity questions. (The right sound bite on an exam is something like "Under the *Midcal* test for determining whether *Parker* immunity applies . . .")

The first prong of *Midcal* requires that the anticompetitive policy originate with the state itself. Importantly, *the state* here means the state legislature, not every organ of state government. Municipalities are not "the state" for purposes of the first prong of *Midcal*.[16] (They *are* the state for purposes of inefficiency, mindless bureaucracy, and corruption). Thus, if a municipality suppresses competition, the policy of such suppression must be traceable to a decision by the legislature; the delegation by the legislature to the municipality of "home rule" powers is insufficient.[17] On the other hand, when a state delegates regulatory powers to municipalities, it need not explicitly permit the displacement of competition through municipal regulation. It is enough that the suppression of competition be a "foreseeable result" of the statutory authorization.[18]

Another question that arises under the first prong of *Midcal* is how coercive the state must be in displacing competition with a different scheme. When the state compels private actors to follow an anticompetitive scheme — as it did in *Parker* — the case for immunity is easy. In other circumstances, the Court merely allows private parties to behave anticompetitively but does not require them to do so. In *Southern Motors*[19] the Court held that, while compulsion is often the best evidence of a state policy to displace competition, it is not strictly necessary to meet the first prong of *Midcal*. Thus, rate-setting bureaus for private motor carriers that were authorized but not compelled by state statutes met prong 1 of *Midcal*.

The second prong of *Midcal* requires that the state actively supervise the administration of the anticompetitive scheme. The basic idea

[14] *California Retail Liquor Dealers Ass'n v. Midcal Alum., Inc.*, 445 U.S. 97 (1980).
[15] *Id.* at 105.
[16] *City of Lafayette v. Louisiana Power & Light Co.*, 435 U.S. 389 (1978).
[17] *Community Commc'ns Co. v. City of Boulder*, 455 U.S. 40 (1982).
[18] *Town of Hallie v. City of Eau Claire*, 471 U.S. 34 (1985).
[19] *Southern Motor Carriers Rate Conference v. United States*, 471 U.S. 48 (1985).

is that a state cannot simply decide that it doesn't like the Sherman Act and tell an industry that it is free to do whatever it wants without fear of antitrust prosecution and without any regulatory action by the state. If the state wants to suppress competition, it must be actively engaged in managing some regulatory alternative. Thus, a "negative veto" system where a state commission has the power to disapprove rates established by private parties does not meet the active supervision requirement.[20] Active supervision "requires that state officials have and exercise the power to review particular anticompetitive acts of private parties and disapprove those that fail to accord with state policy."[21]

A final twist on active supervision takes us back to municipalities, the sources of many of the relevant anticompetitive regulatory schemes. Although municipalities are not the state for purposes of prong 1 of *Midcal*, when a municipality is regulating pursuant to a clearly articulated and affirmatively expressed state policy to suppress competition, there is no requirement that the state be involved in actively supervising the implementation of the municipality's regulatory scheme (which would defeat the purpose of delegating regulatory powers to municipalities).[22]

One way to understand the *Midcal* test is as permission for states to displace competition so long as state politicians take full political responsibility for the decision, and hence render themselves vulnerable to voter displeasure with the consequences of the anticompetitive scheme at reelection time. But this political accountability interpretation of *Midcal* runs into substantial difficulties. In many cases, a political body can get away with an anticompetitive scheme by managing to externalize the costs of the scheme to consumers who can't vote in the relevant jurisdiction. This was glaringly true on the facts of *Parker* itself. As the Court noted, 90 to 95 percent of the raisins grown in California were destined for out-of-state shipment, which meant that most of the consumers paying higher prices because of the proration scheme had no vote in California politics. Some commentators have argued that *Parker* immunity should apply only where state voters fully internalize the costs of the anticompetitive scheme. For better or for worse, however, this is not the law. States are free to enact anticompetitive schemes that externalize costs to nonvoters so long as they meet the minimum requirements of *Midcal*.

---

[20]*FTC v. Ticor Title Ins. Co.*, 504 U.S. 621 (1992).
[21]*Patrick v. Burget*, 486 U.S. 94, 101 (1988).
[22]*Town of Hallie*, 471 U.S. at 34.

3. Interactions Between *Noerr-Pennington* and *Parker* Immunity

The alert reader may have guessed by now that *Noerr-Pennington* and *Parker* issues commonly intersect in the hurly-burly of politics and regulation. Frequently, a firm or firms will pressure governmental decision makers to adopt anticompetitive regulations, and the government will then adopt and implement them with anticompetitive effect. Such scenarios represent both the front end and back end of the political process, and hence entail issues about both kinds of immunity.

A case that well illustrates these interactions is *Omni*.[23] Columbia Outdoor Advertising (COA) controlled 95 percent of the billboard space in Columbia, South Carolina. It was, by all accounts, a "good ole boy" business, deeply connected in Columbia politics. COA didn't take kindly to Omni's efforts to enter the market. According to Omni, COA initially responded by redoubling and modernizing its own billboards and spreading vicious rumors about Omni. When Omni didn't cave, COA allegedly took to political back channels, persuading the city council to pass a new ordinance severely restricting the size, location, and spacing of billboards. Since COA's existing billboards were grandfathered, the ordinance had the effect of entrenching COA's dominant market position and severely hindering Omni's ability to compete.

Predictably, since this is our final story in the book, Omni sued the City of Columbia and COA under the Sherman Act. Also predictably, since this chapter is on immunities, the defendants raised both *Parker* and *Noerr-Pennington* as defenses. And once again predictably, since the trend in the courts in the last few decades has been toward the curtailment of private antitrust suits, the Supreme Court found that both immunities applied and that Omni had no antitrust claim.

Several observations in Justice Scalia's majority opinion are worth noting. First, the Court held that private actors are also protected by the *Parker* state action doctrine. Thus, when private actors like COA participate with the state in the implementation of an anticompetitive state regulatory scheme that satisfies the *Midcal* test, the private actors can claim the same immunity as the state actors.

Second, the Court noted that when the state acts as a commercial actor, it may shed its *Parker* immunity. Thus, if the City of Columbia had decided to raise revenues by going into the billboard business itself, it might not be able to lay claim to *Parker* immunity.

Third, the Court rejected Omni's argument that there should be a conspiracy exception to *Parker*. Omni argued that this case was unlike

---

[23] *City of Columbia v. Omni Outdoor Advertising, Inc.*, 499 U.S. 365 (1991).

3. Interactions Between *Noerr-Pennington* and *Parker* Immunity

Parker because it involved a nepotistic conspiracy between state and private officials. The Court rejected such conspiracy theories as grounds for circumventing *Parker*, fearing that the exception would quickly swallow the rule since plaintiffs could always allege that private interests combined with state actors to bring about the anticompetitive regulation.

Fourth, and in a similar vein, the Court held that mere deviation from state law in the context of exercising delegated power to suppress competition is insufficient to defeat *Parker* immunity. Just as there is no conspiracy exception, there is no corruption exception. Otherwise, small deviations from state procedural requirements could destroy *Parker* immunity and create antitrust liability.

The final two highlights of the case relate to the interaction of *Noerr-Pennington* and *Parker*. Omni argued that even if COA was immunized under *Parker* for its actions to implement the billboard restrictions, it was liable under the sham exception to *Noerr-Pennington* for having induced city officials to adopt the restriction in the first place. The alert reader of this chapter already has all the tools necessary to figure out why this argument failed. To be "sham," the anticompetitive effect would have to be "direct," meaning not achieved through the outcome of the governmental process. But here the only way that the lobbying campaign could have harmed Omni was if the city council adopted the restrictive zoning ordinance. By definition, then, the lobbying couldn't be a sham.

Finally, Omni argued that there should be a conspiracy exception to *Noerr-Pennington* immunity when private parties pull political strings to induce governmental actors to adopt anticompetitive regulations. The Court rejected this argument for the same reason it rejected a conspiracy exception to *Parker* immunity: the exception would swallow the rule.

* * * *

Antitrust immunities are increasingly important in a world of pervasive governmental regulation. Many regulatory schemes have anticompetitive effects, such as entrenching competitors by creating entry barriers or facilitating collusion. The *Noerr-Pennington* and *Parker* doctrines are just one of the analytical categories that courts use to decide whether regulation or antitrust should take precedence. In other circumstances, the courts ask whether a federal regulatory scheme implicitly preempts the operation of antitrust law. Thus, for example, in *Credit Suisse*[24] the Supreme Court held that the practice of initial public offering (IPO) "laddering" — requiring investors to pay surcharges over an IPO share price — was within the regulatory ambit

---

[24]*Credit Suisse Securities (USA) LLC v. Billings*, 551 U.S. 264 (2007).

of the Securities and Exchange Commission and hence not within the ambit of the antitrust laws.

Conflicts between regulation and antitrust are a fitting place to end this book. They remind us that antitrust is just one of the controls on competition in market economies and not the Supreme Law of the Land. Herbert Hovenkamp has aptly referred to antitrust as a "residual regulator,"[25] the regulatory instrument that applies when nothing else does. To be sure, there is an argument for an antitrust role that is more aggressive, both in policing the exercise of privately acquired market power and in preventing regulatory schemes from moving our economy too far from competition as the core driver of economic activity. Whether antitrust should assume that more aggressive posture is for you to decide.

For that matter, it's for you to decide whether we should have antitrust laws at all. After reading this book, you may have come to believe with Justice Oliver Wendell Holmes that the Sherman Act is "a humbug based on economic ignorance and incompetence."[26] In that case, would you do me the favor of burning your copy? I'd hate to see it show up on the resale market and depress my sales.

---

[25] Herbert Hovenkamp, *The Antitrust Enterprise: Principle and Execution* 10 (2005).
[26] Letter from Oliver Wendell Holmes, Justice, U.S. Supreme Court, to Sir Frederick Pollock (Apr. 23, 1910), reprinted in 1 Holmes-Pollock Letters 163 (Mark DeWolfe Howe ed., 1942)

Glossary

Allocative efficiency: A state of affairs where scarce social resources are allocated to their most valuable uses. Achieving allocative efficiency is often considered a principal goal of antitrust policy.

Anticompetitive conduct: Conduct other than competition on the merits that disrupts the proper functioning of competitive markets. Also known as exclusionary conduct. *Alcoa* juxtaposes "superior skill, foresight, and industry," which is not anticompetitive, with deliberately exclusionary conduct.

Antitrust injury: Injury of the kind the antitrust laws were intended to prevent; doctrine similar to standing doctrine that limits private litigants from challenging allegedly anticompetitive conduct that does not injure the plaintiff in a way consistent with the policy objectives of antitrust laws.

Arbitrage: Buying goods in one market and reselling at a higher price in another market. Where arbitrage is possible, it tends to undermine the possibility of price discrimination.

Average variable cost test: A test for defining the appropriate measure of cost in predatory pricing cases, adopted in a majority of federal circuits. Average variable cost is the average of all costs that vary with changes in the level of a firm's output. It excludes fixed costs and is thus considered prodefendant.

Barriers to entry: Market conditions that impede entry. The Chicago School argued that entry barriers only include impediments faced by new entrants that were not faced by the incumbent.

Bertrand competition: An economic model describing the competitiveness of a market based on the assumption that firms sell differentiated goods and compete on price.

Bundling: Selling separate products only in a package. Contrast to tying, where a seller sells two products separately but uses its market power in one of the products to force buyers to purchase a complementary second product as well. Contrast pure bundling, described above, to mixed bundling (or bundled discounting) where the seller offers the buyer a discount if buyer purchases separate products in a package.

Cartel: A group of buyers or sellers operating under a price-fixing agreement, usually in secret.

Celler-Kefauver Act: 1950 federal statute bolstering Section 7 of the Clayton Act by closing the "asset loophole" and making clear that Section 7 applies to nonhorizontal mergers.

189

Glossary

Chicago School: A school of law and economics associated with the University of Chicago, which gained prominence in the 1970s and generally argued for less interventionist antitrust policies based on economic arguments about the efficiency of various competitive practices.

Clayton Act: One of two antitrust statutes passed in 1914 (along with the FTC Act), which strengthened the Sherman Act by adding prohibitions on price discrimination and certain tying and exclusive dealing arrangements, anticompetitive mergers, and certain interlocking directorates, and bolstered the private right of action for treble damages.

Cellophane fallacy: A criticism of the Supreme Court's reasoning in *DuPont* where the Court defined a wide, relevant market because of evidence showing that DuPont could not profitably increase the price of cellophane because customers would substitute other products. If DuPont had already charged a profit-maximizing monopoly price, then other products would appear to be reasonable substitutes because of the high price of cellophane.

Characterization: A stage of Section 1 analysis where a court decides whether a particular practice fits within one of the established per se categories, particularly price fixing. In *BMI*, the Supreme Court admitted that the restraint was literally price fixing, but recharacterized the music copyrights as mere inputs into a new product being created by ASCAP and BMI in order to avoid application of the per se rule, and then applied the rule of reason.

Collusion: Coordinated action by competitors to raise prices or limit output.

Complements: Goods that are jointly used or consumed and therefore exhibit negative cross-elasticity of demand, meaning that an increase in the price of one product results in a decrease in the demand for the other.

Conscious parallelism: Coordination on price or other terms of sale by a group of buyers or sellers who do not overtly agree on coordination. Conscious parallelism is insufficient to show agreement under Section 1 of the Sherman Act.

Consumer welfare: The predominant objective of modern antitrust law. Consumer welfare includes at least the avoidance of deadweight losses resulting from anticompetitive output reductions. It may also include the avoidance of wealth transfers from consumers to producers.

Coordinated effects: One of two theories (along with unilateral effects) of anticompetitive harm resulting from horizontal mergers. Coordinated interaction occurs when the structure of the market makes it feasible for sellers or buyers to engage in conscious parallelism or collusive agreement.

Cournot competition: An economic model describing the competitiveness of a market based on the assumption that firms sell homogeneous goods and compete by making decisions about output levels.

Critical loss analysis: A tool used to define relevant markets under the Horizontal Merger Guideline, by comparing the number of lost unit sales attributable to a SSNIP that would leave profits unchanged with the predicted loss of unit sales from the merger.

Cross-elasticity of demand: The relationship between an increase in the price of one thing and the change in the demand for another. When the increase in price of good A results in an increase in the demand for good B, the two goods exhibit positive cross-elasticity of demand and are substitutes. When the increase in price of good A results in a decrease in the demand for good B, the two goods exhibit negative cross-elasticity of demand and are complements.

Deadweight loss: A loss in allocative efficiency resulting from an increase in price above the competitive level, which induces some customers to not purchase the relevant good.

Differentiated: Heterogeneous or nonfungible; a product is differentiated if consumers perceive significant differences in the quality or properties of goods that they consider to be substitutable. For example, tablet computers are differentiated products because even though customers may chose between different competitive offerings, they perceive each model as distinct from other models based on its capabilities and functionalities.

Direct purchaser rule: A rule derived from *Illinois Brick* allowing purchaser standing to only direct purchasers of an overcharged product, while denying standing to indirect purchasers.

Diversion ratio: The fraction of unit sales lost by one product due to an increase in price that is diverted to a second product; a tool used for determining the likelihood of unilateral anticompetitive effects under the Horizontal Merger Guidelines.

Double marginalization: Successive monopoly mark-ups in the chain of production and distribution, as when a supplier of a raw input with market power marks up the price of the raw input to a manufacturer, who then adds an additional monopoly mark up upon its sale to a retailer.

Economic profit: Returns on capital invested above a competitive level; also known as rents.

Effects test: A test for the extraterritorial application of domestic antitrust law proposed in *Alcoa* and adopted in the Foreign Trade Antitrust Improvements Act; an alternative to a territorial sovereignty approach to jurisdiction.

Elastic (or Elasticity): Sensitive to change in price. Demand is typically said to be elastic if a price increase of *x* produces a decline in the quantity demanded of *x* or greater. It is said to be inelastic if it produces a decline in the quantity demanded of less than *x*.

Elasticity of demand: The effect on the quantity demanded of a change in price. *See* also Elastic.

Elasticity of supply: The effect on the quantity supplied in response to a change in price. *See* also Elastic.

Entry barriers: See Barriers to entry

Equally efficient competitor: A competitor who can produce or sell goods or services at least as cheaply as the dominant firm in the market. Some tests for exclusionary or monopolistic conduct require a showing that the allegedly excluded rival was at least as efficient as the dominant firm.

Exclusion: The condition of being prevented from competing in a relevant market. Exclusion is generally assumed to mean that one or more rivals is prevented from entering or is driven out of a market. However, it can also be used to describe a circumstance where one or more rivals is marginalized in the market, meaning that it remains in the market but is not a full competitive force, for example, because it is confined to a market niche or a very low market share.

Exclusive dealing: Contractual practices that require a seller to deal exclusively with a particular buyer, or a buyer to deal exclusively with a particular seller.

Facilitating practice: A practice that facilitates conscious parallelism among competitors or even collusion. Information exchange among competitors is a class example of a practice that under some circumstances could enable oligopolists to coordinate their pricing or sales practices even without overt agreement.

Fixed cost: A cost that does not vary with changes in the firm's level of output. The cost of building a factory is conventionally described as a leading example of a fixed cost.

Free riding: Partaking of another firm's investment without paying for it. Free riding diminishes the incentives of the "victim" firm to make the investments.

Foreign Trade Antitrust Improvements Act (FTAIA): A 1982 federal statute concerning the extraterritorial application of U.S. antitrust law that, generally, adopts a version of the *Alcoa* effects test, with additional caveats.

Four-firm concentration ratio: The percentage of the market held by the four largest firms in the market. During the heyday of structuralism, the four-firm concentration ratio was considered important to determining whether a horizontal merger should be prohibited.

Glossary

Fungible: Homogeneous or undifferentiated; a product is fungible if consumers perceive that a product sold by one seller is essentially identical to a product sold by another seller. Commodities are examples of fungible products.

Hart Scott Rodino Antitrust Improvement Act: A 1976 federal statute, notable for instituting a premerger notification requirement.

Harvard School (see also Structuralism and S-C-P paradigm): The dominant intellectual school of thought in antitrust law during the 1950s and 1960s, led by economist Joe Bain. A structuralist approach to antitrust. The Harvard School was largely supplanted by the Chicago School, although there continues to be a neoHarvard School that is more focused on institutionalism than structuralism.

Herfindahl-Hirschman Index: A measure of market concentration derived by summing the square of the market share of each participant in the relevant market. The primary tool for assessing market concentration used in the Horizontal Merger Guidelines since 1982.

Homogeneous: See Fungible

Horizontal: The relationship between firms that are competitors, that is, that produce or sell at the same level of production or distribution. *Vertical* relationships refer to the relationship between firms at different levels of production or distribution. *Conglomerate* relationships refer to the relationship between firms that have neither a horizontal nor vertical relationship.

Horizontal Merger Guidelines: Guidelines explaining the approach used to review horizontal mergers, first published by the Justice Department in 1968 and subsequently revised in 1982, 1984, 1992, 1997, and 2010.

Hypothetical monopolist test: An analytical tool used to define relevant markets under the Horizontal Merger Guidelines that asks whether a hypothetical monopolist over a specified group of products would find it profitable to impose a "small but significant and nontransitory increase in price" (SSNIP), generally understood to be 5 percent. Also known as the SSNIP test.

Inelastic: Not sensitive to a change in price. See also Elastic.

Information asymmetry: A circumstance where two parties to a transaction have different levels of information about the transaction. For example, a seller may have better information than a buyer, thus enabling the seller to lock the buyer into anticompetitive terms that the buyer doesn't fully understand or anticipate.

Information cost: The cost of acquiring information, such as a customers' cost of figuring out differences in the cost of servicing a durable good.

Interbrand: Describing effects between sellers of different brands. For example, the introduction of a new Nike shoe affects Adidas's ability to compete, which is an interbrand effect. The Supreme Court has said that the stimulation of interbrand competition is the primary purpose of the Sherman Act.

Intrabrand: Describing effects between sellers of the same brand. For example, competition to expand market share between two retailers of Nike shoes in intrabrand competition. The Supreme Court has said that restrictions on intrabrand competition that stimulate interbrand competition are usually permissible, because interbrand competition is more important than intrabrand competition.

Marginal cost: The cost of producing the next unit of output. Also known as incremental cost. In theory, a firm should consider only marginal cost in deciding whether to produce another unit of output, since fixed or sunk costs already incurred are bygones.

Market power: The power to raise prices above competitive levels or to exclude competitors.

Maverick: A firm that stimulates competition in the market in disproportion to its market share. For example, a small firm that has historically refused to go along with price increases attempted by the larger firms in the market, requiring the larger firms to lower their prices.

Merger: A permanent combination of productive assets through integration of share ownership. Contrast with a joint venture, which involves a temporary combination of some productive assets through contract.

Metering: Charging different effective prices to different customers based on their intensity of use, which is assumed to be a proxy for willingness to pay.

Minimum Efficient Scale: The minimum scale at which a firm's average total cost is minimized.

Monopoly: A market characterized by a single seller or a seller with a high degree of market power.

Monopoly power: A high degree of market power. See also Market power.

Monopsony: A market characterized by a single dominant buyer.

Naked restraint: An agreement having no purpose other than the suppression of competition, which are per se illegal under Section 1 of the Sherman Act and can be contrasted to ancillary restraints that serve some purpose other than suppressing competition and are judged under the rule of reason.

Noerr-Pennington immunity: Immunity from application of the antitrust laws for joint or individual efforts to petition the government to take anticompetitive action. Applies to efforts to persuade any branch of government, including executive, legislative, judicial, or administrative agencies.

Non-fungible: See Differentiated.

Oligopoly: A market characterized by few sellers.

Oligopsony: A market characterized by few buyers.

One monopoly profit theory: A theory advanced by the Chicago School that a seller of complementary products, who has a monopoly over one of the products, would not rationally seek to leverage that monopoly into the other product to extract a second monopoly profit, since the exercise of the second monopoly would cause a reduction in demand for the monopoly product.

Parker immunity: Immunity from the antitrust laws for acts of the state, or private actors acting pursuant to state policy, that suppresses competition. In order for *Parker* immunity apply, the state regulation must meet the two-part *Midcal* test: (1) clear and affirmative expression of state policy to suppress competition and (2) active supervision by the state.

Per se rule: A mode of analysis under Section 1 of the Sherman Act that condemns certain categories of restraint of trade, such as price fixing and market division, without requiring proof of a relevant market, market power, or anticompetitive effects, and without allowing the defendant to offer procompetitive justifications in rebuttal.

Predatory pricing: Pricing below cost in order to exclude competitors and obtain monopoly power. Under *Brooke Group*, a predatory pricing claim requires proof that defendant (1) priced below an appropriate measure of cost and (2) had a dangerous probability of recouping the costs of predation through later supracompetitive pricing.

Price discrimination: Charging different prices to different customers based on their different willingness to pay.

Price squeeze: Predatory strategy by vertically integrated firm that supplies a competitor with an input at wholesale and then prices its own good or service at a retail price that the competitor could not match, given the wholesale price of the input.

Primary line price discrimination: Price discrimination that affects competition at the same level as the firm giving the discount. Under *Brooke Group*, primary line price discrimination is essentially identical to predatory pricing under Section 2 of the Sherman Act.

Procompetitive: Advancing or promoting competition to the benefit of consumers.

Profit Sacrifice/no economic sense test: A leading proposed test for ascertaining when conduct is unlawfully exclusionary of rivals. Under this test, an act is exclusionary if it entails a sacrifice of profits that makes no sense, absent a desire to recoup the lost profits through monopoly pricing.

Productive efficiency: Gains to producers from lowering costs of production or distribution.

Quick look doctrine: A mode of analysis under Section 1 of the Sherman Act that applies to restraints that do not fall within the traditional per se categories, but are of the kind that a person with a rudimentary understanding of economics would understand as posing an obvious risk of anticompetitive consequences. When a court determines that a restraint should be analyzed under the quick look approach, the defendant must immediately offer a procompetitive justification for the restraint; if she cannot, the restraint is treated as per se illegal.

Rapid entrant: Under the Horizontal Merger Guidelines, a firm that is not currently producing or selling in the market, but would do so rapidly and without incurring significant sunk costs in response to a small, but significant and non-transitory, increase in price.

Recoupment: Recovering costs expended in driving rivals from the market, typically by predatory pricing, through later, supracompetitive pricing.

Relevant market: An area of effective competition between rival firms, ascertained by reasonable interchangeability between goods or services from the perspective of customers.

Resale price maintenance (RPM): An upstream firm's dictation of prices that a down-stream firm must use to resell goods sold to the downstream firm by the upstream firm. Typically, this involves a manufacturer telling a wholesaler or retailer the price it must charge for the manufacturer's goods. RPM was *per se* illegal under *Dr. Miles*, but is now judged under the rule of reason following *Leegin*.

Reservation price: The maximum price a buyer is willing to pay, or the minimum price a seller is willing to accept.

Robinson Patman Act: A 1936 statute amending the Clayton Act's price discrimination prohibition. It prohibits discriminatory pricing that may adversely affect competition in the market or competition between an advantaged and disadvantaged firm.

Ruinous competition: An argument classically arising from nineteenth-century economic theory that competition in high, fixed costs industries was inherently ruinous of producers since it drove price to marginal cost. Ruinous competition arguments were advanced to justify restrictions on competition. In its early cases, the Supreme Court rejected ruinous competition arguments as inconsistent with the Sherman Act's assumption that competition is good. Today, ruinous competition continues to be used as an epithet to describe any argument that assumes that competition is harmful.

Rule of reason: The catch-all mode of analysis under Section 1 of the Sherman Act that applies when the per se rule or quick look do not apply. Typically, it requires proof of a relevant market, market power, and anticompetitive effects and permits the defendant to advance procompetitive justifications in defense of the restraint.

Second request for information: A procedural device available to the FTC and Justice Department under the Hart-Scott-Rodino Act to seek further information regarding a proposed merger. When an antitrust agency issues a timely second request, this tolls the waiting period for the parties to close the merger until they have produced the information requested by the agency.

Secondary line price discrimination: Under the Robinson-Patman Act, secondary linie price discrimination injures competition at the level of the firm receiving the discount. For example, if a manufacturer gives a favored franchisee more advantageous price terms than a rival franchisee, the rival franchisee may have suffered secondary line price discrimination.

Sherman Act: The foundational U.S. antitrust statute, passed in 1890, most important today for Section 1, which prohibits contracts in restraint of trade and Section 2 which prohibits monopolization.

SSNIP test: See Hypothetical Monopolist Test.

Structuralism: A school of thought generally associated with the Harvard School, holding that anticompetitive effects invariably followed from concentrated markets. See also Harvard School and Structure-Conduct-Performance paradigm.

Structure-Conduct-Performance or S-C-P paradigm: The core theoretic assertion of the Harvard or structuralist school (see Harvard School and Structuralism). It asserts a deterministic relationship between a market's structure, conduct, and performance, so that simply by observing a market's structure, one could confidently predict whether the market will perform well or poorly.

Substitutes: Two goods are substitutes when an increase in the price of one leads to an increase in the demand for the other.

Tertiary line price discrimination: Under the Robinson-Patman Act, price discrimination that injures competition one or more levels below the level of the firm receiving the discriminatory price. For example, if a manufacturer gives a favorable price to a favored wholesaler, who then passes on the lower price to a retailer, and the retailer's competitor buys from the wholesaler at a higher price and thus loses sales to the favored retailer, the injured retailer may be able to complain of tertiary line price discrimination.

Tying: Using market power over one product to force customers to purchase a complementary product.

Undifferentiated: See Fungible.

Unilateral effects: One of two theories (along with coordinated effects) of anticompetitive harm resulting from horizontal mergers. In differentiated goods markets, a merger between firms whose goods or services are perceived as close substitutes may empower the merged firms to raise price or reduce output regardless of the response of competitors.

Upward pricing pressure (UPP): A model for determining likely unilateral anticompetitive effects under the 2010 Horizontal Merger Guidelines that relies on diversion ratios between products of merging firms and pre-merger incremental cost margins.

Vertical: The relationship between two firms at different stages in a single chain of production or distribution. For example, an automobile parts component manufacturer is vertically related to General Motors.

Wealth transfer: One result of the exercise of market power when consumers pay more than they otherwise would have and thus transfer some of their wealth to producers.

Index

Index

Index